BACK ROADS & BUGGY TRAILS

A Visitor's Guide to Ohio Amish Country

Third Edition

by

Lorraine A. Moore

Front Cover and Maps
by
Debi-Ann Ward
Ward's Computer Works

Illustrations
by
Beth Herman

BLUEBIRD PRESS
Millersburg, Ohio

This edition is published and distributed by Bluebird Press, P.O. Box 371, Millersburg, Ohio 44654.

Additional copies may be ordered by sending a check for $11.95 (postpaid in the continental U.S.) to Bluebird Press. Outside the U.S. add $3.50 for postage.

The author welcomes your comments and suggestions. Write to her c/o Bluebird Press at the above address.

Library of Congress Catalog Card Number: 96-83076

ISBN 1-881122-02-6
$11.95 Softcover

Manufactured in the United States of America.

In loving memory
of my father,
Loren O. Moore,
1919-1993

ACKNOWLEDGEMENTS

As always, my children, Chris and Beth, are a guiding force in my life. There have been moments when I would not have made it without them. *You are the light of my life and at the top of the list of things I'm most grateful for.*

My mother, Ruth Moore, has been a rock, stalwart in her faith in this project—and in me. *This book would not be a reality without you, Mom. Thanks for everything! I hope you know how much you mean to me.*

Of course, if there was no enclave of Amish and Mennonites where I live, this book would be unnecessary. I admire their abilities and hard work as well as their determination to stick to their beliefs in the face of modern temptations. They have reaffirmed my faith in people by their friendliness and willingness to talk to this stranger. I hope their independent enterprises benefit from this publication.

TABLE OF CONTENTS

LIST OF MAPS

WARNING—DISCLAIMER

This book is designed to provide information about the subject matter covered. It is sold with the understanding that the publisher and author are presenting this information purely for the entertainment of readers of this book.

While great effort was expended to gather as much relevant information as available, it should be understood prices and situations change. Every effort has been made to make this book as complete and accurate as possible. However, there may be mistakes both typographical and in content. Therefore, this text should be used only as a general guide to Ohio Amish country, and not as the ultimate source on this area. Furthermore, this book contains information on Ohio Amish country only up to the printing date. It is an ever-changing world, even in Amish country.

The author and Bluebird Press shall have neither liability nor responsibility to any person or entity with respect to any loss or damage caused, or alleged to be caused, directly or indirectly by the information contained in this book.

If you do not wish to be bound by the above, you may return the book to the publisher for a full refund.

INTRODUCTION

What is Amish country?

In the heart of Ohio exists the largest Amish settlement in the world. As you may already be aware, the Amish are a religious sect who disdain most of the modern trappings of life we *English* take for granted. Their roots go as far back as the Reformation in the 16th century. The most noticeable feature about the Amish, the one which attracts the most attention, is their use of horses and buggies for transportation. In addition, most do not have electricity or telephones in their homes.

This eschewing of modern ways has created a unique pocket of almost 19th century-style life existing in the midst of the 1990's.

It's this very reflection of forgotten eras that draws so many people to our rolling, green farmland. Amish country evokes a nostalgic response in those of us steeped in the hustle and bustle of modern cities and society. 'The good ol' days' appear to exist just beyond the window of our automobiles when we see an Amish farmer plowing a field behind his team of horses.

Amish country is a place where morning mist rises in ghostly tendrils from still hollows delineated by the rock-strewn slopes of the terminal moraine. It's a place where the flash of a bluebird's wing and the trill of a song sparrow are as common as the rectangular black shape of a buggy and the jingle of harness. This is a land in which a flock of wild turkeys and the graceful leap of a white-tailed deer can be glimpsed nearly as often as a Holstein cow or a sturdy Belgian draft horse.

Here old ways mingle with the new, yet stand stalwartly resistant to them.

The Amish are a plain people and their ways hark back to our not-so-distant past, to a simpler, less complicated time. They use horses for transportation and farming and gas lanterns to light their homes. They tend orchards and strawberry patches and large gardens from which they harvest fruits and vegetables to can or dry or store in their root cellars. They raise chickens and hogs and gather eggs, stuff their own sausage, and smoke their own hams and bacon. Dairy cows provide fresh milk, butter, and cream. The excess milk is sold for that popular, mild, and nutty-tasting Swiss cheese and the other cheeses made by local companies.

Their clothing is largely handmade and dries on clotheslines in the sunshine. Children and many adults enjoy the wonderful freedom of bare feet during warm weather. How long has it been since *you* wiggled your toes in the cool softness of green grass?

Amish lives are directed by the passing of the seasons, each bringing its own special tasks. Their days are bound by the rising and setting of the sun, although it may be that dark hour before dawn which finds them already at work with the day's first milking, or those last minutes of dusk which catch them trudging toward home behind a weary team after long hours in the fields.

Amish country is a place out of time—not quite in sync with the world most of us experience. Yet it exists in our midst, perhaps as much a state of mind as anything else.

Welcome to this exploration of Amish country! If you're a first-time visitor, you may feel a little overwhelmed by the choices this volume introduces you to. If you've been here before, you may wish to explore new territory. This is a compendium of information about places to see and things to do during your visit.

Need a place to stay? It's in here! If you want to see first-hand some of the cottage industries the Amish thrive on, this will tell you where to locate them. Hungry? Well, the Amish are known for their hearty fare and this will direct you to the nearest restaurant.

Life's a little slower here, so relax and enjoy it. Amish country is a feast for the eyes—and the spirit.

Lorraine A. Moore
Millersburg, Holmes County, Ohio

Ohio Amish Country

Chapter 1

Tips For Travelers

Welcome to this third edition of *BACK ROADS & BUGGY TRAILS*! If this is your first visit, there's a lot to see and do and learn about the area. If you've been here before, you'll be interested in what's new. Since there's so much to tell you, it's hard to know where to start. Let's begin with some basics.

Ohio's largest Amish settlement is not limited by the boundaries of Holmes County. Large portions of Wayne, Coshocton, and Tuscarawas Counties also contain Amish farms and communities.

This is fortunate for travelers because it means you do not have to crowd into one small area. Yes, some locations such as Berlin (pronounced BER-lin) can be very crowded; however, other areas won't be. It all depends on what you're here to see and do.

While this book is designed to get you out into the byways to discover a number of different communities, it cannot possibly explore everything in this vast region. I make no claim to having discovered every cottage industry or interesting business existing here. That's an impossibility. People change their minds; situations change; businesses come and go; signs are put up and taken down, often according to the season. Especially during summer gardening season, Amish women may be too busy to worry about crafting things and will remove their signs. On the other hand, if they've got strawberries to sell or sweet corn and tomatoes, a different sign will be hung. What I find when I do my research may not be exactly what exists 3, 6, or 12 months from now.

Although the Amish are not generally as mobile as some segments of modern society, this region is growing quickly as business people take advantage of our boom in tourism. It's a trend that's bound to continue. All we can hope is that what we value most about the area is not overwhelmed in the process. But the business world is subject to nothing so much as continual metamorphosis, so don't be surprised if you happen across a new or seasonal business which doesn't show up here. Just take advantage of it!

As you're out exploring, keep this in mind: if you can't find exactly what you're looking for, ask. Plenty of artist-craftsmen thrive on the challenge of attempting something they've never tried before. Or they can point you toward someone who does.

Let me add one reminder: Amish cottage industries are real businesses, not tourist attractions. Most of them are small, often only one-person enterprises. The owners are usually willing to answer questions but don't forget that time is money—especially if you've no one to depend upon except yourself. Don't expect them to drop whatever they're in the middle of simply because you show up. And don't be afraid to ask if they've got a moment to chat. They'll appreciate your courtesy.

While the Amish fascinate us, please remember they are just human beings who happen to have different beliefs and values. Some of these may seem silly or irrational to you. The same freedom that allows you to think so, allows them to believe as they choose. All that's asked is that you respect them.

They don't appreciate being stared at or pointed at any more than anyone else. And, while some of them hold very strict beliefs which tend to keep them aloof, many are simply shy. So, offer them a smile and say, "Hello;" feel free to ask questions; and compliment them on their craftsmanship. They are our neighbors.

As a general rule, for religious reasons the Amish prefer *not* to have their pictures taken. I hope you'll respect their beliefs in this regard. After all, there are plenty of buggies and horses and lots of scenery you can photograph.

Speaking of photographs, Amish country's premiere photographer is Holmes County native, Doyle Yoder. His company, America's Amish Country Publications, publishes postcards, calendars, and a coffee-table book he produced with another photographer, *America's Amish Country*. It's 144 pages filled with 313 photos of the Amish from the U.S. and Canada.

His *Amish Country Calendar* grows more popular every year. The 1996 calendar is $9.95 postpaid and the book is $24.95 postpaid.

Orders can be sent to America's Amish Country Publications, P.O. Box 424, Berlin, OH 44610.

One thing folks from urban areas take for granted is businesses open on Sundays. This isn't true among our Amish and Mennonite peoples. Sundays are sacred and spent in church services and with their families. What this can mean for visitors is real disappointment if they're not prepared. See the chapter, "What's Open on Sunday?" and plan ahead. There are places to go and things to do, but you'll need to know where to find them.

A major change taking place as the telephone companies struggle to keep up with the surge in demand for more telephone numbers for fax machines, computer modems, cellular phones, and pagers is the changing of area codes. As of March 9, 1996, Holmes, Wayne, and Tuscarawas Counties will become part of the new 330 area code. I've made the changes and hope there are no snafus on the other end.

Let's talk a little about driving in Amish country. In the hills of Holmes County the roads follow the twists and turns of the terrain. A glance at a county map makes that explicitly clear. Then, of course, we have lots of slow-moving vehicles—horses and buggies and carts and farm wagons and bicyclists—on the roads. Combine those with the volume of traffic from local folks and outside visitors and it sounds like an accident waiting to happen, which it certainly can be. As much as you may want to look at the countryside, please pay strict attention to the highway or gravel road in front of you. Be aware that just over the next rise there could be an Amish child walking or riding a bicycle, a horse and buggy carrying a family, or a team of draft horses pulling a wagonload of hay. If possible, trade driving time with other passengers in your vehicle so one person doesn't have to spend all his/her time behind the wheel. That will allow everyone an opportunity to see the scenery. So, buckle up (It's Ohio law.) and drive safely. We want you to enjoy a carefree visit, not a tragic one.

While on the subject of driving, let me point out that gas stations may be fewer and farther between than you're used to. Gas is readily available in main communities like Sugarcreek, Millersburg, and Loudonville, but less so in small Amish villages since they aren't dependent on automobiles. So, keep an eye on that gauge.

Glancing through this book, you'll notice maps are a necessary part of getting off the beaten path and finding your way around on the back roads and buggy trails in the area. These maps are meant to assist you in locating local businesses. They will help you get from place to place within a specific township, but how much aid they will be as you travel across country is doubtful. If I were doing the driving, I'd prefer to see the *whole* picture vis-a-vis a county map, rather than just a tiny segment of it.

BACK ROADS & BUGGY TRAILS is arranged by sections for each county, and further arranged by chapters on the communities and townships within those counties. An ordinary map of the State of Ohio will not help locate townships, so use the villages as reference points. Most, if not all, should appear on state maps to assist in finding the general areas referred to.

My suggestion, however, would be to get some county maps, at least one of Holmes County. AAA is a great source of free maps and information if you're a member. If not, write to the following:

a) The Holmes County Chamber of Commerce, 91 N. Clay St., Millersburg, OH 44654, (PH: 330-674-3975) sends packets of information on the county everywhere and can supply a map. It's an unsophisticated, black and white map, but it's the same one I used to get myself about. A more detailed, colored map is available by writing to the Holmes County Engineer, 10 S. Clay St., Millersburg, OH 44654. Each map costs $1 plus postage of $.52.

b) The Wayne County Visitor & Convention Bureau, P.O. Box 77, Wooster, OH 44691(1-800-362-6474). Their packet does not include a county map unless you ask for one.

c) The Tuscarawas County Convention & Visitors Bureau, P.O. Box 926, New Philadelphia, OH 44663 (1-800-527-3387). This county recently named all roads and updated maps should be available by June 1996. Ask for one with your information packet.

d) The Coshocton County Convention & Visitors Bureau, P.O. Box 905, Coshocton, OH 43812 (1-800-338-4724).

Berlin, Loudonville, Shreve, and Sugarcreek also have business associations or tourist bureaus which will supply information. See these chapters for more information.

Those manning the phones at 1-800-BUCKEYE have free information about Amish country they'll be glad to send if you give them a call, but these do not include county maps.

Some of you may note the lack of community maps and be disappointed or, worse, panicky. Most of the communities in Amish country are small and easily explored. These are rural villages, not sprawling urban areas, and that's the reason I felt maps were unnecessary. If you do have trouble finding any business listed, don't be afraid to ask. Most shop owners and clerks are local folks who know their way around and will be glad to assist you.

On the subject of maps and roads, I should explain the address shorthand used throughout the book. In Holmes County roads are numbered rather than named. There are state routes, U.S. routes, county roads, and township roads. It's the custom here to abbreviate these and I've used these abbreviations throughout the text. So, when addresses are given, State Route could be St.Rt. but, if I've done my job correctly, should be SR as in SR 39; US Routes will be simply US and the number; County Roads are CR as in CR 212; and Township Roads are TR.

I've added one new feature to this third edition—on the suggestion of several people and because I desire to make this book as easy to use as possible. There's now an alphabetical index of businesses. If you've had a friend or relative visit or have read about some place and you really want to see it but all you know is the name, this feature is for you. Locate the name in the index, turn to that page, and you'll find out just where your best friend Sam's favorite restaurant is or which shop Cousin Louella raved about. Hope it helps!

For an informed overview of the region you might want to consider taking a guided tour. There are now three such services I'm aware of:

1. **Country Coach, Inc.**, is owned and operated by Carol Glessner. It was the first of its kind in the area and, with stops at various Amish cottage industries, may be the most informative about present-day Amish life. She has an air-conditioned, 15-passenger van and will customize tours for group needs. 1, 2, and 2½ hour tours depart Carlisle Village Inn in Walnut Creek at 9 am Mon.-Sat. year 'round and at 3:30 pm on Sun. May-Oct. tours also at 4:30 pm and sunset. From the Dutch Country Kitchen Restaurant, Berlin, her tours depart at noon and 2:15 pm. Sign up at the front desks of each location or call 1-800-619-7795 for reservations. Walk-ons are welcome. A 2-hour tour is $10 for adults and $5 for children.

2. LaVonne Chumney opened **Buggy Trail Tours** in the spring of 1995. She offers a 2-hour backroads tour with a mystery stop for $8 for adults and $4 for children 6-12. Private, custom tours for a minimum of 10 people are also offered with 7 days advance notice. Her 12-passenger bus departs from Der Bake Oven II in Berlin at 10 am, noon, 2, and 4 pm. Purchase your ticket at Der Bake Oven II. For more information contact LaVonne at 330-893-3248 or by writing to P.O. Box 462, Berlin, OH 44610.

3. **Alpine Hills Shuttle** sells tickets from a booth at and departs from the corner of Broadway and Main Streets in Sugarcreek. Offering a 1¼-hour trip Mon.-Sat., May-Oct., from 10 am-6 pm. Ages 11 and older $5, children 3-10 $3, and under 3 free. There may be a wait if they don't have at least 6 passengers.

Another way to see some of Amish country is by bicycle. If you haven't brought your own, you can rent them from **Amish Country Bike Rentals** located at Artisans Mercantile in Sugarcreek. Owner Harry Arnold is an experienced bicyclist and offers suggestions for your trip as well as helmets, safety flags, and maps. A variety of rates is available from $5 for 1 hour to $20 for all-day trips. Call 330-852-2456 for more information.

As you can see, there are plenty of ways to experience the area. So, now that you've got some of the nuts and bolts, let's discover Amish country!

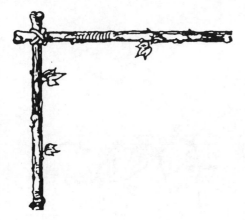

Section I
Holmes County

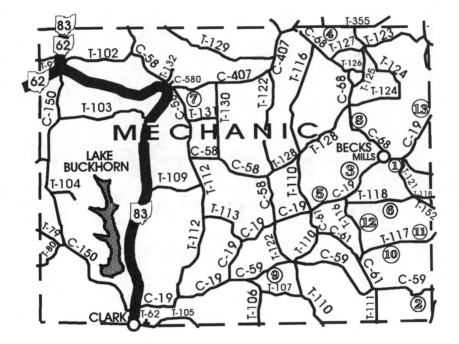

**Mechanic Twp.
Holmes County**

Chapter 2

Beck's Mills and Mechanic Twp.

The hub of Ohio's Amish country is Holmes County. According to the folks at 1-800-BUCKEYE, they get more calls about Holmes County than anywhere else in the state. This means we're one of the top attractions in Ohio.

Named for Major Andrew Holmes who was killed during the War of 1812, Holmes County was formed from parts of Coshocton, Tuscarawas, and Wayne Counties in 1825. The county encompasses about 420 square miles and within that area are four traffic lights (three in Millersburg and one in Nashville), one movie theater (in Killbuck), and nearly 1,000 miles of roads—more than 500 of them unpaved.

If you're into statistics, you might be interested in knowing that in 1992 there were 1,550 farms in the county, averaging 122 acres, and 189,000 acres in the county engaged in farming and agriculture. With so much of our land devoted to agricultural endeavors, it's not surprising that Holmes County ranks near the top in production in the state. Based on 1992 yields, the county was second in hay, third in dairy production with 251.4 million pounds of milk, third in oats harvested, and tenth in hogs.

Visitors used to flock in only during warm weather—and they still do, of course. However, more and more come to Christmas shop or drive in during a sunny winter weekend.

The two things that remain constant here are the Amish going about their daily business and the wonderful scenery. So, whatever season you pick to visit, you'll find both of these in plentiful supply.

If you want to read more about Amish country in the comfort of your own home, no matter what the season, you might find a subscription to *The Holmes County Traveler* informative and enjoyable. Published five times a year and featuring articles about local people, places, businesses, and history, the *Traveler* helps readers discover some of what's most interesting about this area. Subscriptions are available for $12.95 per year by writing to P.O. Box 358, Millersburg, OH 44654.

One of my favorite pastimes is just getting out and driving on roads I'm not very familiar with. I enjoy discovering those nooks and crannies that make this region so beautiful. Now, if I could just master the art of photography and capture some of these images on film....

This section on Holmes County does not include all of the townships. The largest concentration of our Amish population live in the eastern half of the county. The fewest probably live in the southwestern areas of Killbuck, Richland, and Knox Townships. Although I made no attempt to include the whole township, a chapter on the Killbuck area is included since it offers several attractions visitors will find interesting.

I would be remiss, however, if I failed to tell you this southwestern corner of the county offers some of the most spectacular scenery. SR (State Route) 514, particularly from Nashville to Danville in Knox Co., US 62 from Danville to Killbuck, SR 520 between Glenmont and Killbuck, and SR 60 from Killbuck to US 36 in Coshocton Co. present beautiful vistas around every turn in every season. They are some of my favorites, especially when dressed in autumn's patchwork of vibrant colors.

And if these major highways wind through great scenery, imagine what undiscovered delights await those who try the county and township roads. Fairly makes the fingers tingle to grab that steering wheel and get started. So, let's do it!

The southernmost village in Holmes County is Clark, located on SR 83 and sitting right on the Coshocton-Holmes County line. Clark is not, however, the focus of this chapter. I merely give it as a reference point because it's probably the only community in Mechanic Twp. to show up on an ordinary Ohio map. One more reason for getting yourself a Holmes County map if you don't already have one. See Chapter 1 for tips on where to get maps, or struggle along with the map of Mechanic Twp. given here.

Our travels in this township will center around the tiny village of Beck's Mills, northeast of Clark.

The history of Beck's Mills began when the Michael Beck family moved into the area in 1822. Between 1830 and 1850 hundreds of wagons loaded with farm products traveled through the village and it became quite a prosperous place. Unfortunately, the railroad's arrival in Millersburg in 1854 halted the progress of Beck's Mills.

You'll notice how much more rugged the landscape becomes south of Millersburg. The hills are steeper; the valleys deeper. It's beautiful countryside. I love the wild places best of all but there's no way I'd farm some of those slopes like my Amish neighbors do.

If you have time, do some sightseeing in this township. You can see plenty without getting off the paved roads, if you'd prefer not to.

SR 83 has been designated a scenic highway for as long as I can remember. Take it south of Millersburg and turn east onto CR (County Road) 19 just before you enter the village of Clark. You can take this directly to Beck's Mills, or you can take the long way 'round by turning onto CR 59, then north on CR 61 which will bring you back onto CR 19. Take your time and enjoy the view. Depending on your destination, you can take either CR 19 or 59 to CR 600 in Clark Twp., at which point you can travel north toward Charm or south to New Bedford.

When you take CR 19 into Beck's Mills, you'll discover a tiny, quiet, Amish community tucked in the picturesque Doughty Creek Valley. The biggest businesses—in fact, the only businesses—are Beck's Mills General Store and the lumber company across the road.

From Beck's Mills you might want to turn onto CR 68 which you can follow north back toward Millersburg. See if you can spot a green and white marker along this route. It says you're traveling on Old Port Washington Road, the very first state road in Ohio.

I first drove this area on a winter morning when sunlight sparkled on the snow and the sky was a clear, pale blue shell overhead. It reminded me of the northern Virginia mountains. It's just as lovely in the spring when the wildflowers are blooming and the grass is an emerald carpet or in the autumn when the leaves turn the hillsides into brilliant calico.

One of the purposes of this book is to take the mystery out of getting off the beaten path in Amish country. It's my mission to help you feel comfortable taking a few side roads and discovering a corner of the world you haven't explored before. That's why I hope you'll at least get a Holmes County map.

Since this is the first chapter, some explanation of addresses is probably in order. You may notice a wide variety of them in many townships. Most of our small communities don't have the necessary manpower for rural delivery. Townsfolk pick up their daily mail from post office boxes. Outside of town, the mail is delivered from a larger post office such as Millersburg.

In Mechanic Twp. most of the addresses are Millersburg, but a few are delivered out of Baltic which is in Tuscarawas County. Some townships may contain addresses from 3 or 4 post offices outside the immediate area. If you wonder why, this is the reason. I once lived a few miles southeast of the village of Nashville in western Holmes Co. I had a Big Prairie address and a Glenmont phone number. Later, I lived southwest of Nashville with a Lakeville address and a Nashville phone. It all depended on which side of SR 514 one lived. If you want anonymity, it's not a bad idea because no one can find you!

I've made an effort to tell you where to find these businesses, as well as indicate them on the maps. In Amish country an address alone may not make it easy to find what you're looking for, but it's getting better now that the counties have numbered everyone. Imagine the difficulty if the only address you had to go by was a route number, which existed in some places as recently as 1993.

Now it's time to explore Mechanic Twp.

BECK'S MILLS

In Amish country you'll discover that any general or variety store is just that—full of all sorts of stuff. This is for the convenience of our Amish neighbors who can enjoy one-stop shopping between visits to the "big city." Such a store is the **Beck's Mills General Store**. From groceries to dry goods and hardware, this store is a good place to browse. You might want to have a hot cup of coffee or an ice cream cone and they have both here. Located in Beck's Mills on CR 19 across from the intersection of CR 68 at 5330 CR 19, Millersburg, OH 44654. Hours are Mon., Tues., Fri., Sat. from 7 am-5 pm; Wed. until 8:30 pm; Thurs. until noon. PH: 330-893-2303.

MECHANIC TWP.

1. If you enjoy poking around for a bargain, stop in and explore **Buy-Rite**, a store which handles new and used furniture, all sorts of used housewares, bows and archery supplies, and lots of miscellaneous. Travel CR 19 just north of Beck's Mills General Store; turn right onto TR 119, then right again on TR 121. It's on the right at 2761 TR 121, Millersburg, Oh 44654. They tell me they have no hours here. I guess that means if they're home, they're open—except on Sunday, of course.

2. **Atlee A. Barkman** makes benches, porch swings, and those large, martin bird houses. You'll see plenty of these birdhouses in the area because martins eat lots of mosquitoes. Find him at 5020 CR 59, Baltic, OH 43804.

3. Levi N. Raber owns **Beck's Mills Furniture Shop** at 5435 CR 19, Millersburg, OH 44654. He makes custom furniture in oak and cherry—hutches, desks, tables, chairs, bedroom sets, and grandfather clocks. You'll have to get on his waiting list or, if something catches your eye, buy right off his showroom floor. The shop is about ½ mi. west of town.

4. Junior A. Yoder operates **Country Hickory Rocker Shop**, 5798 TR 355, Millersburg, OH 44654. TR 355 is on the township line but this business is on the south side of the road, so it's in Mechanic Twp.

5. **Doughty Valley Crafts** is owned and operated by Lydia Ann Raber. Lydia paints glassware and the wooden toys her father makes. The Noah's ark with pairs of wooden animals would delight a little child, as would the barn, or the team of horses pulling the hay wagon. In addition to these crafts, there's also a variety of household items. Find this shop at 5781 CR 19, Millersburg, OH 44654.

6. Wholesale and retail nylon harnesses are sold at the **H & E Nylon Harness Works**, 5186 TR 118, Millersburg, OH 44654.

7. So many hickory rockers are made in Holmes Co. that some craftsmen have to go farther and farther afield to find the necessary hickory branches. The green wood, bark intact, is steamed and formed, then put together in that traditional rocker form with either oak, cherry, or walnut slats, depending on what the maker prefers or has to work with. If you're interested in trying or buying one, stop in to see Levi C. Miller at **The Hickory Rocker Shop**, 6932 CR 407, Millersburg, OH 44654.

8. **Miller's Custom Butchering** does winter processing of beef, hogs, and deer. Eli D. Miller also makes summer sausage and bologna and buys beef hides. Talk to him at 5491 CR 68, Millersburg, OH 44654, north of Beck's Mills. Open approximately October 1 to May 1.

9. At **Oak Ridge Woodworking** Norman Hershberger specializes in silver and jewelry chests. Stop in to see his handiwork at 6200 CR 59, Millersburg, OH 44654.

10. The Hershberger family operates **Scenic Country Furniture** at 4950 TR 117, Baltic, OH 43804. Most of their handiwork is sold wholesale but they will make some custom pieces. You can't help but notice what a grand view they get to see every day.

11. Another place to locate those hickory rockers is the **Woodland Rocker Shop** owned by Atlee C. Yoder. His father-in-law sells these rockers at his home in Clark Twp. (see the Charm and Clark Twp. chapter for location), but you can also buy one here. Located at 4901 TR 117, Baltic, OH 43804.

12. As you can see, hickory rocker makers are plentiful in this township. Our fourth and final craftsman is Abe J. Yoder, who makes hickory rockers at his home. Find **Yoder's Rocker Shop** on TR 116.

Lodging

13. If you're looking for a quiet getaway where you can unwind, you might want to make reservations at **Tina's House**. This remodeled 19th century home sits about ¼ mi. off the road. You can enjoy the seclusion from the front porch or the deck in back and there is no phone or TV to interrupt it. There are two bedrooms on the second floor with queen and double beds in each room. On the first floor there's a living room, kitchen, and bath with shower. This is not a bed and breakfast establishment, so no meals are served. However, you can bring your own groceries and cook in the furnished kitchen if you'd like to. Note: You need to bring your own towels. Children are welcome. Rates start at $50 for two adults. Tina's House is open from April until after Thanksgiving weekend. It's located on CR 19 northeast of Beck's Mills and about 2½ mi. west of Charm. There's no sign to point it out on CR 19, however, so contact manager Miriam Weaver at 330-674-6268 or 6521 CR 189, Millersburg, OH 44654, for information and reservations.

Please Note: The Amish do not have telephones in their homes. If you want information on products, services, or prices, drop a letter into the mail. Enclose a self-addressed, stamped postcard or envelope for their convenience. They will reply.

Berlin Twp.
Holmes County

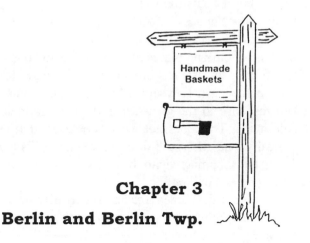

Chapter 3

Berlin and Berlin Twp.

For many years the Mecca for visitors to Amish country has been Berlin. There aren't many days that pass without an influx of people from outside the area, especially on Fridays and Saturdays. More and more it's true even in the dead of winter—if the weather's decent, they'll come!

So, what can I tell you about Berlin that you don't already know? I'll tell you that, if you want to pronounce it like the natives, you say BER-lin with the accent on the first syllable (as opposed to ber-LIN, as in Germany).

Berlin was the first village formed in the county. That was in 1816. It was the site of the first blacksmith shop in the county, owned by one Jacob Korn, a Pennsylvania German. Now a dry town, at one time there were five saloons in the community. Hard to believe these days. Berlin was also the first village to have a factory—the Braden and Hassock (or Hasack) Farm Implement and Iron Company. These and others allow Berlin to claim many of the "firsts" in the county.

When Holmes County was formed in 1824, Berlin competed with Millersburg and the hope-to-be community of Lima for county seat. Millersburg was chosen because of its more central location and abundance of nearby water.

Today, Berlin is home to many interesting businesses which cater to Amish country visitors. Horses and buggies compete with car and truck traffic and parking is admittedly a problem. If you're having trouble finding a parking spot, try the parking lot at the elementary school which is a couple blocks west of downtown. You'll have to walk a little, but it beats the frustration. Of course, this only works when school is not in session. Another place that might have a spot for your vehicle is just north on US 62 on the right. It seems to be a no-man's land of parking places, unattached to any business.

The influx of tourists has brought many changes to this village, especially in the past 10 years. More and more businesses have started in response to the great demand for crafts and all sorts of handmade items. This does not mean, however, that everything in town is locally made as you'll discover when you look around. But, since this is the shopping capitol of Amish country, you'll have lots of fun browsing and buying.

Everyone knew the modern era had finally arrived in Berlin when the county's first Burger King opened on the west edge of town in April 1994.

In 1995 new "Welcome to Berlin" signs were erected to greet everyone. The local paper says the Ohio Dept. of Transportation is making noises—finally—about addressing the parking and traffic problems. Widening SR 39/US 62 through the downtown, providing turning lanes, crosswalks, and traffic lights are much needed in this community of 4,000.

For a packet of information on Berlin, write or call the Berlin Area Visitors' Bureau, P.O. Box 177, Berlin, OH 44610; PH: 330-893-3467. Their brochure includes a map of the downtown area showing many business locations. Lack of a map will not, however, be a hindrance since Berlin is small by urban standards and the majority of businesses are stretched along Main St. which is SR 39 and US 62. These highways divide on the east side of town, SR 39 heading east toward Walnut Creek, and US 62 going north toward Winesburg.

A money-saving tip you might want to consider is Grandma's Book of Savings, a coupon book for stores and restaurants throughout Amish country. Created by Brian Conn, it offers more than $1,000 worth of savings. The $10 booklet is issued each year. It's sold in many local shops but if you're interested in getting one of these before you arrive, contact Brian at 330-893-3399 or write to P.O. Box 422, Berlin, OH 44610.

Well, this is going to be a lengthy chapter, so let's get started. There's more than enough to see right in Berlin to keep visitors busy for a couple of days, to say nothing of everything else in this township. After all, you're in the heart of Amish country now.

BERLIN

The **Amish Collection Country Shoppe** opened a third store in downtown Berlin since the last edition of this book. Their other shops are in Sugarcreek and Hartville. Find dolls, J. Brownberry sweatshirts and jackets, a large selection of goose gear, painted mailboxes, a roomful of baskets and wreaths, and plenty more. PH: 330-893-3711. Hours Mon.-Sat. 10 am-5 pm.

With an eclectic mix of antiques and collectibles, **The Amish Connection** might have just the piece you've been looking for. Proprietor Pat Ashburn specializes in American antiques, particularly Hoosier cabinets, as well as linens, old toys, and decorator accents. Located at 4977 W. Main St. where Country From the Heart used to be. PH: 330-893-3747. Hours Tues.-Sat. 10 am-5 pm.

Paige Pottery, wire art, pierced tin, rugs, Amish prints, Ruth's Amish Dolls, doilies, placemats, and accent furniture are just some of what awaits eager shoppers at **Arvada's Gift Chalet**. Find Arvada Everhart's shop on Main St. PH: 330-893-3124. Open Mon.-Sat. 10 am-5 pm.

If you like antiques, you'll want to be sure to see the new **Berlin Antique Mall**. Vendors have filled it's 8,400 sq.ft. with all sorts of antiques and collectibles. At 4898 W. Main St.. PH: 330-893-3051. Hours are Mon.-Sat. 9 am-5 pm.

Berlin Bulk Foods has all your kitchen staples, over sixty different spices, baking mixes, and an assortment of meats and cheeses. Find this store at 2 N. Market St. PH: 330-893-2353. Hours are Mon.-Sat. 8 am-5 pm.

You'll fall in love with **Berlin Creek Gallery**. Featuring the prints of such artists as P. Buckley Moss, Diane Graebner, Steve Polomchak, Thomas Kinkade, Al Koenig, and N.A. Noel, this gallery is a feast for the eyes. Here, too, is Nancy's Creative Picture Framing. You'll see it enhancing the artwork on display and it can be yours if you bring in a print or photo you want framed. Some artists are occasional visitors to the Gallery. Call ahead to find out when the next artist visit is planned. Located on Main St. at 5042 SR 39 on the west side of town. PH: 330-893-2686. Open Mon.-Sat. 10 am-5 pm and also by appointment.

Originally a barn, **Berlin Country Market** is three levels full of interesting gifts and home decorating items. Lamps, Fenton glass, oak and pine furniture, baskets, wreaths, silk and dried arrangements, Amish-made wooden toys, and lots more would be appreciated in any home. Located beside Dutch Country Restaurant on the east side of town. PH: 330-893-2799. Hours are Mon.-Sat. 10 am-5 pm.

Berlin Gardens is the place to go if you're looking for something to dress up your yard or garden. They have gazebos, bridges, arbors, lawn furniture, windmills, wishing wells, mailboxes, bird feeders, etc. Next to Raber's Nursery & Greenhouse on the west side of town. Answering service: 330-893-3411. Open Mon.-Sat. 9 am-5 pm. Closed in Jan.

Hand-thrown stoneware pottery from Three Rivers Pottery is available at the **Berlin Pottery House** which opened in the spring of 1995. There's a full line of dinnerware with all the accessories and it's microwave and dishwasher safe. Located at 4838 E. Main St. PH: 330-893-4141. Hours are 10 am-5 pm Mon.-Sat.

Berlin Village Mall on the west edge of town is one of the newest additions to the community. Several shops are located in this strip mall which opened early in 1995:

Catalpa Trading Company has fossils, scrimshaw, rocks, jewelry, knives, handmade brooms, canes, and more.

Der Mortar and Pestle is a gift shop featuring cards, glassware, collectibles like thimbles, pewter, mortars and pestles of wood and stone, carved wooden boxes, framed prints, cards, and candies. They have a Christmas room open year 'round. PH: 330-893-3731. Open Mon.-Sat. 9 am-5 pm.

Savannah Sweets can satisfy any sweet tooth with candies—120 different kinds—from chocolates such as macadamia nut truffles and raspberry jellies to gourmet jelly beans, violet pastilles from France, and nuts. PH: 330-893-3737. Open 10 am-6 pm Mon.-Sat.

Spector's moved their Millersburg store to the mall in Berlin and offer a complete line of dry goods from fabrics and sewing notions to quilt patterns, needlework kits, and embroidery floss. They also have some kitchenware, undergarments and socks, books, and baby clothing. Open Mon.-Thurs. 8 am-5 pm; Fri. until 6 pm, and Sat. until 4 pm.

Buggy Trail Tours leaves from Der Bake Oven II's parking lot Mon.-Sat. See Chapter 1, Tips for Travelers, to read more about it.

The **Clutter Box** not only has a new location but a new focus. They moved to 4877 W. Main St. and now have about 30 crafters producing items from handwoven rugs to Amish-made nightware. Upstairs in Elsie's Attic you'll find old bottles, collectibles, and prints. PH: 330-893-3295. Hours are 10 am-5 pm Mon.-Thurs. and until 6 pm on Fri. and Sat.

With a showroom of almost 10,000 sq.ft., **The Colonial House** has plenty of furniture to see. Solid oak and pine are fashioned by Amish craftsmen into cupboards, cabinets, hutches, tables, chairs, and smaller items as well. If you like oak, you'll enjoy this. Located right on Main St. in downtown Berlin. PH: 330-893-2891. Hours are Mon.-Sat. 10 am-5 pm.

Country Casual Shop has a good mix of gifts, crafts, and Shaker-style, Amish-made unfinished furniture. Lots of interesting and fun country items in this old Amish farmhouse. Located just north of the SR 39 and US 62 intersection on the west side of US 62. PH: 330-893-3662. Hours during the summer are Mon.-Thurs. 10 am-5 pm; Fri. and Sat. until 6 pm. They're closed in Jan.; otherwise, they're open during the winter Mon.-Fri. noon-4:30 pm and Sat. 10 am-5 pm.

This store is for serious crafters. **Country Craft Cupboard** has lots of great supplies for all sorts of handmade items. Whether you want to stencil the walls of your home, make floral arrangements, sew your own Amish dolls, paint a T-shirt, or decorate a birthday cake for someone special, you'll find everything you need to do your own creating. Just walking in the door will get those creative juices flowing and now they have two floors! Find this shop on Main St. next door to The Stitching House. PH: 330-893-3163. Open Mon.-Sat. 10 am-5 pm.

Country From The Heart also made a move recently—to 4827 E. Main St. Their country folk art designs are found in Noah's ark items, pigs, cows, sheep, cats, bears, and villages. They also carry handmade dolls, primitive baskets, candles, Attic Babies, dried flowers and wreaths, and much more. PH: 330-893-3555. They're open Mon.-Sat. 10 am-5 pm.

Gift baskets for all occasions are at **The Country Gingerbread Shoppe** located where The Gingerbread House was. They have gourmet food items, jewelry, pottery, and hand-loomed rag rugs and placemats made on their in-store loom. At 4925 W. Main St. PH: 330-893-2088. Open April-December, Mon.-Sat. 10 am-5 pm.

Customers pick the stain and dimensions they desire, so each piece of bedroom or dining room furniture is custom-made just for them at **Country Junction**. In addition, doll collectors will delight in the selections from Zook, Georgetown, Good-Krugar, and others. You can't miss this store on the west side of town because there's a circa 1930 Amish buggy setting in the front yard. At 5039 SR 39. PH: 330-893-3452. Open Mon.-Sat. 10 am-5 pm.

Dad's Toys opened in the Berlin Village Mall but has already moved to the east side of town at 4787 E. Main St. As the name implies, boys of all ages will delight in the farm toys, banks, Breyer horses, tractor-trailer replicas, collectible cars, etc. An 80-page catalog is available. PH: 330-893-4100. Opne Mon.-Sat. 10 am-5 pm.

Der Bake Oven II is the downtown branch of the original Der Bake Oven (see listing in Berlin Twp.). Hungry shoppers can indulge in home-baked pastries, breads, rolls, cookies, cakes, and pies, or have some hand-dipped ice cream, soft yogurt, or old-fashioned custard. Located on the south side of SR 39 at the intersection of US 62. PH: 330-893-3365. Hours are Mon.-Thurs. 6 am-5 pm; Fri. until 5:30 pm; Sat. until 6 pm.

Both antique and reproduction jewelry, particularly marcasites, garnets, and Black Hills gold, is the specialty at **The English Ladies' Nostalgia Shoppe**. They also have toiletries, glass, old books, and Victorian lithographs. You can often shop here to the accompaniment of classical music. I love it! Find this shop at 4840 E. Main St. PH: 330-893-2036. Hours are Mon.-Sat. 10 am-5 pm.

Gas is sold in Berlin at The Dutch Cupboard. See their listing under "Dining" for hours.

German Village is the name of the local IGA. If you're hungry, check out the small cafeteria at the back of the store. There are tables where you can sit and enjoy cabbage rolls, chicken divan, lasagna, or whatever's on today's menu. However, there's more under this roof than just groceries and something to eat. The **Gospel Book Store** is just inside the front door and offers books, office and religious supplies, and some gift items. Then there's **Kandel's V&S Variety Store** which, as the name promises, has a little bit of everything. Finally, there's **Plain & Fancy Fabrics** with fashion and quilt fabrics, notions, patterns, yarn, and craft supplies. German Village IGA is located on Oak St., one block south of SR 39, and is open Mon.-Sat. 7 am-8 pm. The other stores under this roof don't necessarily keep the same hours.

Hartman's Home Fresh Foods is, as the name implies, an emporium of taste treats. What are you looking for? Fudge or hand-dipped chocolates such as turtles with pecans and caramel centers? Maybe jams, jellies, maple or fruit syrups, fruit butters such as apricot or pumpkin, bread and butter pickles, and corn relish are more to your liking. All of these plus muffin and pancake mixes, popcorn, cookbooks, nuts, and homemade ice cream are to be found in this tempting store. Information on mail order is available by writing to P.O. Box 104, Berlin, OH 44610. The store is on Main St. PH: 330-893-3118. Open Mon.-Sat. 10 am-5 pm.

You can observe the quilt-making process on the first and last Tuesdays of each month at **Helping Hands Quilt Shop**. If you can't find a quilt in stock that's quite right, you can get one custom-made. Depending on the pattern you choose, you may wait a year. Helping

Hands was the first craft shop in Berlin. That was in 1974. They have ready-cut quilt kits and all the supplies would-be quilters could ask for. This is paradise for anyone who wants to buy or likes to make any of the needlework crafts. Shoppers can also find wallhangings, pillows, table runners, crib quilts, and other quilted items. One thing you may not know about Helping Hands is that all profits—minus expenses, of course—go to charity. Hats off to owner Alma Mullet! Find this busy shop in the heart of Berlin on Main St. Mailing address is P.O. Box 183, Berlin, OH 44610. PH: 330-893-2233 or 893-2234. Hours are Mon.-Sat. 9 am-5 pm.

John's Wood Shop features rockers from child-sized to hickory, shelving, towel bars and racks, cedar bluebird and wren houses, suet and seed feeders, cedar chests, dining room furniture, and crates to use as storage units. Most of the locally made furnishings are oak, but they also have some unfinished pine pieces. On the porch is outdoor furniture such as swings, gliders, and Adirondack chairs. Located on the left just north of the intersection on US 62. PH: 330-893-3448. Hours are Mon.-Sat. 10 am-5 pm.

The work of contemporary Mennonite and Amish artists is displayed at **Kaufman Gallery**. There's a variety of mediums for sale from artist-designed quilts, great functional pottery, photos, Fraktur painting, to Amish folk art. Those of you expecting to find only conservative artwork will be surprised, so my advice is don't have any preconceived notions. This is a terrific place to browse and decide which piece would look just right in your home. Located on the first floor of the historic Pomerene House on Main St. Address is P.O. Box 85, Berlin, OH 44610. PH: 330-893-2842. Open Mon.-Sat. 1-5 pm from June through Oct. Saturdays only April-May and Nov.-Dec. By appointment Jan.-March.

Some remodeling and a new side entrance have enhanced the offerings at **Nature's Paradise**. Organic and specialty foods, maple syrup, fresh-ground peanut butter, apple butter, bulk foods, dried fruits, and nuts line up in delicious array on the shelves. If you're into homeopathy, herbal medicine, or have considered that there might be a more natural way to treat some ailments, you'll find a big selection of herbal teas, extracts, vitamin supplements, etc., and a book rack containing titles to help you learn more about it. Located on the corner of Main and Market Sts. PH: 330-893-2006. Hours are Mon.-Sat. 8 am-6 pm; until 8 pm on Wed. and Fri.

The place in Berlin for perennials, bulbs, seeds, bedding plants, and all your gardening needs is **Raber's Greenhouse & Nursery**. Scratch your gardening itch here on the west side of town. Closed after Christmas until early Feb. Hours Mon.-Sat. are 8 am-5 pm. Extended hours during the spring gardening season.

Todd and Royce Ann Peck started **Royce Craft Baskets** in the basement of their Coshocton home in 1988. Today the store in Berlin is one of three selling their popular handwoven maple-splint baskets, all designed by Royce Ann. Some have oak handles; some are dyed in combinations of five colors; some have lids or leather "ears." Sizes range from large to tiny. There's bound to be a basket here to charm you. If you're interested in mail order, they have color literature. Inquire at P.O. Box 144, Coshocton, OH 43812. Located on E. Main St. in Berlin. PH: 1-800-882-1128. Open Mon.-Sat. 10 am-5 pm.

Sarah McClure opened **Sara's Folk Art** on the north side of Dutch Country Kitchen (formerly Berlin House Restaurant). This shop features primitive woodcrafts, Raggedy Ann and Amish dolls, bird houses and benches, pottery, and flower arrangements. PH: 330-893-3726. Hours Mon.-Sat. 10 am-5 pm.

Schrock's Heritage House contains 2 floors and 14,000 sq.ft. of showroom to show off locally made solid oak and cherry furnishings and woodcrafts. Find Schrock's just east of the SR 39 and US 62 intersection. PH: 330-893-2242. Hours are 10 am-5 pm Mon.-Sat.

Sol's Exchange expanded by remodeling a 6,000 sq.ft. building right next door into **Sol's Palace**. They're both popular craft malls where everything is handmade. Find primitive, Victorian, and country arts and crafts in a fun mix with something for everybody. Enjoy! Located at 4914 W. Main. PH: 330-893-3134. Open Mon.-Sat. 10 am-5 pm.

Capturing the charm of an old-fashioned mercantile is **Sommer's General Store**. Barrels of candies, leather goods from Weaver

The former Berlin House Restaurant underwent changes in both management and name, reopening as **Dutch Country Restaurant** early in 1995. Breakfast includes all your favorites. On the lunch and supper menu are sandwiches and dinners of broasted chicken, ham, roast beef, pork chops, etc. Currently, they're serving all-you-can-eat fish on Fridays from 4-8 pm for $5.95. A children's menu is available. Located at the intersection of SR 39 and US 62 where you can't miss it. PH: 330-893-4142. Hours are Mon.-Sat. 6 am-8 pm.

I'm putting **The Dutch Cupboard** here because they serve food. They offer daily hot specials for the lunch crowd Mon.-Fri. Cold salads and sandwiches are also available, even on Sat. and Sun. This is a convenience store with grocery items and it sells Shell gasoline. You can get free coffee with a fill-up. PH: 330-893-3125. Fax in your order to 330-893-4140. Hours are Mon.-Thurs. 6 am-11:30 pm; Fri. and Sat. until midnight; Sun. 7:30 am-11 pm.

The Outback & Pizzeria is a good place to satisfy your taste for pizza. They also have subs and other sandwiches, chicken dinners, salads, and a variety of luscious ice cream desserts. Lunch and dinner specials are offered. Located next to the Dutch Cupboard on the west side of town on SR 39. PH: 330-893-3191. Hours are Mon.-Sat. 10 am-10 pm.

Lodging

Berlin Village Inn has 22 rooms in a motel setting. Each room has A/C, cable TV, and phone. Rates are $42 for 1 person; 2 persons with 2 beds are $54. AAA rated. Stay Sundays by reservation only because the office is closed. Located on the west edge of town at 5135 SR 39, Berlin, OH 44610. PH: 330-893-2861 for reservations.

Scheduled to open early in 1996 is **Carriage House Inn**. The four rooms with private baths will be named after a type of carriage and Diane Graebner is doing a special painting for each. A continental breakfast will be served. Rates are expected to be $75-$80 per couple in the summer and $55 in the winter. Located down the street from Donna's Country B&B at 5453 East St. PH: 330-893-2226 for reservations.

If you're celebrating a special occasion with your partner, you might enjoy the romance of the cottages at **Donna's Country Bed & Breakfast**. They have heart-shaped, waterfall Jacuzzis, fireplaces, cathedral ceilings with skylights, kitchenettes, built-in stereo systems, and cable TVs. In addition, there are three rooms with private baths, two of them suites with kitchenettes, in the house. They also have a log cabin on 6 acres about a mile from town which sleeps two. Rates are $65 to $149.95. A full, country-style breakfast is served if you stay in the cottages and a continental breakfast for the other accommodations. Located ½ block south of SR 39 on East St. Write P.O. Box 307, Berlin, OH 44610, or call 1-800-320-3338.

Jake n' Ivy's Overnight Rooms has 3 rooms with private baths and A/C for guests. A continental breakfast is served and children are welcome but there are no TVs. Rate is $60 per couple. Turn north at Berlin Village Mall. Located at 5409 Tom Lion Rd. (TR 356). PH: 330-893-3215 for reservations.

Guests at the **Overnite Get Away** can sit on the porch swing and enjoy the view. By the spring of 1996 they should have added four more rooms, for a total of six. Located behind the Wallpaper Place on the west side of town. Write P.O. Box 416, Berlin, OH 44610, or call 330-893-2529 for information about current rates and reservations.

Paul and Ella Coblentz have changed the location of **Pine Lane Tourist Lodging**. They're farther back the lane in the woods now and have 3 rooms, one with 2 double beds, one with 1 double bed, and the third with a single bed. Kitchen facilities are available. Their rates are the best bargain around—$20 per couple. Children are welcome and ages birth-5 are free. Ask about their family rates. Turn off SR 39 at Raber's Greenhouse, the mailing address is 5011 TR 359, Millersburg, OH 44654. PH: 330-893-2641 for reservations.

If you'd enjoy staying in a home that's on the National Register of Historic Places, **Pomerene House** is for you. This former home of Dr. and Mrs. Peter Pomerene and their 11 children offers a 2-room upstairs suite. The sitting room furnishings were made locally and the bedroom boasts the original interior shutters and Victorian decor. In the bath the original clawfoot tub has been modernized with a hand-held shower. Two single beds for additional persons, A/C, and ceiling fans are available. Rates for 1 or 2 people are $50; 3 or 4 persons $60 or $70. An additional suite with a double bed and kitchenette is available for parties of 5 or 6 persons for $50. Included is a complimentary breakfast at a local restaurant. No children under 6, smoking, or pets. Located above the Kaufman Gallery right on Main St. (US 39). Write to P.O. Box 185, Berlin, OH 44610, or call mornings or evenings 330-893-2842.

One of the new lodging establishments in town is **The Robin's Nest**, located on US 62 about ¼ mi. north, next to John's Woodshop. Four rooms are available—a Victorian Room with king-sized bed, bath, and sitting room; a Country Room with queen-sized bed, bath, and sitting; and two rooms with queen-sized beds, a bath, and sitting room on the second floor. All rooms have private entries, phones, TVs, A/C, microwaves, coffee makers, and refrigerators. Rates $65 to $75. Located at 4727 US 62. PH: 330-893-2045 or 893-3744 for reservations.

Shaver's Bed & Breakfast is currently on the real estate market, so things may change at this location soon. They have 3 rooms—one with a queen-sized bed, one with a double bed, and the third with a single bed. A continental breakfast of coffee, tea, and juice with doughnuts and rolls from a local Amish bakery is offered. Central A/C and cable TV is available. Located just north of the US 62 intersection. Write to Eric and Cheryl Shaver at P.O. Box 286, Berlin, OH 44610, or call 330-893-3061 for rates and further information.

Sommerset Tourist Rooms is another new lodging facility now open. Two rooms are available, one with 2 full beds, the other with a queen-sized bed and a single. A crib can be provided and a TV jack is also available. Private baths. The small kitchen has a refrigerator, microwave, stove, oven and coffee maker. Coffee and tea are furnished. Rates are $50 per couple with additional persons $5. Turn off SR 39/US 62 at Raber's Greenhouse. Located at 5094 TR 359 (Sommerset Rd.). Call 330-893-3130 or 1-800-337-6414 for reservations.

Towne House Bed & Breakfast has two suites in their 2-story house. They have A/C but no TVs. Decorated with Early American and Victorian furnishings, there's room enough for a family in the 3-bed suite. The other suite has one double bed. Children are welcome and, if they're 12 and under, they stay for free. Rates are $55 per couple. Mon.-Sat. guests can enjoy anything on the breakfast menu at Boyd & Wurthmann's Restaurant. On Sundays when the restaurant is closed, a continental breakfast is served. Located next to Berlin Bulk Foods on N. Market St. just off SR 39 within walking distance of all the downtown shops. Reservations can be made by calling Berlin Bulk Foods at 330-893-2353. Evenings call 330-893-2481.

BERLIN TWP.

1. One mile east of Berlin on SR 39 is the **Amish Farm** where visitors can get a guided tour of an Amish home and buggy rides. There is a 20 min. slide presentation about the Amish way of life and both kids and adults will enjoy seeing the farm animals. It's a good introduction to the Amish lifestyle. Rates of $5.50 for adults and $4 for children 2-12 include the tour, slide presentation, and buggy ride and you should allow about 2 hrs. to see all that's here. PH: 330-893-3232. Open April-Oct. Mon.-Fri. 10 am-5 pm; Sat. until 6 pm.

A whole complex of shops have grown up around the Amish Farm, so you'll want to visit these businesses while you're there:

Dutch Heritage Country Store is full of specialty shops: **'Tis the Season** is a year 'round Christmas shop; **I Love Amish Country** is filled with items such as Amish dolls, bonnets, etc., that pertain to Amish country; **A Victorian Summer** is a frilly paradise of Victorian decor; **Birdz-N-Beez Garden Shoppe** appeals to anyone who gardens. One shop runs into another in an interesting series of vignettes that will appeal to shoppers. PH: 330-893-3232. On the opposite end of the building is **Finders Keepers** featuring plenty of decorative wooden items, rag rugs, walking sticks, pierced tin, and stoneware in a rustic setting. PH: 330-893-3528. Hours are 10 am-5 pm Mon.-Fri. and Sat. until 6 pm.

Dutch Heritage Woodcrafts is located in an old barn. Oak furnishings are featured here. Visitors can watch the craftsmen at work through the large windows in the back. PH: 330-893-2211. Hours are Mon.-Sat. 10 am-5 pm.

Gramma Fannie's Quilt Barn offers quilt patterns and kits for the do-it-yourselfer as well as bolts of calico and sewing notions. If you can't find a quilt that suits you on the large display rack upstairs, you can order one custom-made. There is also a large frame upstairs with a quilt-in-progress where you can watch the progress on one of tomorrow's heirlooms. PH: 330-893-3232. From April-Nov. they're open Mon.-Fri. 10 am-5 pm; Sat. until 6 pm. Winter hours are noon-5 pm and Sat. 10 am-5 pm.

Another business at this location is **Hiland Buggy Shop**. You'll see it behind the Dutch Heritage Country Store.

The Leather Shop features leather products from jackets and hats to saddle bags and belts. PH: 330-893-3633. Hours are Mon.-Sat. 10 am-5 pm.

As of this writing, both The Fort and Hoopz Slamball Coliseum, listed in the second edition, have gone out of business.

2. If you've been looking for a unique souvenir of Amish country, stop by **Berlin Furniture** to look at their pens and pencils handmade in 20 different woods. They can be laser engraved if you choose. Berlin Furniture carries a variety of small gift items such as wooden pen boxes, a wooden tape measure, clocks, pocket knives, and toys. They also have oak and cherry furnishings and Berlin Flyer wagons. Located at 5044 CR 120, Millersburg, OH 44654. Turn south at the Baptist Church in Berlin. Market St. becomes CR 120. Hours are Mon.-Fri. 7 am-5 pm; Sat. until 4 pm.

3. **Berlin Shoe Repair** can re-sole, re-heel, and re-stitch seams, of course, but they also sell shoes, boots, and rubber footwear. Find this shop at 5770 CR 77, Millersburg, OH 44654.

4. Custom-made furniture built right on the premises is what you'll find at **Berlin View Woodcraft**. Their specialty is rolltop desks but they also craft bedroom furniture, entertainment centers, tables, and chairs. Owners Terry and Chris Steiner do business at 5520 CR 77, Millersburg, OH 44654. PH: 330-893-2636. Hours are Mon.-Sat. 9 am-5 pm.

5. Find the **Bunker Hill Blacksmith** here on CR 77.

6. A country hardware with plenty of non-electric items is as close as **Bunker Hill Hardware**. Located 1 mi. north of Berlin at 5916 CR 77, Millersburg, OH 44654. Hours are Mon.-Sat. 8 am-6 pm.

7. Gideon Troyer makes **cedar chests** south of Berlin on CR 120 (turn south on Market St.). The sign simply says "cedar chests" and it's the second farm down the lane.

8. **Cedar chests** are also made at the home of Wayne Troyer, 6531 TR 362, Millersburg, OH 44654. It's the first place north of CR 207.

9. There are 12 styles of tables and 13 styles of chairs to choose from at **Country Furniture & Bookstore** and they're all locally made. They also have living room and bedroom suites, mattresses, cupboards, bookcases, hutches, desks, and an interesting selection of books and Bibles. Find this store just east off CR 77 at 4329 CR 168, Millersburg OH 44654. Hours are Mon. and Fri. 9 am-6 pm; Tues., Wed. and Thurs. until 5 pm and Sat. until 4 pm.

10. If you're hungry for some home-baked goodies, stop at **Der Bake Oven**. Bread, rolls, pastries, cookies, donuts, cakes, and pies are available here in mouth-watering variety. Located at the intersection of CRs 207 and 77 north of Berlin. They have a second store, Der Bake Oven II, right in town. PH: 330-893-2114. Hours are Mon.-Sat. 7 am-5 pm. Closed on Saturdays in Jan. and Feb.

11. The home of the original baby Swiss cheese, making about 3,000 small, round wheels each day, is **Guggisberg Cheese**. Before noon you can watch the cheesemakers at work through the large windows at the back of the gift shop. Imported and domestic cheeses of many varieties are for sale and the gift shop has cuckoo clocks, cookbooks, Swiss chocolates and other gourmet-type foods, and many European items. They have a mail order catalog available and ship gift baskets anywhere (PH: 1-800-262-2505). Find this popular business at 5060 SR 557, Millersburg, OH 44654. Hours April-Nov. are Mon.-Sat. 8 am-6 pm; Sun. 11 am-4 pm. Closed Sundays after Christmas.

12. **Handmade baskets** are made by the Eli H.E. Stutzman family on their farm east of Berlin at 4093 SR 39, Millersburg, OH 44654.

They make big and little sizes in all shapes, including egg baskets. A unique double basket made specifically to sit on stair steps is rather odd-looking but quite practical.

13. Visitors to **Heini's Cheese Chalet & Country Mall** can sample over 50 varieties of cheese made here. As you walk around the gallery of refrigerated cases, you can sample all the cheeses. How about chocolate or chocolate mint cheese? (It tastes like fudge.) From sweet to tangy with garlic, pepperoni, and chive—these are just some of the cheeses available. Lowfat yogurt cheese is made here and, yes, the traditional Swiss and other varieties, most of which also come smoked. You'll find bulk foods and meats and there's a large viewing area where you can watch the cheesemaking process. A Tom Miller mural depicts the history of cheesemaking. The Lace Boutique offers curtain and table lace, dolls, candles, Precious Moments figurines, and clothing items. Gift shop hours are 10 am-5 pm Mon.-Fri. Sat. until 5:30. Take US 62 north of Berlin to the blinker light and turn left. Heini's is on your left. They have mailorder and gift baskets available by writing to 6005 CR 77, Millersburg, OH 44654, calling 330-893-2131, or faxing 330-893-2079. Cheese house hours are 8 am-5 pm Mon.-Sat. and until 7 pm April-Nov.; generally open Sun. noon-5 pm.

14. There are always fresh vegetables and fruits for sale during the season at **Hershberger's Truck Patch**. They offer baked goods from their bakery across the highway or you can stop at the bakery, too. Find a taste of country goodness here. Located on SR 557 not a mile south of SR 39. Closed during the winter.

Across the highway from the Truck Patch, blacksmith **Mose A. Hershberger** does business evenings and Sat. by appointment only. Located at 4881 TR 354, Millersburg, OH 44654.

15. Lawn furniture is the specialty at **Hershy Way Ltd.**, 5918 CR 201, Millersburg, OH 44654. PH: 330-893-2809.

16. The Amish frequently use bicycles for transportation. In this area they can get a new Fuji or Shogun bike, a reconditioned one, or have repairs done at **Hiland Bikes**. They also have all those accessories such as bells and horns, lights, racks, mirrors, etc. Located at 4860

TR 367, Millersburg, OH 44654. Open evenings 'til 8 pm; Sat. 8 am-5 pm. Closed Wed. and Sun.

17. Storage barns of all sizes are made at **JDM Structures**, 5840 CR 201, Millersburg, OH 44654. PH: 330-893-3674 (answering service). Hours Mon.-Fri. 7 am-4:30 pm; Sat. until 11 am.

18. If you love different kinds of bread the way I do, you'll want to stop at **Kauffman's Country Bakery**. How about beer bread, cheese, sourdough, herb, vegetable, wheat, English muffin, raisin, French, garlic, rye, onion rye, or cinnamon raisin? Your mouth is watering by now, isn't it? If not, think angel food cakes; fruit and cream pies; pecan, maple, and cinnamon rolls; pudding cakes; donuts; coffee cakes; whoopie pies; brownies; and cookies, cookies, cookies. Have mercy! I think you've got the picture—this is a BIG bakery with plenty of room to roam around and look things over, and we haven't even talked about the non-bakery items. Mail order is available. Located across from Heini's Cheese Chalet. Address is 4357 US 62, Millersburg, OH 44654. PH: 330-893-2129. Open 7 days a week with hours Mon.-Sat. 7 am-6 pm; Sun. noon-5 pm.

19. Just beyond Kauffman's Bakery, north on CR 77, hangs a sign advertising **lawn furniture**. If you have a need for this type of item or want to compare prices, stop by and talk to them.

20. Henry E. Mast operates **Mast's Blanket and Harness** where horse owners can get everything from driving draft harnesses to saddle pads and horse wormers. Find him at 4710 TR 370, Millersburg, OH 44654.

21. If I could advise visitors where to start in Amish country, my recommendation would be the **Mennonite Information Center**. Here the historic and religious heritage of the Amish and Mennonites is illustrated in a 265-foot circular mural, *Behalt*, meaning "to keep or remember." A half-hour guided tour follows their Anabaptist beginnings in Switzerland in 1525 to the present through the colorful mural scenes. This will give you a much clearer idea of the culture which makes Amish country so unique. The mural was painted by German-born artist, Heinz Gaugel, who maintains an office in the

building and may be on hand while you're there. He is also responsible for the magnificent sgraffito plaster mural on the outside of the building. In addition, visitors can see a 20-minute slide show on the local Amish and Mennonite community, and there is always someone on hand to answer questions. A good selection of books will assist in further exploration of the Amish-Mennonite peoples, and a gift shop sponsored by the Mennonite Central Committee provides items made by craftspeople from Third World countries and from local folks, too. Admission for the guided tour and slide show is $5.50 for adults, $2.50 for children 6-12, and under 6 are free. This should definitely be on your must-see list. The Mennonite Information Center is at 5798 CR 77, P.O. Box 324, Berlin, OH 44610. PH: 330-893-3192. Open Mon.-Sat. 9 am-5 pm.

22. The sweet rolls are of gigantic proportions and there are bread, pies, and an unending variety of cookies at **Miller's Bakery**. This Amish bakery also makes cheese tarts which are so wonderful I've developed an addiction. The sugar caramelizes a little on top of the cheese filling and underneath lurks a layer of red or black raspberry, blueberry, lemon, or another fruity flavor, making these irresistibly luscious. Don't even try to resist, enjoy! They also have homemade candies, home-canned goods, and an array of crafts. Located off SR 557 at 4280 TR 356, Millersburg, OH 44654. PH: 330-893-3002. Hours are 7 am-6 pm Mon.-Sat.

23. If you're looking for a storage barn, talk to the folks at **Miller's Storage Barns**, 4230 SR 39, Millersburg, OH 44654. PH: 330-893-3293. Hours are Mon.-Fri. 7 am-5 pm; Sat. until noon.

24. **Quilts and wallhangings** are made to order at Andy Hershberger's, 6024 CR 77, Millersburg, OH 44654. This is just north of Kauffman's Bakery.

25. **Raber's Holz Shop** will do some custom woodworking in oak and cherry but is creating mostly for the wholesale trade these days. By the way, "holz" means wood. Find Ed Raber at 6014 TR 310, Millersburg. OH 44654.

26. Ohio's oldest woolen mill, **Rastetter Woolen Mill,** is no longer

family-owned. Berlin businessman, Alan Zinck, bought the mill at auction in 1995. However, Ardie Rastetter is the manager and makes sure the mill continues to operate with the same high standards. A wool carding machine and a picking machine are more than a century and a quarter old and still used in making warm wool comforters. The machines are in use about twice a week and visitors can watch through a large observation window. Rug-weavers also work at looms, making rag rugs. Hand-hooked and braided rugs are also available as well as Hudson Bay blankets. Wool clothing is now sold at The Woolen Mill (see listing), their store in Berlin. Rastetter Woolen Mill is west of town at 5802 SR 39, Millersburg, OH 44654. PH: 330-674-2103. Open Mon.-Sat. 10 am-5 pm.

27. **Real Wood** is the name Mahlon D. Miller gave to his wholesale and retail furniture business at 6185 CR 77, Millersburg, OH. Stop in to see what he's currently working on.

29. **Stan's Meats, Inc.**, may be just the place if you're looking for freshly frozen cuts of beef or pork, including fresh and smoked casing sausage, to pack in an ice chest and take home. On CR 201 north of Dutch Harvest. PH: 330-893-2818. Open Mon.-Fri. 7 am-5 pm.

29. For your harness needs, talk to Roy A. Troyer at **Troyer's Harness Shop**. Located south of Berlin at 4977 TR 367, Millersburg, OH 44654.

30. There was no one home when I stopped, so interested visitors will have to find out for themselves exactly what kinds of oak crafts Vernon Weaver specializes in at **V-W Woodcraft**, 5071 TR 353, Millersburg, OH 44654.

31. A new complex of businesses opened at **Windmill Village** late in 1994. To keep the map as uncluttered as possible, I'll list the shops at Windmill Village first, then two that are right next door:
   Dad's Oak Furniture specializes in smaller pieces that you can take with you. Everything in the shop is locally made—tables, lamps, bookcases, small rolltop desks, etc. They are not doing any custom work at this time. PH: 330-893-3855.
   Grins & Giggles is a country gift shop that searches for the

different and unusual. Owners Harold and Karla Liggett make some of the items they sell. PH: 330-893-3660.

Holmes County Floral & Gift has cut flowers, fresh and silk floral arrangements, plants, wreaths, prints and stationery. PH: 330-893-3686.

NatureScene is one of those wonderful nature-oriented shops with birdhouses and feeders, books, tee and sweatshirts, and decorative items with a nature theme. Be sure to see owner Kent Miller's paintings on tree fungus, crates, and prints for your walls. PH: 330-893-3040.

Sonia Lee's Coffee Haus serves 8 flavors of dessert coffees and 4 flavors of hot chocolate which you can sit down and enjoy at a small table, then buy to take home. She serves bagels, donuts, and muffins and plans to have ice cream and sandwiches. PH: 330-893-3763.

Sunflower Mercantile is owned by SuAnne Yoder who makes a lot of the painted and quilted gift and decorative items. If she hasn't made it, probably a member of her family has. You'll find hand-crocheted doilies, handmade baby clothes, and lots more in this charming shop. PH: 330-893-3807.

Windmill Village is located at 4481 TR 367 across the road from Hiland High School. All the shops are open in the summer from 10 am-6 pm Mon.-Sat. Close at 5 pm in the winter.

The other two shops at this same map location number are:

Erb's Stoves & Fireplaces specializes in ventless gas fireplaces. They also sell natural gas and electric appliances—washers and dryers, ranges, refrigerators, and freezers. In addition, Edward Erb's oldest son, Duane, makes lawn furniture, swing sets, and play centers for your yard and garden. Located at 4455 TR 367 next door to Windmill Village. PH: 330-893-3903. Hours Mon.-Sat. 9 am-5 pm.

If you've got a baby on the way, you'll be interested in "furniture that grows with your child." You can see it at **Kinder Konvertibles Furniture** where they have a crib which changes to a youth bed, then into a double bed, and changing tables that convert into dressers. Bassinettes, playpens, strollers, tables and chairs, cradles, bedding, handmade wooden pull toys, and even glider rockers for mom can be found in their store next to Windmill Village at 4642 TR 367, Millersburg, OH 44654. PH: 330-893-4101. Hours are 10 am-6 pm Mon.-Sat.; noon-5 pm during the winter.

Dining

32. A popular part of the complex of businesses owned by the Guggisbergs is **Chalet in the Valley Restaurant**. Only lunch and dinner are served here. Chicken, roast beef, and/or Swiss steak with all the trimmings including dessert are served family-style. Also on the menu are Swiss and Austrian dishes such as wienerschnitzel and schwein schnitzel. The Tiroler Wurst Plate is knockwurst and bratwurst with hot German potato salad and sauerkraut. If your tastes run more toward American midwest fare, choose from T-bone and New York strip steaks, beer-batter cod, catfish, baked stuffed flounder, or chicken. On Fridays their special is all-you-can-eat cod with steak fries and salad bar for $5.75. They also offer sandwiches but these are not served after 5 pm. Try the Matterhorn for dessert. It's Swiss meringue, pineapple rings, and ice cream covered with whipped cream. Or try the Black Forest cake, apple strudel, homemade pies, or ice cream. If you're unable to eat dessert now, you can get something sweet to take with you at their bakery and ice cream shop across the highway. There's a special menu for the 10 and under gang with meals $3 or less. Chalet in the Valley is open Tues.-Sat. 11 am-8 pm and Sun. until 3 pm during the summer. They are closed Jan. and Feb. Located on SR 557 across from Guggisberg Cheese. PH: 330-893-2550.

33. **Dutch Harvest Restaurant** has become a popular dining spot since it opened a few years ago. Breakfast is served 7-11 am Mon.-Sat. and 8-11 am on Sun. You can enjoy a breakfast buffet daily March-Oct. and on Sat. and Sun. from Nov.-Feb. Family-style dinners are as popular here as elsewhere with chicken, ham, and roast beef. Currently, Wednesday's special is barbequed pork ribs and Friday's is all-you-can-eat wings or fish. Soups, sandwiches, and salads are on the lunch and supper menu. Of course, they have plate dinners—Swiss steak, pan-fried and broasted chicken, liver and onions, and turkey are among the choices. And there's always dessert if you can hold it. Amish pudding, apple dumplings, fruit and cream pies are just some of the sweet treats to choose from. No room? Buy one of the baked goods on display to enjoy later. They have a children's menu with favorite dinner and sandwich choices. When you're finished with your meal, be sure to wander through their lovely

gift shop with a variety of Victorian, country, and children's items. Located at the intersection of CR 201 and SR 39. PH: 330-893-3333. Hours are Mon.-Sat. 7 am-8 pm; Sun. 8 am-3 pm.

Lodging

Located at #33 beside Dutch Harvest Restaurant is the **Amish Country Inn**. They've added 15 more rooms, so there are now 50 here with A/C, phones, and cable TVs. Rates for standard rooms are $56.95 July through Oct., double occupancy; $6 more for a deluxe room with a balcony or patio; $3 more for a room with a king-sized bed or handicap facilities. Extra persons are $5 for adults, $3 for children 12-17, and under 12 stay free. Cots and cribs are available for $5. They have a VCR and refrigerators to rent. Passes to use The Club are included in the cost of a suite and are available for $4 for adults and $1.25 for children 12 and under. The pass allows you to use the pool, hot tub, and steam room on Mon.-Fri. until 11 pm, on Sat. until 10 pm, and on Sun. from noon-5 pm. Located a mile west of Berlin just north of SR 39 on CR 201. PH: 330-893-3000.

34. Jr. and Wanda Miller built a brand new home and opened **The Cape Cod Bed and Breakfast** in 1995. Located in what seems like an out-of-the-way spot with plenty of peaceful seclusion, it is just minutes from Berlin. Two rooms with private baths, A/C, TVs, and queen-sized beds. A single bed is available for one room. Continental breakfast is served. Rates $55 per night. Located at 6194 TR 362, Millersburg, OH 44654. PH: 330-893-2225.

If staying in a rustic cabin in Amish country sounds like fun, **Countryside Camper's Paradise** is the place for you. There are 4 furnished cabins here with cast iron woodburning stoves, lofts with 2 full-size mattresses, kerosene lamps, and 2-burner Coleman gas stoves. Some have sofa sleepers and can sleep 8. There are picnic tables, a centrally located water pump and toilets outside, and the showers are in the basement of Miller's Bakery. The cabins are furnished except for your food, sleeping bags, and ice for the ice chest. Rates are $16 per adult; ages 6-12 $4, and under 6 free. Special rates are available with 4 adults in one cabin for $12 each or a weekly rate of 6 adults in one cabin for $8.50 each. Ask about other specials. Next to Miller's Bakery (#22 on the map) at 4280 TR 356, Millersburg, OH 44654. You can call for reservations on Mondays at 330-893-3002.

35. **Das Gasthaus** is a home in the country, surrounded by farmland, but only 5 minutes from Berlin. There are 4 bedrooms with queen beds. One room has 2 double beds. The living room and kitchen downstairs are completely furnished and at your disposal. Children are welcome and cots available but, if you need an extra room, it's $25 more. All rooms have private baths. A continental breakfast is furnished. The house has A/C and a large porch and deck where you can enjoy the view. Rate is $50 per couple. Your hosts are John and Barbara Schlabach. Das Gasthaus is at 4821 CR 207, Millersburg, OH 44654. PH: 330-893-3089 for more information or reservations.

36. On a hilltop with a spectacular view and plenty of peace and quiet is **Guggisberg Swiss Inn**. There are 23 rooms with 2 double beds plus a honeymoon suite with a Jacuzzi, kitchenette, and queen-sized bed. A complimentary Swiss breakfast, which usually includes a meat and cheese platter, pastries, juice, coffee, tea, and milk, is served each morning in the lobby. Rates for 2 persons are $79 on the first floor, $84 on the second floor, and $135 for the honeymoon suite. Children under 12 stay free. Sleigh rides in the winter and carriage rides in the summer are available. Guests can enjoy these for $5 per person. Find this inn just south of Chalet in the Valley Restaurant at 5025 SR 557, Charm, OH 44617. PH: 330-893-3600.

37. Another new bed and breakfast establishment is **Katelynn's Cottage**. Right now they have only one room, but may add four more in 1996. This room has a private entrance, bath with skylight and sunken tub, stone fireplace, and king-sized bed. A swim pass at The Club is included as well as either a continental breakfast on premises or the breakfast buffet at the Dutch Harvest Restaurant. Rate is $100 per night. Located at 5734 CR 203 (Honey Run Rd.), Millersburg, OH 44654. PH: 1-800-874-9006.

38. Two private suites above a garage are available for guests at **Traveler's Country Loft**. These suites are spacious and very nicely decorated. Each has a bedroom with double bed; bath; kitchenette

with sink, refrigerator, toaster oven, and microwave; a small table with two chairs; and a living area with sofa, hickory rocker, and cable TV. Coffee is furnished for the coffeemaker, and the rooms have A/C. On the west side away from the road is a small balcony furnished with seating and a table where you can enjoy a peaceful interlude. Summer rates are $60; winter rates are $45. Turn south on SR 557 off SR 39 and it's the first home on your right. PH: 330-674-5854.

Camping

39. **Scenic Hills RV Park** is in the midst of Amish country's busiest area, a mere mile from Berlin. 35 full-hookup sites are open April-Nov. This campground is designed for large units with easy access and 7 pull-through sites. Tents and small campers are discouraged since there are no restrooms with showers. Rates $14.50 per night with a discount if you stay more than 3 nights. Located atop a hill with beautiful vistas. Operated by Sam and Mary Hershberger. Go east on SR 39 to TR 367 and turn south to 4642 TR 367, Millersburg, OH 44654. PH: 330-893-3258 or 893-3607.

Please Note: The Amish do not have telephones in their homes. If you want information on products, services, or prices, drop a letter into the mail. Enclose a self-addressed, stamped postcard or envelope for their convenience. They will reply.

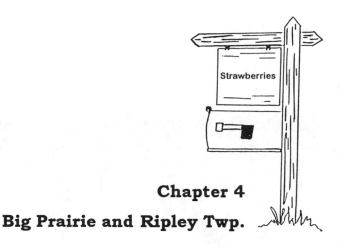

Chapter 4
Big Prairie and Ripley Twp.

Because so much of the land in this area is flat, in olden days it was referred to as "the big prairie." When the post office was established in 1821, it was given that name. Originally, Big Prairie, the only town in Ripley Twp., was named Cannansville after founder John Cannan. The history of this area includes an 1802 visit from Johnny Appleseed who planted orchards in Ripley and Washington Twps.

Big Prairie is located in the very northwest corner of Ripley Twp., so much of our exploration of this area will be done south and east of this community.

A drive along CR 100 from Big Prairie to Lakeville in Washington Twp. will take you past O'Dell's Lake which was once a very well-known, popular, summer resort area. This spring-fed lake is about 2 mi. long and ½ mi. wide and is still surrounded on this southern side by summer cottages and year-round residences.

BIG PRAIRIE

Prairie Station is *the* general store in Big Prairie. In addition to the gasoline, cold drinks, sandwiches, and grocery items a traveler can purchase here, this store has an interesting variety of formerly owned items. Located at 13238 CR 100, just north of SR 226. PH: 330-496-2361. Hours are Mon.-Sat. 8 am-8 pm; Sun. noon-6 pm.

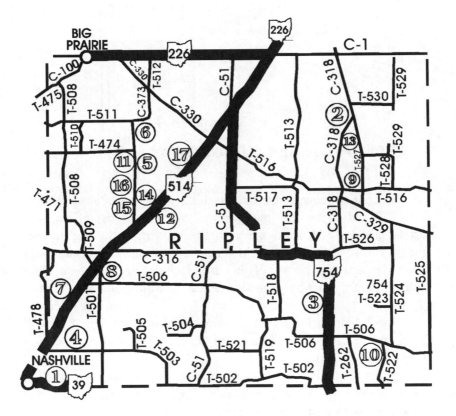

Ripley Twp.
Holmes County

Nancy Davenport operates the **Yarn & Bead Shop** in her home at 9049 TR 1043, Big Prairie, OH 44611. If you like to knit, crochet, embroider, or do any kind of handcrafts, you can find quality yarns, floss, needles, accessories, and how-to books. In addition, Nancy sells Stanley Home Products and does floral arrangements for all occasions. She also offers workshops and free knitting lessons. For more information call her at 330-496-3574. Shop hours are Tues.-Thurs. 11 am-5 pm, or by appointment. Her home is located just off SR 226 on the east edge of town.

RIPLEY TWP.

1. Just east of Nashville on SR 39 is **Amish Traditions**. What started out as a shop full of small crafts has grown over the years. Now, in addition to the large selection of handmade crafts, they also have a big selection of lawn furniture and lawn ornaments; oak furniture for your home; Robinson-Ransbottom crockery, and more. Find this shop at 13231 SR 39, Big Prairie, OH 44611. PH: 330-378-2791. Hours are Mon.-Sat. 9 am-7:30 pm (summer); 10 am-5 pm (winter).

2. Rex and Diane Dye operate **Christian Homestead Bookstore** with Sunday school and church supplies, greeting cards, crafts, and custom-designed wood products. Located at 8655 CR 318, Shreve, OH 44676. PH: 330-567-9933. Hours are Tues. and Thurs. 10 am-8:30 pm; Wed. and Fri. 10 am-5:30 pm; Sat. 9 am-noon. Closed Sun. and Mon.

3. More and more visitors are coming to Amish country at Christmastime. If you're here between Thanksgiving and New Year's Day, be sure to see the **Christmas light display** at the Donald and Mabel Plant residence, 7117 SR 754, about 3 mi. north of SR 39. Open every evening 6-11 pm.

4. A second must-see **Christmas light display** can be found at the Wachtel family's Spring Walk Farm. Their dairy farm is transformed into a Christmas fantasy by 55,000+ lights and you can see it at 13113 TR 503 from 5-11 pm.

5. Levi R. Yoder makes those ever-popular hickory rockers at **Hillside Rocker Shop**. He is also making bird houses and bird feeders these days. Find him at 7990 CR 373, Big Prairie, OH 44611.

6. Cary Hulin throws functional pottery at **Holmes County Pottery**—on the wheel, that is. He had the first firing of his wood-fired kiln in Nov. 1995. By spring the retail shop should be ready so visitors can browse or watch him at work. Everything from dinnerware to planters is offered. I like the earthy, hands-on shapes of his pots. Find this busy pottery at 8500 CR 373, Big Prairie, OH 44611. PH: 330-496-2406. Open Mon.-Sat. 9 am to 5 pm.

7. **Kow Kuntry Station** has groceries, bulk foods, a deli, ice cream cones, sandwiches, Pizza Parlor pizzas, camping supplies, Amish crafts and furniture, and Amish baked goods. What more could you ask for in a store? And, since it's owned by the Langs who've been Holstein dairy farmers for many years, you'll find lots of cow-related gifts. After all, you're in "Kow Kuntry" now! Located about 1½ mi. north of Nashville at 7303 SR 514, Big Prairie, OH 44611. PH: 330-378-4344. Hours are Mon.-Sat. 8 am-6 pm; Sun. 10 am-6 pm.

8. Don't let the name fool you because you can get a little bit of anything in wood at **Kuntry Lawn Furniture**. The most noticeable display of their handiwork will be at father-in-law John A. Weaver's farm at 7488 SR 514, Big Prairie, OH 44611. A little sign says cedar chests and you might want to ask if John has any in stock you can look at. There's nothing like the clean fragrance of cedar and these are finely made. If furniture or custom cabinets interest you, John will send you over to talk to his son-in-law and partner, Ervin J. Raber at 13238 TR 473, Lakeville, OH 44638. Don't be put off by the address since it's just right across SR 514 and down TR 473, probably not a mile distant. Whether you have a Big Prairie or Lakeville address out here depends on which side of SR 514 you live.

9. If it's spring and you're hunting flower or vegetable plants for your garden, you might want to see what the folks at **Miller's Greenhouse** have available. Find this seasonal business south of Shreve at 8231 TR 527, Shreve, OH 44676.

10. Larry Williams makes custom furniture and cabinets at **Paint Valley Wood Works**. He's restored some antique doors and windows for folks who couldn't find anyone to save these treasures, and says he's always willing to tackle 'most anything. Find his shop at 6705 TR 522, Millersburg, OH 44654. PH: 330-674-0535.

11. If you're looking for someone to repair that saddle or make you some harness or tack in leather, nylon, or bio-plastic, try Dan Raber of **Prairie Lane Harness**. Find him on CR 373 just north of Yoder's Shoes and Repair.

12. Two businesses are located here—**Shady Lane Bulk Foods** with hours Mon.-Fri. 9 am-5:30 pm and Sat. until 4 pm. Closed Wed. and Sun. The second business is **Wengerd Wood Shop**. Jonas Wengerd does custom work such as kitchen cabinets and dressers, mostly in oak. He will also do furniture repairs and is open evenings. Find these businesses at 7756 SR 514, Big Prairie, OH 44611.

13. **Shreve Storage Barns** can supply any size storage facility you might need at 8439 TR 527, Shreve, OH 44676.

14. Looking for vinyl or canvas products or repair work? Stop at **Woodland Tarp Shop** on SR 514, just north of Wengerd Wood Shop.

15. Emanuel Yoder has been in business at **Yoder's Shoes and Repairs** for many years. His cider press is up and running again, under the management of some of his grandchildren. He's taught them well and the freshly pressed cider available during the autumn is still the best I've ever tasted. Mr. Yoder carries a good line of work shoes, boots and rubber footwear, and does shoe repairs. Stop in to see him just off SR 514 at 7830 CR 373, Big Prairie, OH 44611.

16. At **Yoder's Archery, Yoder Mfg. & Lumber, and Yoder's Craft Store** you can find everything from hunting and fishing supplies and licenses, to clocks and clock-making accessories. They also have some wooden crafts and supplies. Find them at 7841 CR 373, Big Prairie, OH 44611. Hours are Mon.-Fri. 7:30 am-5 pm. Sat. until 11:30 am.

Dining

The **Ol' Smokehaus Restaurant** at Whispering Hills Campground (location #17) features "Amish country slow-cooked smoked BBQ" and open-air dining in a large pavilion. The homemade barbeque sauces range from Mild Country Hickory to Smokin' Cajun. On the menu are ribs, chicken, beef brisket, pork, and sandwiches with a salad bar and Ruth Saurer's apple dumplings and cobblers as well as Amish-baked pies. There's a Country Breakfast Bar on Sat. and Sun. mornings. Hours are 8 am-9 pm daily from Memorial Day through Labor Day and weekends May 1-Memorial Day and Labor Day-Oct. 15.

Camping

17. Closely associated with Shreve but in this township of Holmes County is **Whispering Hills Campground and RV Park**. With 300 campsites, an Olympic-size swimming pool, fishing, a spring-fed 8-acre lake, tennis courts, hiking trails, and a lot more, this campground has something for everyone who loves to camp. Not sure you're one of those? Never tried it? You could rent a camping trailer, completely furnished except for bedding, towels, and kitchen needs. Rates for a family of 4 are $40. The camper will sleep 4-6 with additional people at $3 each per night. They also have cabins to rent. If you're tent campin, sites are available with no hook-up for $14.50 per day. Complete hook-up sites are $19.50 per day. More than 2 in your party? Children 4 and older are $1 extra; adults $3 extra.

Whispering Hills has a full schedule of activities from hay rides to movies and dances to church services. The Plain and Fancy Fair held in August and the Apple Dumpling Festival held in early October draw people from all over to this lovely campground. Located on SR 514 about 3 mi. south of Shreve. For more information write to P.O. Box 607, Shreve, OH 44676, or phone 330-567-2137 or 1-800-992-2435.

Please Note: The Amish do not have telephones in their homes. If you want information on products, services, or prices, drop a letter into the mail. Enclose a self-addressed, stamped postcard or envelope for their convenience. They will reply.

Chapter 5
Charm and Clark Twp.

Clark Township was originally called German. When the U.S. entered World War I, patriotism demanded names with such close German connections be changed, so the township was renamed Clark.

Two very Amish communities—Charm and Farmerstown—are the focus of this chapter.

First named Stevenson or Stevensville when the village came into existence during the Civil War, Charm has also been called Putschtown (or Putchtown or Pootchtown), taken from the German word meaning small bunch or clump. Some local folks can still be heard calling it that.

On September 30, 1995, Vernon J. Miller's book, *Historical Album of Charm, Ohio*, was released. It's available to anyone interested in the beginnings of this village and the surrounding area. Mr. Miller spent 7½ years researching and completing this written and pictorial history. The book is available in some local shops or by ordering from Vernon J. Miller, Charm Publishing, 4755 CR 19, Millersburg, OH 44654, for $34.50. Ohio residents add $2 sales tax.

Farmerstown was platted in 1827 as Farmersville. History records changes in many community names when they established post offices. Such was the case here. There happened to be another community called Farmersville in Ohio. So, when the post office was established in 1866, the name was changed to Farmerstown.

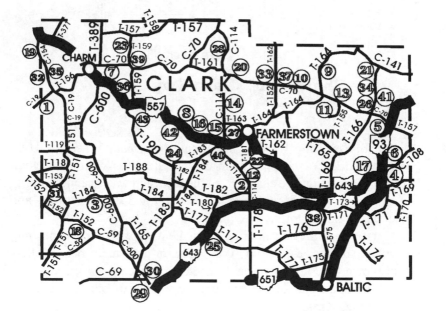

Clark Twp.
Holmes County

Since this area is closely tied to agriculture and Farmerstown is one of those communities which still maintains many businesses necessary to an agricultural population, this is a most appropriate name.

Visitors will not find the plethora of craft businesses in Farmerstown which exist elsewhere. It remains a quiet village serving the needs of the surrounding Amish farmers. In this way it harkens to an earlier era. After all, how many small towns still boast a village blacksmith?

If you like to get out and see the countryside, I suggest you pick up SR 643 south of Farmerstown and take it to New Bedford. It's a winding highway through lovely hills and valleys filled with Amish farms. Some gorgeous views along the way. At New Bedford you can take CR 600 back toward Charm or take SR 651 over to Baltic. Both have their scenic moments, also.

But, if you've got the time, follow SR 643 on south of New Bedford. In the past year I've discovered how beautiful this route is. The driver has to stay alert because of the many twists and turns; however, I haven't experienced much traffic competition when I've been on it. So, you should be able to go slowly enough to enjoy the scenery. It comes out on SR 83 which you can follow north to Millersburg or south to Coshocton. SR 83 is a designated scenic highway but you'll have to keep up the speed because this highway usually has heavy traffic.

CHARM

One note for visitors is that many of the craft shops in Charm are only open Fridays and Saturdays after Christmas until April.

Brook-line Antiques and Museum opens in May on Saturdays. You'll find an ever-changing display of quality antiques, as well as a little museum on the history of Charm for which there is no charge. Claude Ruston Baker painted the large mural on the back wall of the barn which depicts the early days of the village. Since this is an unheated barn, the business closes at the end of October. P.O. Box 111, Charm, OH 44617. PH: 330-276-1203.

Charm Bicycle Shop sells new bikes such as mountain and cross bikes by Diamond Back, Raleigh, and Nishiki, and does repairs. The shop is located at Miller's Dry Goods in the back room of the quilt barn and is open Mon.-Fri. 8 am-8 pm and Sat. until 5 pm.

Tables and chairs for your dining room, hickory rockers, and those popular and comfortable glider rockers can be found at **Charm Furniture**. Find the driveway beside Ole Mill Crafts and follow it up the hill. Located at 4486 SR 557, P.O. Box 33, Charm, OH 44617. Hours are Mon.-Tues. 8 am-6 pm, Wed.-Fri. until 8 pm, and Sat. until 4 pm. Closed Thursdays and Sundays.

You'll find the local grocery at **Charm General Store** right next to The Homestead Restaurant. In addition to grocery items, you can get a hot cup of coffee, tea, or hot chocolate, cold sodas, and sandwiches. Housewares, clothing, gift items, Amish straw and wool hats, and Berlin Flyer wagons are in their basement room. PH: 330-893-2400. Hours are Mon. and Tues. 7:30 am-5:30 pm; Wed. and Fri. until 9 pm; Thurs. until noon; and Sat. until 5 pm.

Not only harness, but buggy robes, a wide variety of footwear, pet and bird feeds, and sleigh bells can be purchased at **Charm Harness and Boot**. Located at 4441 CR 70, P.O. Box 114, Charm, OH 44617. Hours are Mon., Tues., Sat. 7:30 am-5 pm; Thurs. until noon; Wed. and Fri. until 7 pm.

E&E Woodcrafts has unfinished pine pieces for the creatively inclined, including child-sized furniture, folk art dolls, tinware, Amish prints, and a wide variety of little gift items. Address is P.O. Box 70, Charm, OH 44617. PH: 893-3498. Hours are Mon.-Sat. 10 am-5 pm. Closed January and February.

Above Charm Harness and Boot is **Erb's Sports and Archery**. With a complete line of archery supplies, fishing tackle, live bait, ammunition, hunting clothes, and accessories, this shop offers something for every sportsman. P.O. Box 55, Charm, OH 44617. Located in Charm just off SR 557 on CR 70.

While you're visiting Charm, you might want to browse through **Keim Lumber**. Of course, you can find tools, etc., in your own backyard but here you can choose from one of 37 different styles of weather vanes or buy one of those old-fashioned, handcranked ice cream freezers. Stop in and see if Keim Lumber can surprise you—or maybe just bring back old memories. Find it on the hill at the intersection of SR 557 and CR 70. PH: 1-800-362-6682. Hours are Mon.-Thurs. 7:30 am-5 pm; Fri. until 8 pm; Sat. until 11:30 am.

Amanda Miller began selling fabrics and notions from the kitchen of her home and by 1995 **Miller's Dry Goods** celebrated 30 years in business. The horse barn has been converted into the Quilt Barn to display the large variety of quilts and quilted items. The house is now full of bolts of calico, patterns, and everything you could possibly need to make your own quilts. They take orders for custom-made quilts. Located at 4500 SR 557, Millersburg, OH 44654. Open Mon.-Sat. 8 am-5 pm. This is one shop in Charm that's open all winter.

Old Blacksmith Shop Gifts is filled with housewares, locally made bird houses and feeders, horse collar clocks and mirrors, calico photo album covers made in Charm, handmade wooden trains and farm sets with painted barns, animals and fence, doll beds, knickknack shelves, straw hat clocks, games, puzzles and coloring books for the kids, and lots more. Find this shop next to E&E Woodcrafts, P.O. Box 86, Charm, OH 44617. Hours are Mon.-Sat. 9 am-5 pm.

Located in what was once a flour mill, **Ole Mill Crafts** specializes in wooden items cut by owner Rhoda Raber Troyer's new husband, Arlen, in a small workroom at the back of the shop. These pieces are then painted by the multi-talented Rhoda who also stitches "country apparel" such as jumpers and vests and paints denim shirts and sweatshirts. Woven comforters, hoop wall hangings, dolls, and a variety of attractive gift items are also on display. Located at 4492 SR 557, P.O. Box 7, Charm, OH 44617. Hours are Mon.-Sat. 9 am-5 pm. Fri. and Sat. only in Jan. and Feb. PH: 330-893-2388.

There's a good selection of upholstered furniture as well as dining room and bedroom suites in a former grain mill at **Ole Mill Furniture**. In addition to locally made oak rockers and other pieces, there's name-brand furniture from Tell City, Lane, and Kimball among others. Don't forget to check what's on display in the basement. Hours are Mon., Tues., Sat. 9 am-5 pm; Wed. and Fri. until 9 pm; Thurs. until noon. PH: 330-893-2823

Ruthie's Gift Shop has taken the place of Arvada's. Here you'll find nice prints for your walls; some quilts and quilted items; linens and laces; tinware; a large selection of Amish and other dolls; braided rugs, placemats, and chair pads; salt-glazed pottery; hand-thrown stoneware in a choice of blue, green, or brown glazes; and other gift items. Located across the street from the Homestead Restaurant. PH: 330-893-3369. Hours are Mon.-Sat. 10 am-5 pm.

Troyer's Arrow & Supply specializes in custom-made arrows. Just east of downtown Charm at 4433 CR 70, Charm, OH 44617. Below the house, along the road, are several cages of very self-satisfied, fat, little squirrels. A large pen houses three deer—Buster, Doe-Doe, and Bambi. Fun for kids and adults to see.

Dining

Undoubtedly, the hub of Charm is the **Homestead Restaurant**. A busy restaurant is one where the food's good. It's not unusual to see a line of would-be diners waiting to get tables. This non-smoking restaurant serves family-style dinners featuring chicken, ham, and roast beef with all the trimmings, including dessert. If you prefer, order one of the daily specials or a plate dinner, sandwich, soup, salad, or baked stuffed potato. For dessert try a piece of homemade pie—ala mode, of course—or "The Charmer", a sundae of ice cream, strawberries, chocolate, and bananas topped with whipped cream, nuts, and a cherry. Summer hours Mon.-Sat. 7:30 am-8 pm. Winter hours Mon.-Sat. 7 am-7 pm. Fri. until 8 pm. PH: 330-893-2717.

Lodging

Sleepin Inn Charm opened for business in 1995. They have three rooms with queen-sized beds and private baths. A continental breakfast with homemade bread is served. Rates are $65-$80. At 4487 SR 557, Charm, OH 44617. PH: 330-893-3760.

Right across the street from the Homestead Restaurant is **The Watchman's Cottage**. This delightful, one-room Victorian cottage is furnished with antiques, a double bed with a crocheted spread, and lace curtains at the windows. There's a coffeemaker for guests to enjoy, and a gas fireplace adds the final touch of romance to this already romantic setting. The bath has a shower. The nightly charge of $85 includes breakfast at the Homestead. If you're staying on Sunday when the restaurant is closed, you get Sat. supper. The Miller Haus takes their reservations, so call 330-893-3602, or ask at the restaurant.

FARMERSTOWN

You'll find the **Farmerstown Blacksmith Shop** across from the elementary school at 2771 SR 557, Baltic, OH 43804.

Farmerstown General Store is, as its name implies, a place where you can get a wide variety of grocery and other items. There has been a general store in this community since 1855. If you're looking for a snack, they have sandwiches and chicken dinners to go. Located at 2845 SR 557, Baltic, OH 43804, in the heart of Farmerstown. Hours are Mon.-Thurs. 7:30 am-5:30 pm; Fri. until 8 pm; Sat. until 5 pm. PH: 330-897-5844.

Even this tiny village has its well-attended livestock auction. The **Farmerstown Livestock Auction** is held on Tuesdays and has the state's largest weekly feeder pig sale. There's a lunch bar located on the top floor, while produce vendors and a flea market set up outside, weather permitting. This is a good place to browse and observe the Amish as they go about their business. P.O. Box 22, Baltic, OH 43804. PH: 330-897-2275 or 897-6081.

The **Farmerstown Shoe-n-Gift Shop** is one of those variety stores where variety is the watchword. They have a little bit of everything from housewares to shoes, decorative items to games, toys, and infant things. They do offer a free catalog. Visit this store ½ mi. east of Farmerstown at 2701 SR 557, Baltic, OH 43804. Hours are Mon.-Fri. 8 am-6 pm; Sat. until 5 pm. Closed Thurs. and Sun.

Close enough to be considered part of the village, **Farmerstown Upholstered Furniture** is just south off SR 557 at the junction of TR 181. They manufacture sofas and loveseats, swivel rockers, those glider rockers which are so comfortable, and recliners. Here you'll also find lawn furniture including benches and picnic tables, swings, gliders, and porch rockers. Write for a brochure from owner Mose M.E. Yoder at 2791 TR 181, Baltic, OH 43804.

There are more ways than electric or winding to run a clock. Find out how at **Farmerstown Watch & Clock Repair**. Mose E. Barkman has a large selection of clocks on display. Located at 2869 SR 557, Baltic, OH 43804. The sign is a small one above the door, so be on the lookout for it. The small tan building is just west of the elevator.

You can get a smoked turkey or ham for the holidays or have your deer processed at **Gingerich's Farmerstown Meats**. Offering cuts of beef, pork, deer, and lamb, their specialties are bologna and weiners. Located in Farmerstown at 2933 TR 163, Sugarcreek, OH 44681. PH: 330-897-7972. Open October-April.

CLARK TWP.

1. Albert and Mattie Yoder will reupholster that lumpy sofa in the rumpus room at **A & M Upholstery**, 4996 CR 19, Millersburg, OH 44654.

2. All kinds of items for your horse as well as nylon harnesses are at **Beachy's Nylon Harness Shop**. They also carry nylon webbing by the fifty-yard roll. Find them at 2815 TR 182, Baltic, OH 43804.

3. **Bee Supplies & Raw Honey** can be found on TR 184, ½ mi. west of CR 600.

4. **Bixler's Grocery** will supply a snack or cold soda as well as Amish baked goods and other groceries. On SR 93 across from the SR 643 intersection. Hours Mon.-Sat. 7 am-8 pm.

5. The 3500 sq. ft. showroom is full of locally made oak and cherry furniture at **Brookside Furniture**. Custom orders are accepted.

Located 2½ mi. south of Sugarcreek at 2949 SR 93, Sugarcreek, OH 44681. Lest you think otherwise, a glance at your map will show that SR 93 crosses the southeast corner of this township, so don't get confused! Open Mon.-Sat. 9:30 am-6 pm. PH: 330-852-4528.

Also at this location is **Brookside Nursery** (formerly Sunset Hill Nursery). They have shade trees, shrubs, and more during the gardening season. Hours Mon-Sat. 9:30 am-5 pm. Fri. until 8 pm. Closed Thurs. and Sun.

6. If you're looking for something to do in the evenings, on Sundays when most other businesses are closed, or to entertain the kids, you couldn't do better than **Cabin Creek Golf**. Two 18-hole miniature golf courses include 4 bridges, a waterwheel, 2 waterfalls, and a gazebo. Or try your swing at the driving range which just happens to be heated for year 'round use. Sand volleyball ($20 per hr. or $3 per person) and a putting green ($2.50 for ½ hr. or $4 for an hr.) have recently been added. Built on a corner of their family dairy farm, Bob and Lois Schlabach designed the challenging, one-of-a-kind, miniature golf courses. This family-entertainment center includes a snack bar. Price for a round of miniature golf is $4.00 for adults; under 12 is $2.50. Buckets of balls range from $2 to $5.50. Group rates available for 10 or more. Located south of Sugarcreek on the corner of SR 93 and CR 108, summer hours are Tues.-Sat. 10 am-10 pm; Sun. and Mon. 1-10 pm. PH: 330-852-4879.

7. **Charm Rocker Shop** has built a nice new showroom to display their furniture. Dining room chairs and glider rockers are their specialty, but they also have a variety of oak and cherry furnishings made by local Amish families. Hours are Mon.-Sat. 8 am-5 pm. Located ½ mi. east of Charm at 4220 CR 70, Millersburg, OH 44654. Send for their free color brochure.

8. John R. Hershberger does furniture repair, stripping, and refinishing at **Country Furniture Repair**, 3273 SR 557, Baltic, OH 43804. Find John 3 mi. east of Charm if you have a rickety piece of furniture that needs fixed.

9. Leon and Carol Miller sell new and used bikes at **Countryside Bicycles**, 2012 TR 164, Sugarcreek, OH 44681. Their motto is,

"Quality bikes with service." Hours are Mon.-Fri. 9 am-7 pm; Sat. until 5 pm. PH: 330-852-4949.

10. **Erb's Shoe Store** not only has footwear but hats and custom-made rag rugs woven on-site. It's on CR 70 east of the intersection of TR 162 and the last place down the long lane.

11. **Erb's Stove Center** is one of those rather unique businesses which may exist nowhere except Amish country. If you wonder how the Amish manage to keep their food cold without electricity, you can see gas refrigerators here. (Yes, some still do use ice boxes.) Owner, Ed Erb carries what could be considered the leading-edge technology for the Amish lifestyle. There are gas irons, heating and cooking stoves as the name implies, and other appliances. Most of their business these days is done at their new shop near Windmill Village in Berlin Twp. (see that chapter). That's also where the lawn furniture can now be seen. Located south of CR 70 at 3139 TR 155, Sugarcreek, OH 44681.

12. Draft horse supplies and cast iron toys are available at the **E-Z Seat Co.**, 2380 CR 114, Baltic, OH 43804. If you have kids on your Christmas and birthday lists, check this out.

13. **E-Z Spreader Mfg.** specializes in horse-drawn manure spreaders. This may seem an unlikely candidate for our book; however, feed and utility carts, wheelbarrows, wooden hobby horses, and sturdy wagons are also made here. Get the wagons and racks varnished or painted in red or John Deere green and yellow. Their hobby horse comes in black, white, sorrel, or spotted. Write for prices and more information to 1951 CR 70, Sugarcreek, OH 44681. They can also be reached through their answering service at 330-893-2464. Hours are Mon.-Fri. 8 am-5 pm; Sat. until noon.

14. Although the straw is imported from South America, **Farmerstown Book & Broom** makes straw brooms the old-fashioned way. Also find a variety of books, office furnishings, and miscellaneous items. At 3270 CR 114, Sugarcreek, OH 44681.

15. Not only does **Farmerstown Furniture** have a display of oak furnishings for your home, but owner, Junior Hershberger, also makes some custom furniture and does custom finishing. The punched tin or copper panels you'll see in some pieces are designed and made right here. Have an old spinning wheel that needs to be fixed? Find parts for it here or ask Junior to restore it for you. This store has some of the loveliest brass hardware I've seen as well as carved and pressed oak "gingerbread" to dress up your own unfinished furniture pieces. If you are into furniture restoration, send for a copy of their catalog ($2.00) and discover the more than 1000 items available for the refinisher. Order from 3155 SR 557, Baltic, OH 43804. Answering service at 330-893-2464. Store hours are Mon.-Sat. 7 am-5 pm.

16. If you like antique furniture, be sure to stop at **Hershberger's Antique Mall**. They doubled their space, building another 4,000 sq.ft. building, so now have 8,000 sq.ft., most of it filled with furniture. There's enough to see in these buildings to keep an antique lover busy for a couple of hours—at least. One of their specialties is Millersburg Carnival glass. Answering service at 1-800-893-3702, Ext. 300. Located 3 mi. east of Charm at 3245 SR 557, Baltic, OH 43804. Open Mon.-Sat. 9 am-8 pm.

17. **Hickory rockers** are sold at the farm of Atlee C. Miller, 1525 SR 643, Sugarcreek, OH 44681. Find Mr. Miller down the first lane to the right on SR 643 west of the SR 93 intersection. There's a sign at the end of the driveway, so you can't miss it. Mr. Miller's son-in-law makes these rockers of oak, walnut, or cherry at Woodland Rocker Shop. (See listing under Beck's Mills and Mechanic Twp.) Children's rockers and footstools are also available.

18. **Hillside Buggy Shop** may have just what you want if you have a carriage which needs repairs or you've been wanting a new one. Find Emanuel R. and Roman A. Yoder on TR 152 south of Charm.

19. **Hillside Crafts** is making more furniture than ever. Find hickory rockers, oak quilt racks, jelly cupboards, dry sinks, bedroom suites, dining tables and chairs, baskets by the Gingerichs, occasional tables, shelves of all sizes, and wooden toys. Located just off SR 557 north

of Charm at 3080 TR 154, Millersburg, OH 44654. Hours are Mon.-Sat. 9 am-5 pm; evenings by chance. Open all winter.

20. Christ M. Yoder & Sons manufacture **horse stocks, hay racks, and breaking sleds** at their farm on CR 70. Well, you never know what people are looking for and these could be vital items if you've got livestock. Contact them at 2999 CR 70, Sugarcreek, OH 44681.

21. James and Freda Miller own **J & F Furniture Shop** at 3521 TR 166, Sugarcreek, OH 44681. They specialize in oak children's furniture and most of their items are sold wholesale, but they will do some retail sales at their shop. PH: 330-852-2478.

22. Bio-plastic harness for draft and buggy horses is made by Jacob Miller at **J-M-A Halter Shop**. He'll custom make it and ship it to you UPS. Mr. Miller also sells registered Belgians, those big golden draft horses with the blonde manes and tails which are so common in Amish country. Find this shop at 2584 SR 557, Baltic, OH 43804.

23. Bio-plastic, coated, nylon harnesses for shows, parades, pulling, and general farm and driving are made at **J.R. Yoder Nylon Works**. Mr. Yoder has shipped harnesses as far away as Barbados and has even custom-made them for elephants. Now *that's* a harness! Located 1 mi. east of Charm off CR 70 at 3649 TR 159, Sugarcreek, OH 44681.

24. Whatever fencing needs you have, you can probably find what you're looking for in the wide variety available at **Maple Valley Fence**, 2457 TR 183, Baltic, OH 43804.

25. Mose E. Raber does furniture repair, stripping (even painted pieces), and refinishing at **Meadow Valley Furniture Repair**. Mr. Raber also makes lawn furniture. Find this craftsman at 3210 SR 643, Baltic, OH 43804.

26. Emery Miller can make you a road cart, buggy, or cattle/farm trailer at **Miller's Carts & Trailers**. He also sells outdoor furniture, gliders, and swings. Ask to see his buggy wheel coffee table. Located right behind Union Cheese at 3197 TR 166, Sugarcreek, OH 44681.

27. If you're interested in pine furniture with a walnut finish, stop at **Miller's Quality Crafts**. Just ½ mi. northwest of Farmerstown on CR 114, they have shelving, magazine and quilt racks, bread boxes, toy chests, spice cabinets, dry sinks, microwave cabinets, corner cupboards, and a whole lot more. Their address is 2950 CR 114, Sugarcreek, OH 44681.

28. If a trophy or plaque is what you need, **Miller's Woodcraft**, 3767 CR 114, Sugarcreek, OH 44681, may have just what you want since that's all they make here.

29. Mose and Anna Miller make lovely mantle, wall, and grandfather timepieces at **New Bedford Clocks**. All their clocks are available in oak, cherry, or walnut. Send your SASE for their flyer with order form to 1439 TR 183, Baltic, OH 43804.

30. All sorts of fabrics, notions, greeting cards, baby and clothing items, games, toys, school supplies, kitchen and bath towels, bedspreads, rugs, and lots more can be found at **New Bedford Dry Goods**. If you're traveling along picturesque CR 600, find it just before you get to New Bedford at 1409 CR 600, Baltic, OH 43804. Hours are Mon., Tues., Wed., and Fri. 8 am-8 pm; Thurs. and Sat. until 5 pm.

31. This bulk food store seemed really out of the way when I stumbled across it, but it's here for the convenience of our Amish neighbors. These stores are stocked with a little bit of everything. **Raber's Country Store** at 2213 TR 151, Baltic, OH 43804, also sells herbs, Shaklee, Forever Living, and Nature's Sunshine products.

32. **Raber's Shoeing Service** moved from its downtown Charm location to 3739 TR 154. Closed Tues., Thurs., and Sun.

33. John E. and Leroy E. Raber operate **Raber's Wood Products**. They specialize in dinette sets and bedroom suites. If they don't have exactly what you want, ask if they'll custom-make it in oak or cherry. Find them at 2747 CR 70, Sugarcreek, OH 44681. Answering service at 1-800-893-3702, Ext. 444.

Also at this location is **Raber's Kitchen**, serving reservation-only breakfasts and dinners to groups of at least 10. Leave a message at the answering service (number above) for more information.

34. **Rainbow Bedding Co.** has new and rebuilt bedding and can custom-make mattresses and boxsprings to your specifications. Find this business ½ mi. north of CR 70 at 3417 TR 166, Sugarcreek, OH 44681. PH: 330-852-3127. Hours are Tues.-Fri. 8 am-6 pm.

35. Samuel D. Yoder takes custom orders only and will build to your specifications at **Ridge View Furniture**. He doesn't do tables, chairs, or corner cupboards, but can probably make whatever else you want in oak, maple, cherry, or walnut. There is no showroom, but you'll find him at 3482 TR 154, Millersburg, Oh 44654.

36. The tiny district of La Perche, France, was the original home of the Percheron draft horses. Black or dappled gray in color, these huge horses weigh about a ton and are used to plow fields and haul heavy loads. Melvin J.M. Miller of **Sunny Slope Farm** breeds these giants as well as registered Jersey cattle. Find him just east of Charm at 4191 SR 557, Millersburg, OH 44654.

37. In the rear of the Troyer house at 2101 CR 70, Sugarcreek, OH 44681, you'll find **Troyer's Bargain Store**. This is one of those stores offering everything from housewares and gifts to farm supplies.

38. **Troyer's Country Store** is another of those Amish-owned bulk food/grocery stores. Try shopping one of these stores at holiday baking time. When was the last time you tasted black walnuts? I remember their piquant flavor in my favorite childhood ice cream. Does anybody still make black walnut ice cream? This store is conveniently located on the corner of SR 643 and CR 575, 1¼ mi. north of Baltic, at 2119 CR 575, Baltic, OH 43804.

39. Just in case you've wondered, the Amish do have running water—even without electricity. How? To quote the song, "The answer, my friend, is blowing in the wind." Surely you've noticed the many windmills in the area. David Troyer sells and services windmills and towers at **Troyer's Windmill Sales**. This free form of

energy is very popular with our Amish neighbors, and Mr. Troyer has put up windmills as far away as the Carolinas. So, if you're in need, want more information, or even think you'd like a small ornamental windmill for your yard, contact him at 3981 CR 70, Sugarcreek, OH 44681.

40. If you're in the market for a rolltop desk which will become a family heirloom, stop in at **Valley Furniture**. Jonas Yoder offers five sizes from 45 to 66 inches wide and they're made of 1-inch oak. If oak's not your thing, ask to have one made in solid cherry or walnut. To give you an idea of the quality and materials used, an average desk will weigh over 400 pounds. That's a desk! Executive office desks and file cabinets are also available. Located at 2707 CR 114, Baltic, OH 43804, ½ mi. west of Farmerstown off SR 557, south on TR 114 to the first house.

41. Got a picture of something you can't find in a furniture store? Stop in and talk to Jonas A.J. Miller, owner of **Valley View Woodcrafts**, 3274 TR 166, Sugarcreek, OH 44681. From rolltop desks to—well, to whatever you have a fancy for—Mr. Miller can make it for you out of any hardwood. You may have to wait a year but, from what I saw, it would be worth it. PH: 330-852-4353.

Lodging

42. Paul and Naomi Miller are the managers of **Charm Countryview Inn**. This lovely inn sets on beautifully landscaped grounds off the road on a slope overlooking a delightful view. It also has the distinction of having been featured in the August 1991 issue of *Country Magazine*. Each of the 15 guest rooms suggests real country-home comfort with its individual decorating of queen-sized beds covered with handmade quilts and oak furnishings. A full country breakfast is served in the dining room Mon.-Sat., and a continental breakfast on Sun. You can also have an evening snack if desired. Each room has air conditioning and a private bath, and your peace remains undisturbed since there are no TVs here. Rates are $65-$95. Sorry, no pets allowed. Open year 'round. PH: 330-893-3003 for reservations. P.O. Box 100, Charm, OH 44617. The Inn is located on SR 557 between Charm and Farmerstown.

43. Only 2 miles from Charm in a peaceful setting around a fishing pond are **Mel and Mary's Cottages**. Each of the four cabins have two bedrooms, full baths with tub and shower, kitchenette, and sitting rooms with fireplaces. There's no swimming, but a paddleboat is available as are horseshoes and a playground for the kids. The cabins have electricity but no TVs. One is handicap accessible. Rates begin at $75 per couple. Located at 2972 TR 190, Baltic, OH 43804. Open March-Dec. and Jan.-Feb., depending on the weather. PH: 330-893-2695 for reservations.

Please Note: The Amish do not have telephones in their homes. If you want information on products, services, or prices, drop a letter into the mail. Enclose a self-addressed, stamped postcard or envelope for their convenience. They will reply.

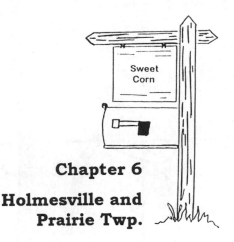

Chapter 6
Holmesville and
Prairie Twp.

Holmesville claims the distinction of being the place where the first white settlers chose to locate in the county. Jonathan Grant and his son walked from Pennsylvania in 1809. They carried with them a gun and ammunition, seeds to plant, a few tools, and some cornmeal. The cabin they built was about a mile from the site of the present village. The first white male and female children born in the county were born in Holmesville in 1817.

Several industries are located in and around Holmesville today. SR 83 used to make a left-hand turn and go through the heart of town. Rerouting it straight through eliminates the glut of traffic and has allowed the community to retain its quiet character.

HOLMESVILLE

Sid Hackaday operates the **Citgo Station** right beside the Holmesville Market at the intersection of SR 83 and Main St. It's open from 5:30 am-8 pm Mon.-Fri. and 8 am-8 pm on Sat. Closed Sun. PH: 330-279-2008.

Sandwiches, cold and hot drinks, grocery items, and Amish baked goods can be procured at the **Holmesville Market**, the local convenience store. Located right on SR 83 just north of the Main St. intersection. Hours are Mon.-Sat. 9 am-11 pm; Sun. noon to 11 pm.

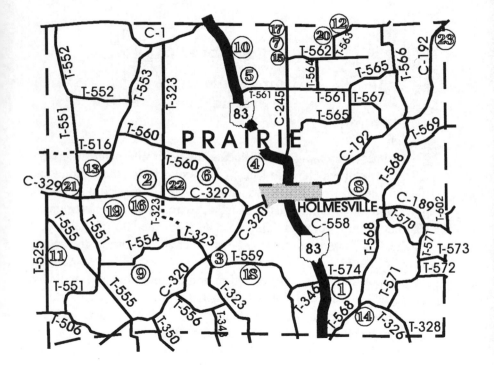

Prairie Twp.
Holmes County

Dining

I guess dining isn't the right word for **Main Street Pizza** since they don't have a dining room. However, you can take out pizza, subs, sandwiches, salads, and frozen yogurt. It's pretty popular with the locals. Located at 102 W. Main about a block east of SR 83. PH: 330-279-2765. Hours are Mon.-Thurs. 10 am-10 pm; Fri. until midnight; Sat. 11 am-11 pm; and Sun. 3-9 pm.

PRAIRIE TWP.

1. **A&M Country Woodworking** specializes in custom-made furniture. They take orders for "grandma rockers" with upholstered seats and head rests, footstools, and glider rockers. They also have a large selection of Vanguard paints. Stop in and talk to owner Andrew Miller about your needs at 7920 TR 574, Holmesville, OH 44633.

2. Urie and Martha Byler will "turn your ideas into customized furniture" at **Byler's Handcrafted Furniture**, 9545 CR 329, Holmesville, OH 44633. PH: 330-279-4142.

3. You can find **Chupp's Buggy Repair Shop** on CR 320 at the intersection of TR 323.

4. Antique lovers will delight in **Croco House Antiques**. First of all, there's the house itself, a circa 1850 brick with 10 rooms, walnut and chestnut woodwork, red oak floors, and a cupola with a widow's walk. Once part of that chain which comprised the Underground Railroad, Croco House is a registered National Historic Landmark. These days, the house is filled with antiques, glassware, and collectibles. One room is devoted to the Paint Valley Workshop's woven rugs, placemats, and table runners in plaids and with colorful country stenciling. You'll also find baskets, fringed lampshades, and wreaths. If antique dresses and turn-of-the-century hats are your interest, they may have several to choose from. Lots of interesting pieces and much to see, so take your time and enjoy. Located just ½ mi. north of Holmesville at 8147 SR 83. PH: 330-279-2461. Hours are Mon.-Sat. 11 am-5 pm. Usually open Sun. 1-5 pm. They are closed during January.

5. **83 Crafts & Furniture** was opened by Eva Miller in 1995. She sells country decorations, gift baskets for all occasions, glassware, Victorian mirrors, and Amish-made oak furniture. 8935 TR 561, Holmesville, OH 44633 (right on SR 83). PH: 330-279-3031. Hours Mon.-Sat. 10 am-6 pm.

6. If you want to honor someone with a plaque or trophy, give **Hilltop Trophy Shop** a call at 330-279-2852. They also engrave medals and name plates for desks, make rubber stamps, supply business cards, and sell Mason shoes. They are located at 9000 TR 560, Holmesville, OH 44633. Hours 1-8 pm Mon.-Fri., until 6 pm on Wed., and 8 am-2 pm on Sat.

7. Well, if you're going to shop at this store, gird your loins for their l-o-n-g driveway. Don't bother to stop at that first set of buildings. You ain't even close yet! Just keep going. **Hilty's Shoe Store** is worth the effort if you're in need of work shoes, boots, jogging-type shoes, or rubber footwear, so enjoy your off-road adventure.

8. Here's one of those businesses which may exist nowhere else in the country. **Holmes Wheel Shop** makes all kinds of buggy and cart wheels from about 20 to 50 inches in diameter. They have them lined up by the dozens, wooden spokes attached to hubs, waiting for rims, and looking like nothing so much as rows of Tinkertoys. Most of their business is wholesale, but they will do retail sales. They also have a free wholesale catalog available which will describe the different types of wheels they make. If you would like a copy, write to them at P.O. Box 56, Holmesville, OH 44633. Find this interesting business at 7969 CR 189. PH: 330-279-2891.

9. For custom-made tarp needs for your boat, pick-up, or camper stop in and talk to Crist Yoder, owner of the **Holmesville Tarp Shop**. Located at 9760 TR 554, Holmesville, OH 44633.

10. Custom handwoven items, yarn, books, and other equipment as well as classes in weaving, spinning, knitting, and crocheting are available at the **Homespun Shed**. There is also a 1600 sq.ft. flea market on the property at 8830 SR 83, Holmesville, OH 44633. PH: 330-279-2079. Hours Fri. & Sat. 10 am-5 pm.

11. One of those Amish stores with a little bit of everything from school supplies to housewares to crafts is **Miller's Housewares & Crafts**. Find this store at 7150 TR 525, Holmesville, OH 44633. Hours are Mon.-Sat. 8 am-5 pm; Fri. until 8 pm.

12. **Nisley's Harness Shop** can help you with your harness needs at 7901 TR 563, Holmesville.

13. There are enough deer, elk, emus, lamas, buffaloes, horses, and ponies to delight the kid in everyone at **Pioneer Acres**, 8017 TR 553, Holmesville, OH 44633. Warning signs tell you NOT to feed or touch the animals, so get out the camera and enjoy!

14. Offering all sorts of produce in season is **Schlabach's Produce** at 6850 TR 326, Holmesville, OH 44633.

15. **Shetler's Bulk Food and Book Store** at 9099 CR 245, Holmesville, is *the* place in this area for all your bulk food needs. They are closed on Thurs.

16. For furniture and miscellaneous items, stop by **Spookhollow New & Used Furniture**, 9728 CR 329, Holmesville, OH 44633. It's the first place down the driveway. Closed Wed. and Sun.

17. The **T-Town Mart** sells groceries, meats, cheese, and ice cream at their location on CR 245.

18. **Troyer's Homemade Candies** were so much in demand that Lydia and Sarah Troyer's sweet treats are mostly made to sell wholesale these days. Find their chocolates at the Gallery of Crafts in Millersburg. If you want to see about placing an order, they are located at 8830 TR 559, Millersburg, OH 44654.

19. **Wengerd Furniture** is now open for business. They advertise "custom furniture in traditional Amish styles." While most of their business is for the wholesale market, they will custom-make pieces in their shop at 9784 CR 329, Holmesville, OH 44633. Voice mail 1-800-893-3702, Box 329.

20. Wm. C. Yoder makes **gliders, swings, and martin houses** at his residence at 7951 TR 563, Holmesville.

21. At the home of Andy M. Yoder, 10219 CR 329, Holmesville, OH 44633, you'll find **Yoder Bakery** open on Tuesdays.

22. The folks at **Yoder's Upholstery** will tackle just about any commercial or residential project that requires upholstery. Find them at 9368 CR 329, Holmesville, OH 44633, 2 mi. west of town.

Dining

23. The **Horse 'n Harness Pub** is located in the northeast corner of Prairie Twp. However, it's closely associated with the village of Fredericksburg, so find more information about it in that chapter in the Wayne County section.

Please Note: The Amish do not have telephones in their homes. If you want information on products, services, or prices, drop a letter into the mail. Enclose a self-addressed, stamped postcard or envelope for their convenience. They will reply.

Chapter 7
Killbuck

Killbuck is the second largest community in the county. Originally known as Shrimplin's Settlement for Abraham Shrimplin, the first settler in the area, Killbuck has also been known by the names of Oxford and Palladium.

Early American Days are held in Killbuck every Labor Day weekend and this is the village's largest celebration.

Although not in the heart of Amish country, Killbuck has some unique features which this chapter will reveal so you can find and enjoy them for yourself.

Surrounded by the marshes of the Killbuck valley, this community has often been susceptible to the flood waters of Killbuck Creek which flows along the western side of town. These marshlands may look forbidding and worthless; however, they are a valuable wetlands resource. If you're here when the wild roses are blooming, stop and sniff the air. If a breeze is coming from the right direction, you'll be able to smell the sweet fragrance of these pink blossoms.

South of Killbuck on SR 60 travelers can glimpse Killbuck Creek in its wild state. It's a lovely, winding drive. This is probably the only portion of the creek which hasn't been dredged and channeled. The Killbuck twists and turns its way into Coshocton County and eventually empties into the Walhonding River near where SR 60 intersects US 36.

KILLBUCK

We're reaching just outside of Killbuck to tell you about **Bittersweet Farm**. If you like herbs and everlastings, you'll enjoy this shop housed in a 100-year-old bank barn. From antique wooden bowls filled with fragrant dried lavender blossoms to bunches of statice, sweet Annie, money plant, cockscomb, yarrow, artemesia, tansy, rose hips, and bittersweet hanging from ceiling beams to herb vinegars and wreaths by the dozens this is a feast for the senses. Owner Mary Lou Crowe is now serving luncheons in The Farmhouse. She says they're not reservation-only but advises you to call ahead. Served Tues.-Fri. 11 am-2 pm, Sat. 'til 3 pm, and Sun. noon-3 pm. Herbs and perennial plants are on sale in the greenhouse in the spring, and Mary Lou's getting some gardens going for visitors to wander through. To find Bittersweet Farm, take SR 60 about 1½ mi. south of Killbuck. The sign and driveway are on the left. Address is 1720 SR 60, Millersburg, OH 44654. PH: 330-276-1977 for more information or luncheon reservations. Hours are Mon.-Sat. 10 am-5 pm; Sun. noon-5 pm. Closed Jan. and Feb.

Our second reach outside of town is to **Country Greens**. Visitors will find 18 holes of miniature golf, a batting cage, driving cage, game room, and snack bar here. Adults pay $2.50 for a game of miniature golf and those under 18 pay $1.50. Take SR 60 north of Killbuck to the first township road. You'll see the large sign. Located at 3338 TR 90. PH: 330-276-0225. Hours are Mon.-Thurs. and Sun. 2-10 pm; Fri. and Sat. until midnight.

The ONLY movie theater in Holmes County is the **Duncan Theater** in downtown Killbuck. Built in the 1940's, the Duncan shows movies nightly at 7 pm and Saturdays also at 9 pm as well as Sunday afternoons at 2 pm. Admission is $3 for adults and $2.50 for children 12 and under and senior citizens. Owner Henry Yoder has established a large video rental business here as well. Located on the square at 110 N. Main St. (SR 60 is Main St. and runs north to south through the middle of town.) PH: 330-276-7231.

Advertising "Dream Cars of Yesteryear," **G & H Collectible Cars** is a trip down memory lane, particularly for those over thirtysomething.

More like a museum than a used-car business, G & H Collectible Cars has at least 50 classic automobiles inside a large building. These are museum-quality cars and, although the prices certainly reflect that, they are well worth seeing. My 24-year-old son has had a lifelong love of automobiles, especially those of pre-1970 vintage, and these were enough to make him drool. They are gorgeous! Find G & H at 165 Spring St., (4 blocks south of the square), or write P.O. Box 447, Killbuck, OH 44637. PH: 330-276-7875. Hours Tues.-Fri. 10 am-4 pm; Sat. until 2 pm. Open evenings by appointment.

The newest business in Killbuck is **Indian Valley Florist Gallery and Gifts**. A full-service florist with plants and cut and dried floral arrangements, the shop also features handmade gifts by local artisans, including baskets, jewelry, Indian art, and pottery made on location by Brett Sammons. Address is 257 N. Railroad St. Railroad St. runs along the tracks one block east of Main St. PH: 330-276-2006. Hours Mon.-Sat. 8:30 am-5:30 pm, Sun. noon-4 pm.

The **Killbuck Valley Natural History Museum** tells the history of this area of Holmes County with bird, mammal, rock, mineral, and fossil displays; a full-scale model of a rockshelter as used by Native Americans in the area for thousands of years, and a pictorial history of two local railroads. This is a nonprofit museum operated by the Killbuck Valley Historical Society. Museum Curator, Dr. Nigel Brush, led the Martin's Creek mastodon excavation near Berlin in July 1993. The results of this excavation determined that early man used flint chips to butcher the mastodon. Located in the center of town on Front St., the museum is open from 1-5 pm Fri., Sat., and Sun. May-October. Admission for adults is $2; children 6-12 get in for $.50. Groups of 10 or more can make arrangements for weekday and weekend tours by calling Helen Smith at 330-377-4572 or Jim Weiss at 330-276-8025.

George and Caroline Smith feature lots of toys and glassware at **Palladium Antiques**. In addition, there are books and other collectibles. Antique hunters will enjoy these two crowded rooms. Caroline and George say visitors should ask if they're looking for something specific because not everything they have is out on shelves. Caroline collects antique textiles but does not have them on display,

and there is also a separate roomful of "roughs." I first met George
when we were both writing for the now-defunct *Auction & Antique
Buyers Guide*, so this is an extremely knowledgeable couple. Located
at 402 S. Main St. PH: 330-276-5111. They are open 7 days a week
by chance or appointment.

Ronald Rippeth is a master craftsman specializing in Tiffany-style
stained glass lamps at **Rippeth Stained Glass**. The lamp bases are
antique reproductions and with Ron's colorful shades, they are
stunning. He also creates windows so, if you have a desire for
beautiful stained glass in your home, get in touch. Since Ron does not
have a shop, he prefers you call for an appointment at 330-276-7215.

You'll have to get out your county map for this one, unless you just
happen to know where *French Ridge* is in Holmes County. It may not
be fair to stick **Wilson's Country Creations** in this chapter on
Killbuck because it's closer to Glenmont. However, since there is no
chapter on the Glenmont area, this seemed the best place. You may
already have seen some of this company's handiwork because, if
you've seen concrete lawn ornaments in area shops, chances are they
were made here. About 250 different items of concrete statuary are
made, from a 2 inch mouse to a 600 lb. fountain. Most of their
business is wholesale but they will do retail sales and going to the
source is one way to see every item in their inventory. They also have
goose gear for those popular critters and clothes to fit both a rabbit
and teddy bear they make. So, if you want to go to Wilson's Country
Creations, take CR 6 off SR 520 west of Killbuck until you get to
13248 CR 6. It's on the corner of CR 6 and CR 25, so it might be
easier to take CR 25 north of Glenmont. Either way, it's a pleasant
drive. Hours are Mon.-Fri. 9 am-5 pm. Closed Sat., but open some
evenings and Sundays. Call ahead (330-377-4190) to be sure.

Dining

Home-cooked food made from scratch is featured at **Gallion's Front
Street Restaurant**. There are daily specials at lunchtime or try
something from the list of sandwiches. On the dinner menu are Italian
favorites such as ravioli and stuffed shells; flame-broiled steaks,
including 8- and 12-oz. Boston strip steaks; seafood such as batter-

dipped fish, lake perch, clams, and shrimp. They have a special menu for the under 12 crowd. At 142 Front St. next to the Killbuck Museum. PH: 330-276-0024. Hours are Tues.-Thurs. 11 am-7 pm, Fri. until 8 pm, Sat. 9 am-8 pm, and Sun. 11:30 am-3 pm. Sat. is the only day they serve breakfast. Closed Mon. The restaurant is for sale as of this writing so, if sold, the menu and hours may change.

Known in the area for great pizza, **Pizza Parlor II** does not have a dining room but, if you're hungry and plan to be in town to see a movie, take your pizza and sodas up on the hill past the elementary school to the park and relax at a picnic table. Not a bad way to spend a warm evening. They also have sub sandwiches, an Italian salad, garlic bread, and hot chicken wings. Located at 124 Front St. PH: 330-276-5661. Hours are 4-10 pm Tues.-Thurs., until 11 pm Fri. and Sat., and until 10 pm on Sun. Closed Mon.

Subway has opened in the Quick Chek on Front St. with a couple of booths for diners. Hot and cold subs are served on their freshly baked rolls. They also serve breakfast until 11 am. Open Mon.-Fri. 6 am-11 pm; open Sat. at 7 am and Sun. at 9 am. PH: 330-276-4511.

The **Sweet Shoppe** has a small dining area and serves meals, sandwiches, ice cream, etc., during warm weather. Located on N. Main St. It's currently up for sale, so one can only speculate that it will continue to be open spring through autumn. Hours have been Mon.-Sat. 9 am-9 pm. Closed Sun. PH: 330-276-7885.

Lodging

Jacqueline and Christopher Thorne operate **Minnow Run Bed and Breakfast** about 1½ mi. north of town at 3989 SR 60, Killbuck, OH 44637. Accommodations in this Victorian farmhouse include private bath, A/C, fireplace, and continental breakfast. Rates $60 per night. PH: 330-276-7605 for more information and reservations.

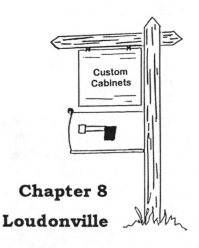

Chapter 8
Loudonville

In our country's earliest history, the only roads known to white men were the rivers. Much exploration was first done by pushing a canoe into the water and paddling into the inner reaches where no one but the Native Americans had gone before.

With its abundance of navigable streams, the Loudonville area demanded exploration by those ever-curious souls who felt compelled to see what was over the next hill and beyond their limited horizons.

In 1810 James Louden Priest recognized the possibilities in this location, made a land deal with two settlers in the area, and the three men laid out town lots and streets. They called the proposed settlement Loudenville. Although the spelling changed somewhere along the way, all the streets Priest laid out are still there today.

With its streams and scenic beauty the Loudonville area was a natural to attract those who enjoy outdoor activities. In the past twenty-five years or so the area has grown from a quiet, out-of-the-way community into the canoe and camping capitol of Ohio. I wonder if Mr. Priest would approve? This emphasis on canoeing the rivers, camping under the stars, and photographing the many scenic views helps ensure the landscape is not spoiled. I'm sure he would approve of that.

Originally the roadbed for the Toledo, Walhonding Valley and Ohio Railroad built in the 1890's, Wally Road is just one of those historic thoroughfares every visitor ought to explore. Closely following the course of the river, the road usually has water on one side and a steep, wooded hillside on the other.

I'm enchanted each time I drive along it, no matter what the season. Somehow, it's almost as if the spirits of those early explorers speak to me and I can imagine what this magnificent country must have looked like to those who first saw it. This is one road which should give you a real feeling for the area and I'd urge you to take the drive leisurely, savoring the green shadows, wildflowers, and possible wildlife as well as the woodsy, crisp pine fragrance, or scent of the river in the air.

Find Wally Road south of town, east off SR 3. It begins here as Ashland CR 3175; leaves Ashland Co. to become Holmes CR 23 where it travels across a corner of Knox Twp.; becomes TR 359 at the Knox Co. line; and ends up as TR 357 in Greer at SR 514. Go ahead, take it to the very end, then turn around and head back. It's as beautiful coming as going! Or, take SR 514 north to Nashville, turn west on SR 39, and you'll be back in Loudonville before you know it. SR 514 is also a scenic favorite of mine.

Before we explore the Loudonville area, let me add one note. I'll say more about this in my "What's Open on Sunday?" chapter, but I'll stress here that practically everything in town is open on Sundays, particularly in the summer. If you've got the children along and spent Saturday exploring Amish country, you might want to treat them to the sights, sounds, and activities of Loudonville on Sunday. There's a lot to see and do here, so let's find out what interests you most.

One thing visitors need to be aware of is the fact that since so many of Loudonville's attractions depend on the outdoors and the river, the weather plays a critical, deciding factor in what's open and what's not. Dry spells aren't a problem. The river runs a little lower and your canoe may scrape bottom occasionally, but that's part of the game. However, rainfall—and this area often sees plenty of it—can shut the whole place down. Rafts, tubes, canoes, and kayaks are available for fun-seekers, depending on the condition of the river and sometimes the temperature.

All the livery owners are concerned with your having fun and being safe. So, wear your life jacket because it's for your protection,

and be prepared with an alternate plan in case the weather isn't
cooperative. High water is dangerous and the canoe liveries are closed
when conditions warrant it.

Of course, we hope your visit finds the sky bright with sunshine.
If it does, wear your swimsuit or old clothes—and an old pair of
shoes—because half the fun of being on the river on a hot summer
day is getting wet! A dry change of clothes is advisable, and don't
take *anything* into the water that you can't afford to get wet or lose.

Loudonville's summer schedule is full of all sorts of special
events such as the Great Mohican Indian Pow-Wow and Rendezvous
which draws Native Americans from all over the country. This is a
wonderful occasion for the whole family to observe, enjoy, and learn
more about our Native American neighbors.

A whole week in early October is devoted to the Loudonville Free
Street Fair, the largest street fair in the state. Downtown streets are
filled with tents, food stands, and carnival rides. 4-Hers bring their
animals and there are all sorts of exhibits. It's a great way to celebrate
autumn.

For more information about the Loudonville area call the
Mohican Tourist Association, 138 N. Water St., Loudonville, OH
44842, at 1-800-722-7588. If you're planning to spend your vacation
here, they also have a Mohican Travel Coupon Book available for
$11.95 which can save you more than $1,000 on camping, canoeing,
meals, entertainment, etc.

Ashland County information can be obtained by contacting the
Ashland Area Chamber of Commerce, 47 W. Main St., Ashland, OH
44805 or calling 419-281-4584.

Loudonville

Over 4500 sq.ft. of oak furniture handcrafted by the Amish of Wayne
and Holmes Counties is at **Amish Oak Furniture Co.** Most of it is
also available in cherry or walnut, if preferred. This is a lovely
showcase for furnishings and includes crocks and pottery, tinware,
comforters, and an upstairs art gallery. In downtown Loudonville at
268 W. Main St. PH: 419-994-3721 or 1-800-686-8855. Hours are
daily 10 am-5:30 pm; Fri. until 8 pm; Wed. and Sun. 12-5 pm.

The **Art Depot**, located below Raby Hardware, is sure to tickle the fancy of artists with their art and craft supplies. You might consider getting some paints and finding a quiet corner to paint one of the magnificent landscapes you'll discover in the area. They also have supplies for air-brush fanciers and do custom matting and framing. Located at 223 W. Main St. PH: 419-994-4430.

Like horseback riding? The only stable in Mohican Forest is **Bit 'N Bridle Stable**, offering guided rides on 5 trails of varying lengths. Group rates are available. Take SR 3 south of Loudonville, then take the first right after you pass the SR 97 intersection. Located about 3½ mi. down a scenic road at 996 CR 3275, Perrysville, OH 44864. PH: 419-938-8681. Open rain or shine February-November.

The Mohican Historical Society was bequeathed funds by Cleo Redd Fisher for a museum. So, the **Cleo Redd Fisher Museum** came into being. With two floors of diplays, this small, attractive museum is worth spending some time in to get a feel for the history of the community. Located at 203 E. Main St., it's open Sat. and Sun. 2-5 pm, and holidays from May-mid-Oct. Admission is 50 cents for adults and 25 cents for children 6-12.

The genius behind the **Creative Outlet** is Vikki Roberts who designs and makes much of the jewelry. You'll be struck by the difference here as soon as you walk in the door. Crystals and stone specimens, T-shirts, and ponchos are abundant. Upstairs is an art gallery featuring works by Native American artists. Books always attract me and their selection of titles is intriguing. The background music may be Native American flutes, piping peaceful, enchanted melodies. And there's that jewelry—lots of it, with silver and turquoise abundantly featured. Take time to enjoy because this shop is crowded with delights you won't find elsewhere in the area. Located at 226 W. Main St., Loudonville, OH 44842. PH: 419-994-5092. Hours are Mon.-Thurs. 10 am-6 pm; Fri. and Sat. until 8 pm; Sun. 11 am-6 pm.

In addition to being a full-service grocery store, **Gribble's IGA** has an in-store bakery stocked with fresh bread, bagels, apple fritters, and donuts. Best of all, if you're looking for a ready-made picnic lunch, their deli can supply sandwiches, salads, and desserts; or call ahead and order a bucket of chicken. Take SR 3 through town, follow its right turn at Heffelfinger's Marathon, then turn left onto Jefferson St. Located at 430 N. Jefferson St. PH: 419-994-3204. Hours are Mon.-Sat. 8 am-9 pm; Sun. 9 am-6 pm.

Hidden Treasurers is a gift and card shop at 234 W. Main St. They also have some antiques, mostly toys, and Christmas items in rooms at the back of the store. PH: 419-994-4567. Open Mon.-Sat. 10 am-6 pm; Fri. 'til 8 pm; Sun. noon-5:30 pm.

The first canoe trip I made way back in the 60's was from the bridge right in the heart of town at the **Loudonville Canoe Livery**. These days, in addition to canoes, they have rafts, kayaks, and tubes to rent. Find this one at 424 W. Main St.—still at the bridge. PH: 419-994-4161 or 419-994-4561. Open mid-April-Nov. from 9 am 'til dusk.

Miner's Sparkle Market has all your grocery needs and a small deli at the back of the store. Right downtown at 128 W. Main. PH: 419-994-3351. Open Mon.-Sat. 8 am-9 pm and Sun. until 8 pm.

Are you ready for some fun? Doug and Patty Shannon have just the place for you. **Mohican Canoe Livery & Fun Center** is a great place for the whole family. This canoe livery bills itself as Ohio's first, having started in 1961. Trips of 2 hrs. (7 mi.) or 6-8 hrs. (15 mi.) are available as well as 2-day trips for the adventurous. They also have rafts, kayaks, and tubes.

If you haven't had enough water by the time you return from a trip down the river, go over and try out the **Mohican Waterslide**. You're probably wet anyway, so why not enjoy the four, twisting, turning slides and the plunge into the pool at the end? The age requirement at the Waterslide is 4 yrs. and 42" tall. Hourly rate is $7 on weekdays, $8 on weekends. All-day rates are available. Open 10 am-8 pm weekdays; until 9 pm weekends. PH: 419-994-3103.

Waterlogged by now? Go on to the **Mohican Riding Stable** with its one-hour guided rides. Open 10 am-7 pm, this attraction costs $16 per horse for 1-2 horses; $14 for 3-9 horses, etc. Age limit is 6 yrs. old and no double riding is allowed by decree of insurance carriers. The sign at the waterslide will direct you.

Looking for something else to do? Well, **Loudonville Go-Kart**

& Mini-Golf awaits. Open 10 am-10 pm with lighted courses. There are now 2 mini-golf courses available. The Level Skill Course is $4/adult, $3/child (6-12). The Adventure Course features caves and waterfalls and is $6/adult, $5/child. Or play both courses—$9 and $8. There are also two tracks for the go-karts. The Family Track for ages 10 and older is $4 per ride. Ages 3-10 ride as passengers in double karts for $1. The Fast Track has an age requirement of 16 or older and is $5 per ride. Each ride is 4 min. PH: 419-994-4020.

If you've got the kids along and everyone's interested in these activities, they have a fun package available which includes a 2-hr. canoe trip, all day watersliding, 2 Family Track go-kart rides, and 18 holes of miniature golf on the Level Skill Course for $19 per person. Group rates for 20 or more are available. Located south of town on SR 3. For more information call 419-994-4097 or 1-800-662-2663.

If your passion is dolls, you'll want to stop at **Mohican Valley Dolls**. These folks restore and dress old dolls, as well as make their own porcelain dolls and carousel horses. These dolls are poured, fired, handpainted, and dressed, some in Victorian style, right on the premises. Find them on Pine and Haskell Avenue, Loudonville. PH: 419-994-4243.

What is now called **The Ohio Theatre** is the original Loudonville Opera House at 156 N. Water St. Constructed as part of a complex which still includes the Mayor's Office and the Police Department, the opera house opened to its first performance December 27, 1910. With two balconies, private boxes, a fly loft, tiers of dressing rooms 4 stories high, and ornate plaster ornamentation, this is a wonderful example of a Victorian theatre. The theatre got new managers, Randy and Pam Burson, in 1995, but movies are still shown at 7 pm weekdays, at 7 and 9 pm Fri. and Sat., and on Sun. at 2 and 7 pm. Admission is $3 for adults and $2.50 for children 12 and under. The Bursons plan to have live entertainment approximately every third weekend (more during the summer). Call or write them for a calendar of events. PH: 419-994-3750. Hey! Don't wait for a rainy evening to enjoy this historic treasure.

Woodcrafts, sweatshirts, gift baskets, handmade jewelry, and a large selection of bisqueware and paints are available at **P.J.'s Ceramics**

& Crafts at 409 W. Jefferson St. across from Gribble's IGA. Hours Mon., Fri., and Sat. 9 am-6 pm; Tues.-Thurs. until 9 pm.

The Piecemaker Fabric Shop has a small selection of quilts and quilted items on display. Also, bolts of fabric and all sorts of sewing supplies. Find them at 249 W. Main St. PH: 419-994-5179. Hours are Mon.-Sat. 10 am-5 pm; Wed. noon-5 pm. Closed Sun.

We're going just outside of Loudonville to Perrysville to catch the **Pleasant Hill Canoe Livery/Mohican State Park Canoe Livery**. Mel Reinthal, who owned Pleasant Hill has leased his property to the State Park Canoe Livery which lost its former location. So, Mike Dresch is now running the operation. This is the only livery operating on the upper part of the Black Fork of the Mohican. Canoe and kayak trips from 1-50 miles are available at rates from $7 to $28 per person. Children under 12 canoe free with two paying adults. This is now the home of the "Moonlight Canoe Trips" held on the Sat. closest to the full moon June-Sept. Cost $8.99 per person per canoe. Flashlights required and reservations advised. Canoers can enjoy a picnic lunch and volleyball while they're here. Season passes available. Open May-Labor Day daily 9 am-5 pm. Located on SR 39 at the edge of Perrysville, 914 SR 39, P.O. Box 10, Perrysville, OH 44864. PH: 1-800-442-2663.

Second Chance is a new and used children's shop at 153 W. Main St., Loudonville. Check this out if you have kids or grandkids. PH: 419-994-9983. Hours Mon.-Sat. 10 am-5 pm. Closed Sun.

Named for a quilt pattern, **Squash Blossom Square** is a lovely shop with some differences. From folk art and pottery to birdhouses and handpainted slate, this store is a treasure trove of interesting decorative and gift items. Be sure to give it time for a proper visit. Located at 251 W. Main St. PH: 419-994-5505. Hours are Mon.-Sat. 10 am-5:30 pm; Fri. until 8 pm; Wed. and Sun. noon-5 pm.

Do organic foods, healing herbs, and aromatherapy interest you? Then, you'll want to visit **Stony Mountain Botanicals**. They emphasize women's natural health care and items to nurture the spirit such as books and crystals. Located at 141 N. Water St.. PH: 419-

994-4857. Hours Mon.-Fri. 10 am- 5 pm; Sat. 'til 4 pm. Closed Wed. and Sun.

Looking for a leather jacket or one of those long dusters? See if the **Thunderbird Indian and Western Wear Gallery** has what you want. They also have Minnetonka moccasins, totem poles, and many decorative items if you want something to add to your southwestern decor. Located at 307 W. Main St., Loudonville, OH 44842. PH: 419-994-4679. Hours are Mon.-Thurs. 10 am-5 pm; Fri. and Sat. until 7 pm; Sun. noon-7 pm (April-Dec.). Close at 5 pm rest of year.

If Indian crafts and accessories are your passion, stop at **Two Rivers Indian Shop**. Owner Allen Combs is principal organizer of the summer pow wows and an interesting man to talk to. Suncatchers, Indian weapons and tools, jewelry, T-shirts, blankets and rugs, arrowheads, moccasins, and bear and elk hides are just some of what's to be seen. Located south on SR 3 in front of the go-kart track. PH: 419-994-4987. Summer hours weekdays 12-5 pm; weekends 12-7 pm. Winter hours Tues.-Sat. noon-5 pm; Sun. 12:30-5 pm. Closed Mon.

Mohican State Park

In 1949 **Mohican State Park** was created from the woodlands of the Mohican State Memorial Forest which still surround it. A trip here to see the fall foliage and maybe have a picnic was a real treat as a youngster. It holds a special place in my heart and I still think the scenery is incomparable. The National Park Service must agree with me because they've designated the Clearfork Gorge and the hemlock forest as a Registered National Natural Landmark. Visitors can enjoy the picnic areas and miles of hiking trails with attractions like Big and Little Lyons Falls where time has obliterated the name and date carved by John Chapman in the early 1800s. Johnny Appleseed, as he is better known, was a frequent visitor to the region because of the apple tree nurseries he planted and tended in this area.

All the camping facilities in the park were closed for renovations during the '95 season. They reopened in October, so here's the scoop: The Class A **Family Campground** has 123 campsites, each with electric, a fire ring, and picnic table. Price per night is $18 for 6 people. An additional 33 sites in this campground now have water and sewer hookups and are $24 per night. An Olympic-size swimming pool is available for use by Family Campground and cabin guests. **Hemlock Grove Camping Area** (Class B) offers 24 primitive campsites with a $9-per-night cost for 6. A **Group Camping Area** which can accommodate 100 is for organized groups only.

Located along the Clearfork River in a wooded area are 25 deluxe housekeeping **cabins**. Each can accommodate 6 people. They have electric heat in the winter and air conditioning in the summer, and contain cooking utensils, dishes, bed linens, blankets, towels, gas fireplaces, and color TVs. The kitchens include microwaves and the bathrooms are newly remodeled. Current winter rates start at $75 for one night. They tell me rates are going up in March but are not known at this time. Call 419-994-4290 for reservations in the campgrounds and cabins.

Mohican State Park Resort and Conference Center offers a secluded setting with a beautiful view of Pleasant Hill Lake. There are 96 rooms with A/C, color TVs, radios, phones, and balconies. This lodge also has 2 swimming pools, one an indoor, heated pool; a sauna; 2 lighted tennis courts; rental bicycles; and nature trails. The lodge is lovely and has a cocktail lounge and a dining room overlooking the lake. Conference rooms available for groups up to 250. Rates April to October are $89 weekdays and $99 on weekends. Children under 18 stay free in parents' room. Discounts for seniors. AAA rated. Located on the west side of the park. Take SR 3 south to SR 97. Follow the signs and enjoy the forest view. Turn north on McCurdy Rd. Although it's about 17 mi. from Loudonville, the lodge is worth the trip. For reservations contact them at 419-938-5411 or in Ohio dial 1-800-282-7275.

Dining

Three sisters operate **D's Dari-Ette** at 305 W. Main St. Good place to grab a quick bite if you're starving after that canoe trip—and who isn't? Sandwiches, ice cream, and all the normal fare are available. In business almost 30 years. Closed in the winter.

Gotta craving for pizza? Call **Downtown Pizza** and order a large with all the toppings to satisfy that hunger. They also have gyros, hoagies, and stromboli. Located at 235 W. Main St. PH: 419-994-3911. Hours are Sun.-Tues. 4-11 pm; Wed.-Thurs. 11 am-11 pm; Fri. 11 am-midnight; Sat. 4 pm-midnight.

East of Chicago Pizza Company has risen from the ashes of the former Mohican Country Store on SR 3 south. In addition to pizzas they serve salads and subs, spaghetti, and barbequed wings. At 3052 SR 3, Loudonville. PH: 419-994-5561. Hours in the summer are Sun.-Thurs. 11 am-11 pm; Fri. and Sat. until midnight. In winter they close at 10 pm Sun.-Thurs.

Giacomo's Brass Plate has an all-new Italian menu with the restaurant's recent change of ownership. They have soups, salads, and sandwiches on the lunch menu (served 11-3) as well as lasagna, spaghetti, and all those great Italian dishes. The supper menu includes steaks, chops, and prime rib in addition to lobster and a variety of pasta. For dessert there are cheesecakes and spumoni ice cream among the offerings. They also serve beer, wine, and alcoholic drinks. Find the Brass Plate at 267 W. Main St. PH: 419-994-5588. Open Tues.-Sat. 11 am-11 pm; Sun. 'til 7:30 pm.

The **Heinz Restaurant** serves three squares a day and has carry-out service. Try their granola with honey for breakfast or scrambled eggs, home fries, biscuits, and sausage gravy for $2.95. The morning meal is served from 8-11 am Mon.-Fri.; until noon on Sat., and 9-11 am on Sun. There are plenty of sandwiches on the lunch menu as well as homemade soups and salads. The dinner menu offers such entrees as lasagna, liver and onions, pot roast, cabbage rolls, roast pork, and the Heinz special—barbequed baby back ribs. On Fridays they have a fish fry for $5.45. Located at 146 N. Water St. next to the Village offices and the Ohio Theater. PH: 419-994-3669. Hours are Mon.-Thurs. 8 am-9 pm; Fri. and Sat. until 10 pm; Sun. 9 am-5 pm.

In an 1853 historical setting with one of those old-fashioned embossed tin ceilings, **Lee's Pub & Grill** offers lunch and supper. For $3-$4 you can enjoy a nice lunch of soup, salad, quiche, or a sandwich. Lunch is served from 11 am until 2 pm. Supper hours are 5-8 pm (Fri. and Sat. until 9 pm) and the menu features such things as pork chops, orange roughy, baked chicken, and prime rib, or specials like parmesan crust salmon quiche with frest fruit. Located at 206 W. Main St.. PH: 419-994-5336. Reservations may be a good idea, especially on weekends. Closed Sun.

You can order hillbilly steak and eggs for breakfast at the **Loudonville Inn Restaurant**. That's fried bologna! The owner must be a football fan because you'll find such sandwiches as the left tackle and right end offered here. You'd have to be a left tackle to eat a half-pound sirloin burger with bacon, cheese, and all the trimmings. For dinner the menu includes spaghetti, chicken and veal parmesan, liver and onions, steaks, perch, and shrimp. There's a menu for the under 10 crowd. Open Mon.-Thurs. 5:30 am-9 pm; Fri. and Sat. 'til 10 pm; Sun. 7:30 am-2 pm. At 258 W. Main St. PH: 419-994-5227.

That fast-food giant, **McDonald's**, is located on SR 3 on the south edge of town. You know the menu here. PH: 419-994-4794. In summer the dining room is open 6 am-11 pm Sun.-Thurs. and Fri. and Sat. until midnight. In the winter the dining room closes an hour earlier, but the drive-thru is open until 11 pm and midnight.

It's with regret that I must inform you **Mohican Manor** is no longer serving meals to the public. But I'm sure the Bright family is enjoying their lovely historic home and we wish them the best.

You might want to see the **Mohican State Park Resort** and there's no better way to check it out than to have a meal in their lovely dining room with its view of Pleasant Hill Lake. The house specialty for breakfast is a freshly baked malt flour waffle with butter and warm syrup or warm fruit. For lunch you'll find a Reuben, Mohican burger, French dip sandwich, Teriyaki chicken sandwich, and a daily special among the menu offerings. Dinner entreés include prime rib au jus (Fri. and Sat. only), filet mignon, oriental pork stirfry, salmon with dill sauce, lemon trout, and angel hair pasta with a choice of three sauces. For dessert you can try Polly Kunkle's grasshopper pie. There is a children's menu available. Breakfast is served 7 am-11 am and they usually serve buffet-style on Sat. and Sun. mornings; lunch from noon-2 pm; dinner Sun.-Thurs. 5-8 pm and until 9 pm on Fri. and Sat. Call 419-938-5411 for dinner reservations.

Rader's Family Restaurant serves a breakfast buffet on Sat. and Sun. during the summer. They are open for breakfast from 7 am-noon seven days a week. In addition to all the regular breakfast fare, they serve corn, buckwheat, oat bran, and regular pancakes. There is no separate children's menu; however, they offer a wide selection of sandwiches including Reuben's and a ¼ lb. Super Dog. Now that's a hot dog! Diners can enjoy a New York strip or rib eye steak, ham, chicken, shrimp, clams or any of their other dinners with 2 side dishes, roll or biscuit for $6.95 or under. They have 15 kinds of homebaked pie to choose for dessert as well as hand-dipped ice cream cones. Located on SR 3 south of town. PH: 419-994-5155. In the summer Rader's is open until 8 pm Sun.-Thurs. and until 9 pm Fri. and Sat. Closing time during winter is one hour earlier.

The **Riverwagon Restaurant** is now open year 'round under new ownership. Their specialty is homemade pizza but they also serve barbequed ribs, sandwiches, subs, and calzones. Located south of town at 3059 SR 3. PH: 419-994-4664. Open daily 11 am-11 pm in the summer. Winter hours may vary.

At the Duke gas station on SR 3 south they have a **Subs-n-Such** where you can get a variety of hot or cold subs on freshly baked French bread. They start serving pastries and donuts at 6 am and are open until 10 pm 7 days a week. PH: 419-994-4032 or 994-3066.

Old enough to remember when drug stores and restaurants had lunch counters? Well, the **Village Pantry and Soda Shoppe** has one in the back, along with booth and table space. Shades of the 1950's! A jukebox plays hits for a quarter while customers enjoy malts, sodas, flavored Cokes, phosphates, shakes, sundaes, and banana splits. With 20 flavors of ice cream and frozen yogurt, these sweet concoctions go on and on. If you prefer, choose a sandwich, soup, salad, or the daily special. And in the front of the shop? Bulk foods and candies, gourmet condiments and coffees, and chocolates. Find this old-fashioned soda shoppe at 153 W. Main St. PH: 419-994-4271. Hours are Mon.-Thurs. 8 am-9 pm; Fri. and Sat. 9 am-10 pm; Sun. 1-7 pm.

Remember the drive-ins of the 50's and 60's where you pulled your car in, ordered a meal, and ate it while sitting behind the wheel? Well,

Zimm's Drive Inn used to be one of those. These days, however, all the dining is done inside. At the time I visited, the restaurant was for sale, so everything may change. Right now it's open seven days a week from 7 am-2 pm. You can start with breakfast or get any of their sandwiches later in the day. There's no separate menu for the kids but plenty for them to choose from. Breakfast is served until 11 am. Located on SR 3 on the northeast side of town at 523 Wooster Rd. PH: 419-994-4551.

Lodging

Albertson's Guest Cottage will accommodate up to 8 people. With 3 bedrooms and 2 baths, this might be the perfect getaway for your family. Weekend rates for 6 are $195. Extra persons $25 each to the maximum of 8. Weekly rates for 6, $395. Everything is furnished except your food and dish soap. Fishing available in the stocked pond. Located on SR 97 near the park entrance. Contact the Albertsons at 115 Hoffman Rd., Loudonville, OH 44842, or phone 419-994-4543.

I love old houses of all kinds, so visiting lodging places like **The Blackfork Inn** is always a pleasure. This circa 1865 brick Victorian townhouse is listed on the National Register of Historic Places. The Inn has six guest rooms, each with its own bath, furnished with antiques. A complimentary full breakfast is served. Rates from $65-$85. The Blackfork Inn is located at 303 N. Water St., Loudonville, OH 44842. PH: 419-994-3252 for reservations.

Plans call for **The Blackfork Inn II** to open in the spring of '96 right across the street. It will have two suites and a new "Ohioana" shop filled with arts and crafts. Call the number above for more information.

Want a place all to yourself where the whole family can relax? Might want to consider **The Bunkhouse**, a cottage with 3 bedrooms and 2 baths which sleeps up to 8. Fully furnished with TV, ceiling fan, screened porch, and electric heat. Take SR 3 south to first right beyond the SR 97 intersection, then right again onto TR 3286. Address is 977 TR 3286, Perrysville, OH 44864. PH: 419-589-2677 for reservations and rates.

Right on the square in downtown Loudonville is **Cannon House Bed and Breakfast**. This residence of Betty and Donn Kieft is a beautifully decorated, 1823 Georgian cottage built as a stagecoach stop on the road between Mt. Vernon and Wooster. Guests can enjoy a suite on the first floor or one of two bedrooms on the second, each with private baths. Rates begin at $55. Guests enjoy a breakfast buffet with fresh fruit, juice, rolls, cereal, and coffee. Located at 109 S. Market St., Loudonville, OH 44842. PH: 419-994-5546 for reservations.

Motel accommocations are available at **Little Brown Inn,** which is under new management. There are 20 rooms with cable TVs, A/C, and phones. May 1-October 31 rates during the week are $40 single and $45 double. Weekends it's $10 more. Winter rates are $35 and $40. Children 12 and under stay free. Located on SR 3 south of town at 940 S. Market St. For reservations call 419-994-5525. Rader's Family Restaurant located next door.

Murder Mystery Weekends are very popular from October-May at **Mohican River Inn**. The 50 rooms have private balconies, A/C, and color TVs. Nine efficiency units with kitchenettes are among them. Conference rooms seating up to 175 are available. Rates for a double are about $47.50. Ask about their special rates for the murder mystery weekends which include 2 nights' lodging, a wine and cheese reception, Sat. meals, and Sun. brunch. Take SR 3 to Wally Road to 16024 CR 23 (Wally Rd.), Loudonville, OH 44842. Make reservations or get further information by calling 419-994-5579 or 1-800-228-5118.

See the Mohican State Park section for information on the **Mohican State Park Resort and Conference Center**.

Camping

Arrow Point Camping & Canoe is located about 4½ mi. south of SR 3 on Wally Rd. At this 34-acre campground you'll find riverfront sites with water and electric and special camping areas for families and singles. Primitive sites at $13 for a couple. Sites with water and electric at $15. Discounts are given on canoeing through the

Loudonville Canoe Livery for those who camp here. Please note that they do not have showers available. Arrow Point's address is 3208 CR 3175, Loudonville, OH 44842. PH: 419-994-5374 for more information and reservations.

Located on the site of an Indian village governed by Chief Mohican John, **Mohican Reservation** is also 1000 feet south of the Greenville Treaty Line. After General Anthony Wayne defeated the Native Americans at the Battle of Fallen Timbers in 1795, this treaty was drawn up and signed, giving lands south of the line to the United States while the lands north of the line remained, temporarily only, in the hands of the Indians. There are 175 campsites, 125 with water and electric and 50 primitive. Open April to Nov., this campground offers quite a line-up of entertainment, including an American Indian Days Program in June. Tents, campers, and teepees are for rent. There is a ball diamond, soccer field, volleyball court, playground, game room, etc. A Good Sampark and AAA rated. Guests get a special rate on canoeing, rafting, kayaking, or tubing available at the campgrounds. Located 7 mi. south of SR 3 at 23270 Wally Rd., Loudonville, OH 44842. PH: 614-599-6631 or 1-800-766-CAMP for reservations.

See the section on the **Mohican State Park** for information on camping within the park.

Riverfront camping is available at **Mohican Valley Camp & Canoe** between April and Nov. Each site has a picnic table and fire ring and some have electricity. Kayaks and canoes are available for 3-6, 9-12, or 18-mile trips, or ask about overnight river trips. When you get back, enjoy a hot shower. Guests are invited to entertain themselves in the game room or on the volleyball court. Located at 3069 SR 3 just south of the Wally Rd. intersection. PH: 419-994-5204 or 1-800-682-2663.

Mohican Wilderness is as far out as we're going—at least in this edition. Located on Wally Rd. 9 mi. south of town, this one is almost to the little community of Greer. In addition to camping, they offer canoeing, horseback riding, and miniature golf. They also have a calendar of special events scheduled here such as the Mohican Trail 100-Mile Run (You read it right. Time limits is 30 hours!), a

Boomerang Contest, and a Bluegrass Festival. Located at 22463 Wally Rd., Glenmont, OH 44628. PH: 614-599-6741.

Molasses Holler's 66 sites all have electric, water, and sewer. This one's not for tents. There's a well-stocked lake, a picnic pavilion, and it's within walking distance of many of the attractions south of town. Rates $14 per day. The entrance is located across from the Riverwagon Restaurant at 3058 SR 3, Loudonville, OH 44842. PH: 419-994-5150 or 419-994-5553 for information or reservations.

There are 500 sites at **Rainbow Springs Family Campground** with water and electric, so this is a big campground. Hayrides, a stocked fishing lake, a swimming lake, paddleboats, a playground, and game room are among the many enticements. Rates about $18 per night for a family and $15 for a couple. Located 4 mi. south of the State Park at 3435 SR 3, Loudonville, OH 44842. PH: 419-994-5095 for information and reservations.

Riverfront campgrounds are numerous in this area and the first one south of SR 3 on Wally Rd. is **River Run Family Campground**. There are 160 campsites here, many with water and electric. Canoeing and tubing are available at a discount for their campers. Sand volleyball, basketball, a game room, and playground are part of the fun. Riverfront sites about $17.50 per night. Located 1½ mi. south of town at 3064 CR 3175, Loudonville, OH 44842. PH: 419-994-5257 for reservations and more information. Open May 1-Oct. 15. AAA rated.

Smith's Pleasant Valley Family Campground has campsites along 1 mile of the river for tents and RVs. Riverfront sites $19 per night. Off river, $17. There are also fully furnished cabins available at $65 per night. Those who stay here get special rates on canoeing. Campers can also enjoy volleyball, horse shoes, hiking, a swimming pool, game room, and playground. All the usual camping amenities are here. Open April 1-Nov. 1. Located 5 mi. south of SR 3 on Wally Rd. Contact P.O. Box 356, Loudonville, OH 44842, or call 419-994-4024 or 1-800-376-4847.

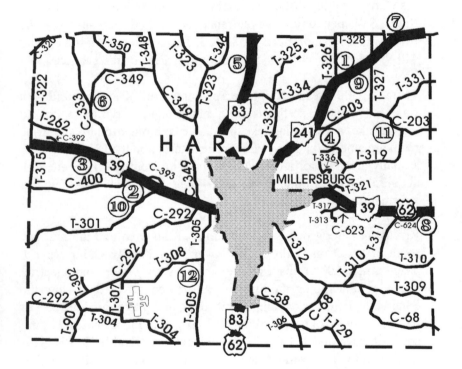

Hardy Twp.
Holmes County

Chapter 9
Millersburg and Hardy Twp.

Millersburg is not only the largest town and county seat of Holmes County, but its downtown shopping district is a gold mine of Victorian architecture. There are so many nice buildings here, including many large, elegant homes. Of course, the centerpiece of Millersburg is the Court House. Listed on the National Register of Historic Places, the Court House was constructed in 1885.

If you're a first-time visitor to this community, you can't fail to notice this impressive stone structure on the square. Since this is a public building, it's open during the day if you want to see it up close and personal. Liberty, holding the scales of justice, is in the lobby outside the courtroom on the second floor.

Take some time to walk through the downtown shops. Many have high, embossed tin ceilings intact and other architectural details which offer their own show-and-tell lesson in history. I'm continually surprised by their spaciousness, so different from what we've come to expect today.

Anyone who enjoys historic buildings must take time to tour the beautiful Victorian House, operated by the Holmes County Historical Society. See below for hours and admission.

A couple of nice things have happened in downtown Millersburg in the past year. Painter, Diane Graebner, opened an art gallery last spring and in the autumn David and Sharon Jones opened Three Feathers Pewter. It's great to have these talented artisans in our midst. Their presence can only enhance the community and, hopefully, draw other craftspeople to locate here. Our Victorian storefronts filled with one-of-a-kind specialty shops would renew the vitality of the downtown as well as attract more visitors to its old-fashioned charms.

To provide some reference points for getting around Millersburg, SR 39 and US 62 are Jackson St., running east to west through the center of town. SR 83 is the main north-south route, called Clay St. until it merges with S. Washington St. south of the square.

Pilots of their own aircraft, can take advantage of this form of transportation to Amish country by flying into the Holmes County Airport located off CR 292 southwest of Millersburg. The airport was opened in 1966 and is a Civil Air Patrol base as well as a refueling stop for Life Flight and National Guard helicopters.

Small twin-engine jets and prop aircraft are provided with safety services such as a non-directional radio beacon, VOR two-instrument approach system for inclement-weather landing, air traffic monitoring by Akron-Canton radar, weather information from Cleveland Flight Service, and all-night runway lights.

Once you're on the ground, there is hangar space, tie-down service, and both courtesy car and rental car availability. The folks at the airport are interested in upgrading services and safety measures for those who use the highways in the sky. For more information call them at 330-674-2686.

Visitors may want to come to Millersburg during its two big annual events—the Holmes County Fair and the Antique Festival.

The fair is held the third week of August, just before school starts, and brings out many involved in agriculture in the County, particularly 4-H youngsters. Did you know Holmes County is one of the top counties in Ohio in number of dairy cows and pounds of milk production? And you thought we were just another scenic wonder.

The Holmes County Antique Festival is the first weekend in October. 1996 will be the 34th year for this event which includes live entertainment, parades, and an antique market where you can shop for furniture and collectibles. The downtown businesses turn their display windows into a Main Street Museum, inviting everyone to stroll the sidewalks and see reminders of the past.

For more information about these annual events and anything else you want to know about Amish country, you should contact the Holmes County Chamber of Commerce. Director Jack Craig is a one-man information center, probably possessing more overall knowledge of the area than anyone else in the county. Feel free to stop by the office at 91 N. Clay St. between the hours of 9 am-5 pm Mon.-Fri., or call 330-674-3975. There is a large rack of free brochures on the front porch and the porch door is open even when the office is closed.

MILLERSBURG

The **Antique Emporium** just keeps growing. They started out with one store, expanded into the building next door, opened a back room, then put an overflow of "roughs" upstairs. What can you find here? Maybe a better question is: What *can't* you find? Old books, linens and textiles, a rack of old clothing, glassware galore, jewelry, kitchenware, crocks, old advertising art and bottles, tools, antique furniture in all sorts of styles, collectibles, and more collectibles. You'll need plenty of time to see everything because there's so much, and it's constantly changing as things are sold and new items brought in. Antique lovers will have a ball! Co-owner/manager, Caren Starr, was also instrumental in organizing and promoting a trio of Antique Markets held at the fairgrounds in 1995. Dealers from across the state brought their wares. For information about future Antique Markets, contact her at 113 W. Jackson St. PH: 330-674-0510. Open Mon.-Sat. 10 am-5 pm; Sun. until 4 pm.

In Amish country this is the one that started it all. **Gallery of Crafts** took the building that once housed Rodhe's IGA, divided the space into booths, and invited area craftsmen and artists to rent space to show and sell their work. Now about 165 participants offer a little bit of everything in the way of handcrafted items. "Goods from the Woods" is here with great-looking painted furniture items, each one a work of art, and a warehouse of unfinished cabinet doors. They're at the back of the building. If you love handcrafted things, this is the place for you! Allow plenty of time to wander and browse through the store. Located at 75 E. Clinton St., one block north of Jackson St. PH: 330-674-5300. Hours are Mon.-Fri. 9 am-5:30 pm; Sat. until 8 pm; Sun. noon-5 pm. Friday hours during the summer until 8 pm.

Are you a bargain hunter? **Goodwill Thrift Shoppe** has an ever-changing inventory of formerly owned items at their store at 16 S. Crawford St., about ½ block south of SR 39 across from the SR 241 intersection. There could be a great buy just waiting for you. PH: 330-674-9222. Open Mon.-Sat. 9 am-6 pm and Sun. 11 am-6 pm.

Award-winning artist Diane Graebner has opened **Graebner Gallery and Framing** at 138 W. Jackson St. This former high school art teacher is well known for her portrayals of Amish life. In addition to her own work, the gallery houses the work of other internationally known artists as well as her husband's framing expertise. It's a lovely, bright showcase of talent. PH: 330-674-6755. Hours Mon.-Sat. 10 am-5 pm. Fri. 'til 8 pm.

The Grocery Bag is a convenience store famous around here for its b-i-g hand-dipped ice cream cones. Trust me, don't order a large one unless you're prepared to eat a *lot* of ice cream. The 75-cent "baby" cone is enough for me. Great cones at great prices! The Grocery Bag is at 189 N. Clay St. PH: 330-674-0833. Open 7 days a week—Mon.-Fri. 6 am-midnight and Sat.-Sun. 7 am-midnight.

Ohio's oldest family-owned clothing store is **Maxwell Brothers Clothiers**. In business since 1866, walking through the door of this store is like a step into the past. There's the attractive, embossed tin ceiling, hardwood floors, and an airy spaciousness which reminds us how grandly past generations planned. John Maxwell is the fourth-generation owner of this shop which sells men's and women's clothes. Be sure to stop by at 45 W. Jackson St. PH: 330-674-4936. Hours are 9 am-5 pm Mon.-Sat. Open Fri. until 8 pm.

In the hands of a fifth generation, **Millersburg Furniture** has been doing business at the same location on E. Jackson St. across from the Courthouse since 1913. They offer a full line of upholstered furnishings and accessories, plus a big selection of Cat's Meow, baskets, comforters, and more. This is a store with plenty of interesting things to see, so take your time. PH: 330-674-3881. Hours are Mon.-Sat. 9 am-5 pm; Fri. until 8 pm.

At 173 W. Jackson St. shoppers will find four businesses under one roof—**Patchwork Place, Book Nook, Etc. Unlimited,** and **Jackson St. West**. Patchwork Place does custom quilting including wallhangings, quilts, and pillows. They also have some things on display. If you want a quilt made to your specifications, expect to wait 6 months to a year. Book Nook sells a good variety of hardbound and paperback books including children's books. Etc. Unlimited sells gourmet foods, gift baskets, balloons to celebrate special occasions, party accessories, gift wrap, cards, and gift items such as Smith & Vandiver toiletries. The fourth enterprise, Jackson St. West, features needlework supplies—fine yarns, floss, counted cross stitch, instruction books, and patterns. It's an interesting, enjoyable mix. PH: 330-674-2076 or 674-0853. They're open Mon.-Fri. 9 am-5 pm and Sat. until 4 pm.

As far as I know, there's only one 24-hour business in Amish country. It's here at the **Shell Food Mart**, 1618 S. Washington St. (SR 83 on the south edge of town). You can get snacks and sandwiches, a newspaper, oil and other auto supplies, and gas for that low tank 7 days a week. PH: 330-674-7344.

Sharon and David Jones have opened **Three Feathers Pewter** at 12 E. Jackon St. Their work has won many awards, and now visitors can watch them practice the nearly vanished art of spinning pewter into beautiful plates, goblets, candlesticks, porringers, and bowls. They also cast this tarnish-free metal into spoons, jewelry, buttons, Christmas ornaments, and more. In addition, their gallery showcases the handmade art of their friends—willow furniture, woven rugs, wood carvings, furniture, jewelry, blown glass, and dipped candles. It's a little gem of a shop, so be sure to put it on your itinerary, or send $3 for a catalog of their pewter items. PH: 330-674-0404. Hours Tues.-Sat. 10 am-5 pm. Sun. and Mon. by chance or appointment.

Thoughts That Count is a veritable treasure trove of delightful, quality gifts and craft supplies. Be sure to allow enough time to dawdle over the selections. If you want a gift for yourself or someone special, you're bound to find something irresistible. If you're a crafter, you'll be captivated by the beads, paints, stencils, small unpainted wooden items, wreaths, swags, and baskets waiting to be anointed with your personal touch. They have linens, doilies, comforters, pillows, prints, candles, etc. Located at 88 W. Jackson St. PH: 330-674-6900. From April-Dec. hours are Mon.-Sat. 10 am-5:30 pm; Fri. until 8 pm; Sun. noon-5 pm.

A 28-room, Queen Anne-style mansion listed in the National Register of Historic Places is home to a wonderful Victorian museum. The **Victorian House** is owned and operated by the Holmes County Historical Society. Built in 1902, this house is a beauty from its parquet floors of oak, walnut, and cherry to its parlor with hand-painted ceiling. There are leaded, stained glass windows, an ornate staircase, and four fireplaces with imported English tiles. Holmes Countians donated the majority of interesting items to be seen in this lovely setting. Located 4 blocks north of the square on SR 83 at 484 Wooster Rd. The Victorian House is open from May through October, Tues.-Sun. from 1:30-4:00 pm. Closed Mon. Admission is $3 for adults; ages 13-18 are $1.

Okay, this isn't a fancy craft shop, but it's the only large chain store between New Philadelphia and Mansfield. **Wal-Mart** is at 1640 S. Washington St. and sometimes folks just want to know where to find a store like this. PH: 330-674-2888. Currently, their hours are 7 am-11 pm Mon.-Sat. and 9 am-9 pm on Sun.

Willie Coblentz's shop is popular with those who are interested in sports memorabilia. Find clothing, collectibles, and cards at **Willie's Sports Stuff**, 79 W. Jackson St. PH: 330-674-9950. Open Mon.-Fri. 2-8 pm and Sat. 10 am-6 pm. Closed Sun.

Buy a bucket of chicken and some jo-jo potatoes or something cold to drink at **Yoder's Market**. Find it at 187 E. Jackson St. PH: 330-674-1845. Hours are Mon.-Sat. 6:30 am-9 pm and Sun. 8 am-9 pm.

If you're musically inclined—or wanna be—you'll enjoy **Young Music & Sound**. They have musical instruments of all kinds. There's a rack full of songbooks, another with sheet music, and CDs, too. Radio Shack electronics and Tandy computers are sold here as well as grandfather and wall clocks. Find Young's at 20 E. Jackson St. PH: 330-674-4076. Hours are Mon.-Fri. 9 am-5 pm; Sat. until 8 pm.

Dining

Birdies Family Restaurant serves daily specials, broasted chicken, a big list of sandwiches, pies, and ice cream. I'm a long-time sandwich fan and their chippy sandwich is scrumptious as is their hoagie with grilled onions and cole slaw on top. Tues. evening enjoy all-you-can-eat beer-batter fish for $5.25. There's always something cookin' at Birdies, 214 W. Jackson St.. PH: 330-674-4851. Open 7 days a week, 6 am-10 pm Sun.-Thurs.; until 11 pm Fri. and Sat.

Fast-food franchises have finally discovered Amish country and keep springing up. Holmes County's second **Burger King** opened in Millersburg in 1995. Located south on SR 83 at 1095 S. Washington St. PH: 330-674-5466. Hours are 6 am-11 pm every day with the lobby closing at 10 pm.

Crossroads Pizza is a take-out restaurant with no dining area but they have all sorts of pizzas, subs, salads, and one of my favorites, breadsticks, which I order with mozzarella cheese to dip in their sauce. Stop at the shop across from the courthouse at 34 S. Clay St., or call in your order to 330-674-7500. Open Sun.-Mon. 3-10 pm; Tues.-Thurs. 11 am-10 pm; Fri. 'til 11 pm; and Sat. 3 pm-11 pm.

Ice cream goodies galore are always on sale at **Dairy Queen** as well as a menu of sandwiches, etc. Find them at 890 S. Washington St. (SR 83 south). PH: 330-674-3064. Hours are 10 am-10 pm every day.

The **Dutch Buffet** opened in September 1995 in the Gallery of Crafts building at 86 N. Monroe St. As the name implies, they always have a buffet open but there's also a limited menu you can order from. The breakfast buffet is served until 11 am. Sat. is a seafood and prime rib buffet, and Sun. is a brunch buffet. PH: 330-674-2424. Hours Mon.-Sat. 7 am-8 pm; Sun. 11 am-5 pm.

Although they're not up and running yet, there is supposed to be an **East of Chicago Pizza** franchise going in at 1653 S. Washington St. behind Pizza Hut. Check it out if you've got a craving for something on their menu. PH: 330-674-1717.

The **English Tea Room,** located in the Bigham House Bed & Breakfast, serves an English high tea by reservation-only. The Tea Room accommodates up to 16 diners, so it's a quiet, intimate setting in the historic Victorian home. Since John is a Brit, he knows a proper tea is served with finger sandwiches, scones with butter, jam, and cream, other desserts, and authentic English tea. For us Americans he also offers coffee. Cost is $6 per person. At 151 S. Washington St., 2 blocks south of SR 39. The Tea Room is open Tues.-Sat. from 1-4 pm. PH: 330-674-2337 or 1-800-689-6950 to make reservations.

Located in Sunshine Villa at 149 E. Jones St. (north of the square, turn east off SR 83 at Village Motors) is **Georgie's Room**. It's open for lunch Mon.-Fri. and Sun. from 11 am-2 pm. They have daily specials as well as soups, salads, sandwiches, entreés for the hearty appetite, and desserts. On Sundays they serve a buffet with two meats and all the trimmings. PH: 330-674-5500.

Historic **Hotel Millersburg** offers dining in The Tavern in addition to upstairs lodgings (see below). They are not open for breakfast but serve lunch from 11 am-2 pm and supper from 5-10 pm. The lunch menu features some tasty salads or you might prefer the "Millersburger," ground beef stuffed with Trail bologna and Swiss cheese. For supper you can start with an appetizer such as their French onion soup. Then enjoy a charbroiled steak or other menu entreé. The kitchen closes at 10 pm, but the bar usually remains open. You might want to call ahead (330-674-1457) for dinner reservations. Lunch served Mon.-Fri.; dinner, Wed.-Sat. Closed Sunday.

Rodhe's IGA Super Center can fill all your grocery needs and has a full-service floral shop but, since this is the dining section, I'll tell you about their restaurant, the **Lovin' Oven**, which serves three squares a day cafeteria-style. They serve breakfast 6:30-10:30 am and on Sun. from 8-11 am. For lunch and supper they always have broasted chicken and jo-jo potatoes, but the rest of the menu varies daily. You can get such dishes as cabbage rolls, ham loaf, baked fish, and lasagna as well as their salad bar. The Lovin' Oven is open until 8 pm and Sun. until 3 pm. Rodhe's is open Mon.-Sat. 8 am-9 pm and Sun. 9 am-6 pm. Find this large store at 2105 Glen Drive off S. Washington St. (SR 83). PH: 330-674-7075.

Another place for take-out is **Mark's Pizza**. In addition to the pizza menu, they have subs, sandwiches, salads, and appetizers. Find Mark's at 815 S. Washington St. PH: 330-674-2378. Open for lunch Wed.-Fri. 11 am-1 pm. Then open 4 pm-10 pm Sun.-Thurs. and until 11 pm on Fri. and Sat., but closed Mon.

It was a plunge into the 20th century the day **McDonald's** opened in Millersburg. You know the menu; you know what to expect. Enough said. Find this McDonald's—one of three across Amish country—at 1586 S. Washington St. PH: 330-674-5334. The restaurant is open 6 am-11 pm and the drive-thru until midnight Sun.-Thurs. They stay open an hour later on Fri. and Sat. nights.

Tantalizing aromas have been emanating from **Norman's Bake Shop and Deli** since before World War II. Despite the fact that Joe Norman sold his business to Dan Stadler in 1995, Joe's hands are still blending all the right ingredients as he teaches Dan the baking art. All sorts of pastries, bread, cakes, and cookies are available. You'll also find cold drinks, assorted chips, sandwiches, salads, soups, and other dishes to take out during lunchtime from 11 am-2:30 pm Mon.-Sat. The bakery is open Mon.-Sat. at 6 am and closes at 5 pm. PH: 330-674-2036.

Is there anybody out there who doesn't know there's delicious pizza, pasta dishes, and a salad bar waiting for them at **Pizza Hut**? Pizzaholics can get their fill at 4388 SR 83 on the south edge of town. PH: 330-674-6688. Hours are 10:30 am-11 pm Sun.-Thurs.; Fri. and Sat. until midnight.

Lodging

Millersburg has many century homes and a few have been turned into wonderful B&B establishments. The **Bigham House Bed & Breakfast** is owned by a Gloucester, England, native and a Canton, Ohio, lass. John and Janice Ellis recently added their own living quarters at the back of the lovely brick home built in 1869 by Dr. Jonathon and Nancy Bigham. So, there are four beautiful guest rooms with private baths, ceiling fans, A/C, and cable TVs in the original home. Summer rates are $75 per couple; winter rates are $65. Not designed for children under 12. Find the Bigham House at 151 S. Washington St. about 2 blocks south of W. Jackson St. (SR 39). It's also the site of the English Tea Room (see the dining section). PH: 330-674-2337 or 1-800-689-6950.

"Because a place like this only comes along once in a blue moon," owners Doug and Melody Burgess named their bed and breakfast **The Blue Moon**. Guests have exclusive use of a 2-bedroom apartment on the second floor of a renovated carriage house. A full-size bed, single bed, and sofa bed offer accommodations for up to five people in this retreat decorated in primitive country style. Rates are $80 per couple and $10 for each additional person. Preschoolers are free, but you'll need to bring your own crib for infants. A continental breakfast is served. Take SR 39 east of the square and turn north on SR 241. Turn into the first alley on the right. At 47 N. Crawford St. PH: 330-674-5119 for reservations.

Kyle and Ty Allison are your hosts at **The Flower Bed & Breakfast**. Guests enjoy the privacy of a suite with living area with kitchenette and bath down and bedroom with queen-sized bed upstairs. There is a sofa bed so this will sleep 4. A/C and TV available. Ty serves a continental breakfast. Rates $65-$80. Find this B&B behind the Victorian House at 241 Walnut St. For reservations call 330-674-7662.

The 3-story **Hotel Millersburg** was built in 1847 with an 1864 addition. The original structure is intact even after extensive renovations. There are 23 rooms on the second and third floors with a sprinkler system, and fire and smoke detectors for your protection. All rooms have A/C, telephones, private baths, cable TVs, and daily maid service. Note: there is no elevator or bellboy, so you'll have to trek up the stairs with your luggage. Summer rates for a single room with single bed are $30; double room with 1 bed, $49; with 2 beds, $59; and a suite with 2 double beds and a sofa sleeper for up to 4 adults, $80-$90. Roll-away bed or crib is $5. Children under 12 stay free with parent and no extra bed. Downstairs is The Tavern. See above for more information on meals. However, they do not serve breakfast in the hotel. Instead, you get a coupon good for 10% off on breakfast at Birdies.

There are 9 rooms at **Traveler's Rest Motel**, 1 with a double bed, 2 with queen-sized beds, and 6 with two double beds. Summer rate for a single is $44.95; 2 people are $54.50. Winter rates are $24.50 and $29.50, respectively. Find this motel at 4316 SR 83 on the south edge of Millersburg. PH: 330-674-6811.

HARDY TWP.

1. If you've an old piece of furniture that needs recovering, see the folks at **Country Upholstery**, 6351 SR 241, Millersburg, OH 44654.

2. **Hershberger Lawn Structures** makes storage buildings and playground equipment for the kids from swingsets to play houses. Stop by and see what they have to offer at 8990 SR 39, 1½ mi. west of Millersburg. PH: 330-674-3900. Hours Mon.-Fri. 8 am-4:30 pm; Sat. 10 am-4 pm.

3. Want to find the best price on cheese? You can't beat the per-pound cost at **Holmes Cheese Company** and their Swiss cheese is really tasty! No fancy gift shop here, just cheeses and Trail Bologna. Find them on SR 39 a couple miles west of town. PH: 330-674-6451. Hours are Mon.-Fri. 8:30 am-5 pm.

4. If you haven't gotten yourself a hickory rocker yet, you can buy one at **Honey Run Hickory Rockers**. Jacob J. Kurtz is the craftsman here and you'll find him at 7426 CR 203, Millersburg, OH 44654.

5. If you like flea markets and garage sales, you'll enjoy **Midway Supply Flea Market**. Located about 3 mi. north of Millersburg on SR 83, the whole building is full of flea-market finds, so you never know what little gem you may run across.

6. Halters, buggy harness, robes, stable blankets, and horse supplies are available at **Miller's Country Harness**. Abe D. Miller also does harness, saddle, and shoe repairs. Find him at 5931 CR 349, Millersburg, OH 44654. Open Mon. and Wed. 7 am-5 pm; Tues. and Fri. until 8 pm; and Sat. until 4 pm. Closed Thurs. and Sun.

7. If you're visiting on a Saturday during nice weather and happen to be on SR 241 traveling between Millersburg and Mt. Hope, look for **Miller's Family Bakery** to be set up under the shade trees in their front yard, selling bread, pies, cookies, and maybe even pizzas.

8. Joan Snyder is the creative force behind **The Petalers Greenhouse**, 6584 SR 39, east of Millersburg. She started with just annual flowers. Then, she expanded into vegetables, a few perennials, and herbs. Now Joan's creating fantastic hanging baskets as well. These are like you see in gardening magazines and books, not the often insipid-looking single plants stuck in plastic pots, but great wire baskets lined with spaghum moss and planted with several varieties and colors that look so wonderful. Stop by and see if you agree. The Petalers is open approximately mid-April through June. General hours are 9 am-5 pm but they stay open later during peak season. Closed Sun. PH: 330-674-2251.

9. For your bulk food needs and a pair of comfortable casual shoes, head to **Weaver's Bulk Foods** at 6440 SR 241, Millersburg, OH 44654. Open daily 8 am-5 pm. Closed Thurs. and Sun.

Dining and Lodging

10. **The Hickory Bed Guest House** is named for a bed crafted by an Amish furniture maker. It's not the only bed available, however, in this guest house which can accommodate up to two families. Proprietors are Rev. Jim and Susan Hayes. Rates for a couple begin at $50. Breakfast is served, except on Sundays, for an additional $5 per person. Bath facilities are shared. Located on a quiet country road at 9101 TR 301, Millersburg, OH 44654. Make reservations by calling 330-674-4214.

11. Planned as an oasis of tranquility where guests can unwind and forget about the world outside, **The Inn at Honey Run** has developed a reputation for the excellence of its facilities since opening in 1982. Owner Marge Stock has planned wisely and well to provide guests with a relaxing experience. The original inn contains 24 rooms; a private lounge with fireplace, library, TV, and game tables; and conference facilities. The Honeycombs are 12 earth-sheltered rooms

added in 1988. Located on the hill above the inn, each of the rooms in The Honeycombs has a private patio, fireplace, and bath with whirlpool. In 1993 Cardinal and Trillium Houses were constructed. These 2-bedroom mini-homes are completely furnished and feature cathedral ceilings with skylights, stone fireplaces, and large windows which look out over spectacular woodlands. The Inn at Honey Run is a very special place. Rates in the Inn begin at $79; rooms in the Honeycombs begin at $125; and a 2-night stay (required) in the guest houses are $200 per night Sun.-Thurs. and $275 Fri. and Sat. Winter discounts offered.

Reservations are required for the Inn's dining room. Lunch is served 11:30 am-2 pm and dinner hours are 5:30-8 pm Mon.-Sat. It is closed on Sundays except for guests. Luncheon menu items include sandwiches or dishes such as salmon pot pie, pan-fried or poached trout, vegetable lasagna, and beef stroganoff. On the dinner menu you might find sesame or buttermilk pecan chicken, marinated London broil, and a New York strip steak. Bread pudding with orange sauce and chocolate silk pie are only two of their taste-tempting desserts. The Inn is known for well-prepared meals and they're always trying new recipes to add to their repertoire, so dining here is a real treat.

For more information on all the Inn's features, write 6920 CR 203, Millersburg, OH 44654, call 330-674-0011, or FAX 330-674-2623. Call toll free 1-800-468-6639 for reservations.

12. A contemporary saltbox home with a wide front porch in a secluded wooded setting is offered at **Woodwind Hollow Bed & Breakfast**. Your proprietor, Janice Thomas, has two guest rooms with private baths. Rate is $75 per couple which includes a full breakfast. Located at 4659 TR 305, Millersburg, OH 44654. PH: 330-674-4113 for reservations. Closed mid-Nov. to mid-March.

Please Note: The Amish do not have telephones in their homes. If you want information on products, services, or prices, drop a letter into the mail. Enclose a self-addressed, stamped postcard or envelope for their convenience. They will reply.

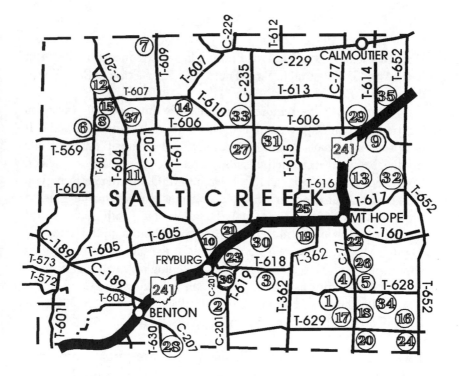

Salt Creek Twp.
Holmes County

Chapter 10

Mt. Hope and
Salt Creek Twp.

Mt. Hope was formed in 1827. Because of its central location between Benton, Berlin, Winesburg, and Mt. Eaton, it was originally called Middletown.

Today, Mt. Hope is probably best known for its weekly auction. Attending one of the area's auctions is probably the best way to meet and talk to our Amish citizens. In addition to the regular Wednesday livestock sale, the Mt. Hope Auction Barn is also the site of several special auctions selling such things as draft horses, farm machinery, and exotic animals as well as annual sales for such charities as the Rainbow of Hope and the Kidney Fund.

Normally a quiet community, Mt. Hope really bustles on sale days, and not all of the action's in the sale barn. Vendors set up outside to sell everything from produce to flea market items. Put one of our auctions on your schedule and go enjoy the sights, sounds, and festival atmosphere.

We can't, however, let Mt. Hope steal all the attention in this chapter because the small community of Benton played an important role in Holmes County's early history. Located about half-way between Millersburg and Mt. Hope, Benton was originally called Martinsburg. Eight grist mills, a woolen mill, saw mills, two stores, a soda pop factory, hotel, two blacksmith shops, a school, church, and wagonmaker were, at various times, businesses which made this village a commercial center in the county. Benton was also the site of the first post office in Holmes County.

Long-time Benton resident, Clayton Miller, has written a book about the community. The *History of Benton 1810-1995* actually began in 1950 when the Millers moved to Benton and Clayton began collecting old letters, articles, and photos. Copies of the book are available for $20 postpaid from Clayton Miller, 6336 CR 207, Millersburg, OH 44654.

Today, Benton is pretty quiet and even the store has closed since the previous edition of this book. I guess it's resting on its laurels.

MT. HOPE

In Mt. Hope, if you need groceries or a snack, you go to **Country Mart**. The store now includes a room for Marcella's Gifts & Crafts where handcrafted items can be found. Country Mart is less than half a block south of SR 241 on CR 77. PH: 330-674-9775. Hours are Mon.-Thurs. 7 am-5:30 pm; Fri. until 8 pm; Sat. until 5 pm.

Lehman's Hardware has a branch of their wonderful store in Mt. Hope for the convenience of the Amish community they've served for so many years. Recently, they expanded the store, nearly doubling the floor space. Shoppers can find many non-electric items such as a grain mill, ice cream freezer, pea sheller, or butter churn. Of course, that's only the beginning of what you'll find here. PH: 330-674-7474. Located right at the square in Mt. Hope, Lehman's is open Mon.-Thurs. 7 am-5:30 pm; Fri. until 8 pm; Sat. until 5 pm.

If your feet get tired walking around the auction, replace your old shoes with a new pair at **Marty's Leather and Shoe**. Athletic and work shoes are most popular with the Amish and most comfortable on tired tootsies. Marty's is located in downtown Mt. Hope, right on SR 241. Open Mon., Thurs., and Sat. 7 am-5 pm; Tues. and Wed. until 5:30; Fri. until 7 pm.

On Wednesdays at 10:30 am, the hay, straw, and grain sale starts at the **Mt. Hope Auction**. Produce, including eggs, chickens, and vegetables, as well as livestock starts selling at 11 am. When you get hungry, buy lunch for $3-$5 in the auction barn. Ask for one of their free calendars listing the year's special sale dates. On CR 77 in Mt. Hope. PH: 330-674-6188 or 674-3017.

The auction barn isn't the only crowded place on auction day. The horses are always lined up at the **Mt. Hope Blacksmith Shop** on sale days. Blacksmith David Beachy is an AFA Certified Farrier and his shop is just south of SR 241 on CR 77 across from the auction grounds.

The **Mt. Hope Cabinet Shop** offers custom-built kitchen cabinets, furniture, and grandfather clocks. Stop in at the shop on the west edge of Mt. Hope at 8041 SR 241, Millersburg, OH 44654.

Are you into healing herbs or just interested in taking better care of yourself? There are enough health food products in the **Mt. Hope Country Health Store** to make you feel better just walking in the door. They also have bulk foods and you can top lunch off with a frozen yogurt cone. Located at 8129 SR 241, P.O. Box 49, Mt. Hope, OH 44660. Hours are Mon., Wed., Thurs., and Sat. 8:30 am-4:30 pm; Tues. until 6 pm; Fri. until 5 pm. PH: 330-674-2202.

Although most of you aren't interested in animal feeds and supplies, the **Mt. Hope Elevator** is right on SR 241 in the middle of Mt. Hope. You might, however, enjoy the horse-drawn wagons which load and unload here. In the little village of Overton in northwest Wayne County where I grew up the local grain and feed elevator's patrons drove up in pickup trucks. Although that one is gone now, I've fond memories of its whirring motors and dry, dusty fragrance.

Mt. Hope Fabrics and Gift Shoppe has a new brick building to do business in these days. Fabrics and notions, infant needs, clothing, toys and books for the kids, and some crafts are available. Right on the corner of SR 241 and CR 77. PH: 330-674-5292. Hours are Mon.-Sat. 8 am-5 pm.

Mt. Hope Harness is just south of town on CR 77. But comfortable shoes and harness aren't all you can get. The back of the building is home to **Lone Star Quilt Shop** with its bolts of calico and sewing notions, as well as quilted items. I'd love to own one of their lone star quilts in rainbow colors. Maybe someday. But even the quilt shop isn't the complete story. Behind this building is **Homestead Furniture** where you can see locally made oak and cherry furniture for the whole home. Located at 7700 CR 77, P.O. Box 32, Mt. Hope, OH 44660. Hours for the furniture and quilt shops are Mon.-Sat. 8 am-5 pm. The harness shop opens at 7:30 am.

If you want to see an interesting craftsman making an interesting product, stop in at **Raber's Cart Shop** in downtown Mt. Hope. Mr. Raber makes two-wheeled draft and show carts. He's even made special-order carts for people in wheelchairs. Mailing address is P.O. Box 17, Mt. Hope, OH 44660.

Dining

Mrs. Yoder's Kitchen begins serving breakfast at 6 am. Breakfast prices are some of the most reasonable around. They serve a buffet on Wed. and Sat. until 10:30 am for $4.95. Family-style dinners are on the menu and they offer daily specials. Good food Mon.-Sat. until 8 pm. Right in Mt. Hope at 8101 SR 241. PH: 330-674-0922.

Lodging

A room for up to 6 people is available at **Mt. Hope Village Lodging**. Private bath with whirlpool, private outside entrance, 2 queen-sized beds and sleeper sofa are available. Rates for single person $39, additional adults $9, and children 3-12 $4.50. PH: 330-674-0922 or 674-6044 for reservations.

SALT CREEK TWP.

1. The sign says "65 carriages and sleighs on display." **A&D Buggy Shop** specializes in restoring horse-drawn carriages and also builds new ones. Located at 4682 TR 628, Millersburg, Oh 44654. PH: 330-674-4053.

2. If your organization occasionally looks for banquet facilities, you might want to consider **Benny's Carriage Haus Banquets**. Arie Coblentz and her daughters do the cooking for a minimum of 20

people and serve by reservation only on Tues., Thurs., Fri., and Sat. Breakfast is now on the menu. Dinners include two meats, dressing, potatoes, vegetables or noodles, salad, dessert, and beverage. There's also a soup and salad menu for those who want a lighter meal. Price is slightly higher if your group is less than 20. Contact Ben and Arie Coblentz at 7089 CR 201, Millersburg, OH 44654, or call 330-674-1523.

3. New and used furniture and appliances are on display at **Bowman Sales**, 5150 TR 618, Millersburg, OH 44654. Open Mon.-Fri. 7 am-8 pm; Sat. until 2 pm. Closed Thurs. and Sun.

4. Waterproof horse blankets are made at **Buckeye Blanket Shop** and right next door is Simeon R. Miller's **Collar Shop**. Both these businesses on TR 628 are typical examples of the cottage industries that thrive here.

5. **Burkholder & Sons Buggy Shop** will make you a new buggy and sell you a trampoline or a fake fur buggy robe. Located at 7400 CR 77, Millersburg, OH 44654.

6. Daniel R. Byler operates **Byler's Buggy Shop & Wheel Repair** at 85ll TR 601, Fredericksburg, OH 44627. New buggies are made to order here and Mr. Byler also does repairs to buggies and wheels, buggy painting and will condition the oil cloth.

7. Monroe E. Chupp operates **Chupp's Blacksmith** at 9107 TR 609, Fredericksburg, OH 44627.

8. **Coblentz Dry Goods** is a large dry goods store catering to our Amish friends. It's full of the "plain" fabrics they wear, all sorts of sewing notions, infant items, and even clothing. Located at 6583 TR 606, Fredericksburg, OH 44627.

9. I love plants of all kinds—indoor and outdoor ones. This is the only place where I've ever found bougainvillea for sale. **Country Corners Greenhouse & Garden Store** also sells trees and shrubs, perennials and seeds. Find this business at the corner of SR 241 and TR 606 north of Mt. Hope at 4401 TR 606, Fredericksburg, OH 44627.

10. If you'd like to give a one-of-a-kind wedding gift of custom-etched glass, or have the glass doors etched in that new gun cabinet or the mirror hanging in the hall, **Country Glass & Crafts** is the place to go. They have glassware, mirrors, etc., and books of designs for you to choose from, or bring your own ideas. Located at 7510 CR 201, Millersburg, OH 44654, just north of SR 241. Hours are Mon.-Fri. 9 am-5 pm; Sat. until noon. PH: 330-674-5429.

11. **Country Hill Farm Fresh Produce** sells fresh fruit and produce in season, and baked goods on Fridays and Saturdays. Located 2 mi. north of Fryburg on CR 201. PH: 330-674-1552.

12. Looking for a good bulk food store? Stop at **The Country Pantry** where you'll find not just a wide variety of bulk items but also ice cream, snacks, cheeses, and lunch meats, and coloring books for the kids. Located at 8861 CR 201, Fredericksburg, OH 44627. Take CR 201 at Fryburg north of SR 241. Open 8 am-6 pm.

13. **Country View Oak** specializes in dining room tables and cedar chests. Owner Owen Mast makes beautiful things. Stop in and see for yourself at 8368 SR 241, Fredericksburg, OH 44627, ¾ mi. north of Mt. Hope.

14. You can buy an authentic Amish black fur or wool hat at several different shops in the area. The label may say they were made locally at **Flying Eagle Hats**, which also has straw hats as well at hat stretchers and plastic hat covers. They will clean and reblock hats, too. Mailing address is 6000 TR 607, Fredericksburg, OH 44627.

15. **Handmade baskets** are for sale at the farm on CR 201 across from Gilead's Balm Manor B&B.

16. **Hillside Harness Hardware** makes all kinds of nickle, chrome, and brass hardware for harnesses at 4205 TR 629, Millersburg, OH 44654. Anyone know what swedge means?

17. Buggy harnesses are in stock at **J.H. Bowman & Sons**, but that's not all. Find horse blankets, buggy robes, riding tack, sleigh bells, horse supplies and accessories, and more. Located at 6928 CR 77,

Millersburg, OH 44654. Hours are Mon.-Fri. 7 am-5 pm; Sat. until 11:30 am. Open the second Sat. of each month until 5 pm.

18. **J.H. Watch Repair** sells all kinds of clocks and watches as well as some furniture items such as cedar chests, magazine racks, recliners, hassocks, and rocking chairs. How about a horse-collar clock for the wall or a painted sawblade clock to sit on a table? Located at 6954 CR 77, Millersburg, OH 44654. Hours are Mon., Tues., Wed. 7:30 am-5 pm; Fri. until 7 pm; Sat. until 3 pm. Closed Thurs.

19. The Mitchel Millers sell **llamas** at 7719 TR 362. You'll see many llamas throughout the area if you take the time to get off the beaten path.

20. This is one of those stores where you can find just about anything, but housewares are the specialty at **Miller's Country Store**. Located south of Mt. Hope at 6888 CR 77, Millersburg, OH 44654. Open Mon., Tues., Wed. 7:30 am-5 pm; Friday until 7 pm; Sat. until 4 pm. Closed Thurs.

21. **Mt. Hope Bike Shop** sells new bicycles as well as doing repair work. Have you seen those bikes where you sit on what looks like a tractor seat and pedal with your feet out in front of you? I'd only seen the homemade kind until I stopped at Mt. Hope Bike Shop. These are supposed to be very comfortable. Find the shop at 7635 SR 241, Millersburg, OH 44654, 2 mi. west of Mt. Hope. There is no sign advertising it, but in the house next to the bike shop Katie Mast takes orders for custom-made quilts and wall hangings. Sounds to me like **Katie's Quilts & Wall Hangings** is keeping really busy, and the samples I saw were gorgeous.

22. Have you seen the new fencing made of vinyl? It's good-looking and maintainence-free but, of course, a little more expensive than wood. **Mt. Hope Fence** not only has this latest innovation but fencing as old-fashioned as split-rail and barbed wire. Whatever your need, stop in and talk to the folks at Mt Hope Fence located at 7468 CR 77, Millersburg, OH 44654. PH: 330-674-6491.

23. Just north of the intersection of CR 201 and SR 241, is a place where kitchen dreams come true. **Mullet Cabinet** has a wonderful showroom to inspire your imagination of what your kitchen *could* be. My favorite, of course, is the cherry cabinets. They also make desks and hutches. In business since 1964, Mullet Cabinet is located at 7488 SR 241, Millersburg, OH 44654. Hours are Mon.-Fri. 8 am-4:30 pm; Sat. until 11 am. PH: 330-674-9646.

24. Get your harness needs met at **Raber's Harness Shop**, 6753 TR 652, Millersburg, OH 44654.

25. Don't let the country location of **Schlabach Sporting Goods** fool you. They have everything for the sportsman: guns and ammo, hunting supplies and fishing tackle, muzzle loaders and accessories. They also do custom reloading. Find them at 5004 TR 616, Fredericksburg, OH 44627. Hours are Mon.-Fri. 5-9 pm; Sat. noon-5 pm. Closed Wed. and Sun.

26. **77 Coach Supply** makes formed wooden parts for horse-drawn vehicles. If you have a need for such an item, talk to them at 7426 CR 77, Millersburg, OH 44654.

27. What little girl wouldn't like a dollhouse? That's only one of the nice things you'll find at **Troy Acres Crafts**. I particularly liked Abe Troyer's wooden, perennial calendar with scenes to change as the seasons do. Find this shop at the Troyers' home northwest of Mt. Hope at 8393 CR 235, Fredericksburg, OH 44627.

28. **Troyer's Arts, Inc.**, is a commercial and fine arts studio, home of Farm Boy collectibles and fine art prints by Wayne Troyer. He says he also does hand-lettered signs; pinstriping on carriages and sleighs; and saves old furniture by stripping, refinishing, and giving it a decorative coat of paint. Since Mr. Troyer does not have a retail shop, be sure to call for an appointment. PH: 330-674-4324. Located at 6014 CR 207, Millersburg, OH 44654.

29. Wayne Troyer operates **Troyer's Lawn Furniture** at 4525 TR 606, Fredericksburg, OH 44627.

30. **Used furniture** is on sale at the Firman and Mary Ellen Miller residence at 7670 SR 241, Millersburg, OH 44654.

31. David A. Swartzentruber operates **Valley Harness Shop** at 5150 TR 606, Fredericksburg, OH 44627.

32. **Valley View Oak** specializes in oak furniture for the dining room. They have a nice showroom where you can see their workmanship. Located 2 mi. northeast of Mt. Hope at 8235 TR 652, Millersburg, OH 44654. PH: 330-359-5375. Hours are Mon.-Sat. 10 am-3:30 pm.

33. **Weaver's Produce** does its business out of a semi trailer. Find fresh produce in season at this roadside stand on the corner of CR 235 and TR 606.

34. Ivan Burkholder specializes in restoring horse-drawn vehicles and has many on display at **Woodlyn Coach Co.** If you want to visit one these craftsman, this one is highly recommended. Find Woodlyn Coach Co. at 4410 TR 628, Millersburg, OH 44654.

35. Abe A. Yoder & Sons keep busy at **Yoder's Porch Swings**. See their selections 2 mi. north of Mt. Hope at 8884 TR 614, Fredericksburg, OH 44627.

Lodging

36. **Fields of Home Guest House** is a lovely log B&B. There are two suites with kitchenettes which can sleep 6, and two efficiency units. One room is handicap-accessible. All rooms have private baths. There's a wide front porch with rockers, inviting you to sit and relax. A large continental breakfast is served. Rates are $65-$95 per couple with extra persons $15. Children are welcome. Located at 7278 CR 201, Millersburg, OH 44654. Call Mervin and Ruth Yoder at 330-674-7152 for reservations.

37. David A. and Sara Mae Stutzman are your hosts at **Gilead's Balm Manor**, another B&B new to the area. Each of their four suites are sumptuously decorated and have Jacuzzis, fireplaces, A/C, TVs,

and kitchenettes. The rooms all overlook the lake and open onto a deck. Continental breakfast is served. Rates $125 per couple with extra persons $10. Children are welcome and stay free. Located at 8690 CR 201, Fredericksburg, OH 44627. PH: 330-695-3881.

I'm not giving **Scenic View Guest House** a map number because it's very close to #36, Fields of Home Guest House, and my map doesn't have room. Myron and Eileen Stutzman have opened the basement suite in their home to guests. There's a bedroom with double bed, kitchen, family room with sofa bed, and private bath. It will comfortably sleep 4. A continental breakfast is served. Rates are $50-58 per couple with extra persons, $5. Find Fields of Home and go north on CR 201 to 7376 CR 201, Millersburg, OH 44654. PH: 330-674-6167 for reservations.

See map location #28 for **Troyer's Brookside Guest House**, operated by Wayne and Mary Troyer. They have a private apartment with one bedroom with a full-sized bed, suitable for two persons. There is a complete kitchenette, A/C, and TV, and guests are welcome to enjoy the picnic area next to the creek. Rate is $40 per couple. Located at 6014 CR 207, Millersburg, OH 44654. PH: 330-674-4324.

Please Note: The Amish do not have telephones in their homes. If you want information on products, services, or prices, drop a letter into the mail. Enclose a self-addressed, stamped postcard or envelope for their convenience. They will reply.

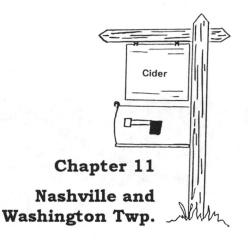

Chapter 11
Nashville and
Washington Twp.

I chose Nashville as the touchstone for this chapter. Since Loudonville is such a big area, the rest of the township would have gotten lost, so it was given its own chapter.

This corner of Holmes County was settled by the Drakes. Eliphalet Drake was deeded land, which included the site of Nashville, by his father in 1827. On a crossroads of Eliphalet's property which visitors traveled north to Wooster, south to Zanesville, and east to Millersburg, he platted the town. In 1840 the population of Nashville was 100. Today, it's approximately 181.

If you like driving around to see the scenery, take SR 514 south of Nashville to Danville in Knox Co. or try CR 22 which winds through both Drakes and Green Valleys. Drakes Valley lies between SR 39 and SR 514 and Green Valley follows the Black Creek between SR 514 and CR 50. These are lovely valleys with some historic homes and, for those looking at their maps, they are in Knox Twp. not Washington Twp.

NASHVILLE

From bird feeders to lawn ornaments to mailboxes to wishing wells, **Dutch Country Crafts** offers all sorts of wooden decorative items for your yard and garden. Some are painted in bright, appealing colors, and some are given a rustic look by charring with a torch. This

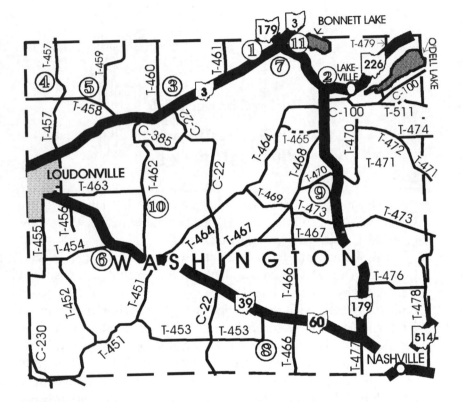

Washington Twp.
Holmes County

home-based business is located at 209 S. Monroe St., P.O. Box 432, Nashville, OH 44661. Monroe St. is CR 52 south off SR 39 at the Buckeye Deli. PH: 330-378-3695. Hours are Mon.-Fri. 4-8 pm.

You can find **Squaw Valley Country Barn & Greenhouse** about 2½ mi. south of Nashville at 5417 CR 52. There's a barnful of antique and used items as well as a greenhouse, selling perennials, bedding plants, hanging baskets, etc. Open April-Oct. Hours are Tues.-Sat. 11 am-6 pm and Sun. until 3 pm. PH: 330-378-2260.

Dining

If you're working on a pizza craving and have no idea where to find a pizza place in this neck of the woods, stop in Nashville at the **Buckeye Deli and Grocery**. Owner Steve Miller is a recent OSU graduate, as you might guess from the OSU decorations and paraphernalia all over the dining area. The guys make a pretty mean pizza here and, if that tantalizing smell doesn't make your mouth water when you walk in the door, your olfactory nerves are dead! They also make subs, tacos and sandwiches, serve ice cream, and have groceries. Located at 124 E. Millersburg Rd. (SR 39), Nashville, OH 44661. PH: 330-378-5663. Hours are Mon.-Thurs. 8:30 am-9 pm; Fri. until 10 pm; Sat. 10 am-10 pm; Sun. 11 am-9 pm.

WASHINGTON TWP.

1. Five miles north of Loudonville on SR 3 is the only canoe livery on the Lake Fork branch of the Mohican River. **Lake Fork Canoe Livery** is open May 1 to Nov. 1, weather permitting. If you'd like to avoid some of the crowds on the Black Fork, this is the place. Six, 10, and 16 mile trips are available, or ask about two- and three-day trips. In addition to canoes, they have single and double kayaks. Rates range from $18-$25 to $60 for 3-day canoe trips, while the kayaks rent for $12-$18. This canoe livery is operated by Britt and Nancy Young of Camp Toodik. Located at 14765 SR 3, P.O. Box 177, Loudonville, OH 44842. PH: 419-994-5484; off-season PH: 419-994-3835.

2. If you've got a Friday night on your hands with nothing to do, head over to **Lakeville Speedway**. This 3/8 mi. dirt track will be howling as the sprint, pro-stock, and pure stock car drivers race for prize money. A list of events for the 20-week schedule that runs from April-Oct. is available by calling 419-827-2160. Admission for a regular night's racing is $8 for grandstand seats and $15 for the pits. Kids under 12 get in free. Located just west of Lakeville on SR 226. Gates open at 5 pm and racing begins at 7:30 pm.

3. **Out On A Limb Wood and Gift Shoppe** is a great place for those who love antiques. This little shop is full of interesting antique furnishings, collectibles, and gifts. Located north of Loudonville at 15285 SR 3, Loudonville, OH 44842. PH: 419-994-4225. Hours are Mon.-Wed. by chance or appoinrment; Thurs.-Sun. 11 am-5 pm. Closed Jan.-March.

4. You don't need a license to catch a trout at **Rainbow Valley's Trout Ranch**. All you need is a desire to get out in the open air and test your luck. Two ponds are available, one with mainly rainbow trout, and the second with several other varieties. One is wheelchair accessible. There's no limit on the catch but you must keep what you catch. Cost is based on a price-per-pound, live-weight basis. So, bring your poles and catch supper! Hours are from noon to dark (about 7 pm) Wed.-Sun. Also open on Monday holidays. Located on TR 457. PH: 419-994-4605 or 994-4872.

5. **Richardson's Greenhouse** sells annuals, perennials, shrubs, trees, and vegetable plants. They usually have a good selection of scented geraniums and herbs available. Located at 8489 TR 459, Loudonville, OH 44842. PH: 419-994-3740. Open Mon.-Fri. 8 am-5 pm; Sat. until 4 pm.; Sun. noon-4 pm.

6. Owner Jane Knight weaves rag rugs on her grandmother's loom and crafts baskets in her gift shop, **Woven Memories**. There's a large variety of gifts and handcrafted items, many displayed on antiques, to see while a player piano tinkles in the background. Jane will also do custom rugs and baskets if you've got your heart set on something specific. Located on SR 39 at 15824 SR 39, Loudonville, OH 44842. PH: 419-994-5007. Hours are Mon.-Sat. 10 am-5 pm.

Dining

7. On the northern edge of Washington Twp. at the intersection of SRs 3 and 179 hungry visitors can get their tummys filled at **Charlotte's Cozy Corners**. The breakfast menu has all the usual fare. For lunch or supper you can choose pizza or one of their sandwiches, or have one of the entreés from the menu. There is also a drive-thru here for beverage purchases. Located at 14660 SR 3, Lakeville, OH 44638. PH: 419-827-2142. Open Mon.-Thurs. 6 am-8 pm; Fri. and Sat. until 10 pm; Sun. 8 am-8 pm.

Lodging

8. Looking for a peaceful getaway? Try **Quiet Country Bed and Breakfast**. For adults only, this residence sets on 98 acres. There's a stocked pond for some fishing and a hiking trail through the woods. You can watch the horses graze in the pasture, see the deer glide out of the woods at dusk, and enjoy the songbirds which come to the feeders. A sport court invites you to enjoy a game of shuffleboard, badminton, tennis, or basketball. Karl and Nancy Tysl are the owners of this smoke-free home. Double or twin beds are available at $60 per night. Located 2 mi. west of Nashville off SR 39 at 14758 TR 453, Lakeville, OH 44638. PH: 330-378-2291 for reservations.

9. Sandy Humphrey operates **Sandy's Place Bed & Breakfast** in her home on a quiet back road near Lakeville. Sandy has two rooms, one with a queen-sized bed and the other with twin beds. Each room has its own bath. Children are welcome and she serves a full breakfast. Rates are $65 per couple. Find Sandy at 7952 TR 470, Lakeville, OH 44638. PH: 419-827-2165.

Camping

10. Named for a Delaware medicine man, **Camp Toodik** occupies more than 100 scenic acres. There are plenty of campsites here, from primitive to full hook-up, shaded and open. Bicyclists and hikers can camp for $5 a night. Primitive sites start at $17 for 2; complete hook-up sites start at $25. Owners Britt and Nancy Young provide transportation for campers to their Lake Fork Canoe Livery several

times a day. Rental units are available for those who don't have tents or campers of their own. Remember to bring your bedding, towels, cooking and eating utensils. Ye Olde Summer Cottage is in a 150-year-old log structure and sleeps 6-8. Rates start at $60. Travel campers and tent trailers can also be rented. The usual campground amenities are available, plus a heated swimming pool. Located south of SR 39 at 7700 TR 462, Loudonville, OH 44842. For information and reservations call 419-994-3835 or 1-800-322-2663.

11. The closer you get to Loudonville, the closer you get to the camping capital of the state. Even if you don't want to camp, your family can still enjoy **Long Lake Park & Campground**. For $2.50 per person you can spend the day swimming, fishing, and picnicking at Long Lake Park. Tues. and Wed. are Family Days where a carload gains admission for $7 (no buses or vans, though). If camping's your game, there are 225 sites with electric and water available May 1-October 15. A family of 4 can spend the night for $18. The 60-acre, spring-fed lake is waiting for your boat (electric motors only) or you can rent a rowboat or canoe for $3 per hour (all day for $20). Since this is a private lake, you can fish with no license and they have bait. Located 6 mi. north of Loudonville just off SR 3 at 8974 Long Lake Dr., Lakeville, OH 44638. For reservations and more information call 419-827-2278.

Please Note: The Amish do not have telephones in their homes. If you want information on products, services, or prices, drop a letter into the mail. Enclose a self-addressed, stamped postcard or envelope for their convenience. They will reply.

Chapter 12

Walnut Creek and
Walnut Creek Twp.

You'll know where the Carlisle name comes from when you learn that Walnut Creek was first known as New Carlisle. Platted in 1827, New Carlisle's name was changed—once again—by the postal system. Because of the abundance of walnut trees in the area and the creek by that name, Walnut Creek was the choice.

This community has been a drawing card for visitors for many years because of Der Dutchman Restaurant. The additional enticements of craft shops, bed and breakfast establishments, a motel, a museum, and a new inn mean Walnut Creek is more popular than ever.

WALNUT CREEK

The **Carlisle House** is a beautiful setting in which to shop. The only question when you walk through the door is where to start? They feature wicker, oak, and cherry furnishings, tables set with English bone china, laces, baskets, lamps, tapestry pillows, a large selection of woven comforters, and many framed prints to decorate your home—and this is just on the second floor! On the first floor are candles and toiletries, a garden room with silk flowers and arrangements, kitchenware, and a big variety of delightful Gnomes.

On the lower level is **Global Crafts**, another of those shops featuring unique gifts from around the world and run by the

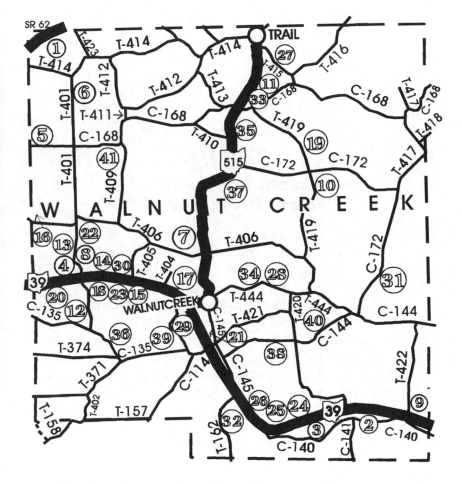

Walnut Creek Twp.
Holmes County

Mennonite Central Committee. There are carved wooden items from boxes and animals to a three-panel, intricate wooden screen made in India; stone figures; brass; painted pottery; and handwoven fabrics and baskets. Also on this level is their Christmas display and a small section devoted to children with toys and personalized items. Located in the heart of Walnut Creek across the street from Der Dutchman Restaurant. PH: 330-893-2535. Hours are Mon.-Sat. 10 am-8 pm.

The fragrance of sumptuous chocolate will smack you right in the nose at **Coblentz Chocolates**. Rich semisweet and creamy milk chocolate are wrapped around a variety of delicious centers—nuts, jellies, flavored creams, and mints among them. There are also several kinds of fudge available, roasted nuts, and gift items. Located on SR 515 just after you turn off SR 39. You can't miss it. PH: 330-893-2995 or 1-800-338-9341. Hours are Mon.-Sat. 9 am-5 pm.

Country Coach, Inc., tours leave from the Carlisle Village Inn at 9 am Mon.-Sat. See Chapter 1, Tips for Travelers, for more information on Carol Glessner's scheduled tours.

Located next door to the Carlisle House in a white frame building is the second of Walnut Creek's gift shops. **The Farmer's Wife** features lots of teddy bears in all sizes, some dressed to the nines in lace and ruffles and earrings. They also have T- and sweatshirts, pottery, craft kits, floss, and needlework patterns. Located at 4952 Walnut St., P.O. Box 151, Walnut Creek. PH: 330-893-3168. Hours are Mon.-Sat. 10 am-8 pm in the summer; until 6 pm in winter.

During his presidential campaign, Ohioan William McKinley spent a night in the circa 1850 home now houseing the **German Culture Museum**. The museum offers an authentic, documented account of the German and Swiss heritages of the area. Furniture, quilts, photographs, folk art, textiles, and documents are displayed. New exhibits are planned each year. No admission charge but donations are accepted. Find it in the heart of Walnut Creek on Olde Pump St. next door to the post office. Open June through Oct. from Tues.-Sat. 12:30-4:30 pm and Fri. evenings 6:30-8 pm. PH: 330-893-2510.

You can take a break from shopping in Walnut Creek at **Happy Pastime Miniature Golf**. Located between the German Culture Museum and Schlabach's Store, this will not only entertain the kids but provide fun for all ages. Weather permitting, they're open daily except Sunday from May-Oct. Adults can play the 18-hole course for $2; students and senior citizens for $1.50. PH: 330-893-2510.

Hillcrest Orchard is open August-April. The Hershberger family's specialties are apples and cider but they also grow melons and peaches. Other items in stock are nuts, honey, candies, and jams, and their own copper-kettle-cooked apple butter. Where SR 515 makes a 90-degree turn past Der Dutchman, take Walnut Street straight east until you find the orchard at 2474 TR 444. PH: 330-893-9906. Hours Mon.-Sat. 8 am-5:30 pm.

Schlabach's Store is *the* general store in Walnut Creek with everything from dry goods to photo supplies. In addition, a grocery, Miller's Foods, is in the same building. Find them at 1 Pump St., Walnut Creek 44687. PH: 330-893-2510. Hours are Mon.-Sat. 7:30 am-5:30 pm; Fri. until 8 pm.

You can get gas, a soft-serve ice cream cone, or another quick snack at the **Walnut Creek BP Food Mart** at the intersection of SRs 39 and 515. Open Mon.-Fri. 5 am-10 pm; Sat. until 11 pm. Closed Sun.

Our final stop on the shopping circuit in town is **Walnut Creek Country Store**. It's located beside the Carlisle House and offers souvenirs as well as all sorts of gift items like Fenton glass, kitchenware, cards, candies, gourd bird houses, and one section of Christmas items with decorated trees. Open Mon.-Sat. 10 am-8 pm.

Dining

Der Dutchman Restaurant has been issuing a siren call to hungry diners since it opened in 1967. Breakfast is served 7-10:30 am and there is the usual fare on the menu, including fried mush. A breakfast buffet is served on Fri. and Sat. mornings. Family-style dinners with pan-fried chicken, ham, or roast beef are available for lunch or supper and include all the trimmings plus dessert. They also offer sandwiches, soups, a salad bar, and plate dinners. Of course, the dessert list features pies, pies, and more pies. There's a children's menu for the under-10 crowd. Next door to the restaurant is a very busy bakery which opens at 6 am and has jams and jellies, cookie cutters, cookbooks, noodles, salad dressings, angel food cakes, pies, cookies, breads, pastries, and donuts. PH: 330-893-2981. Restaurant hours are Mon.-Sat. 7 am-8 pm.

Lodging

There's a 6-mile view from the guest room at **Butler's Quarters**, according to Helen Butler. She and her husband, Bob, offer a non-smoking room with 2 queen-sized beds, which has its own bath and a private entrance. No breakfast is included but they bring in a coffee tray. Children are welcome. Rates $55 per couple with extra persons $5 each. At 2621 Walnut St. (TR 444). PH: 330-893-3208 for reservations.

Karen's Kountry Komfort Bed & Breakfast offers a relaxed atmosphere for guests. A traditional B&B establishment, there are shared bath facilities for the two upstairs guest rooms, perfect for two couples traveling together. One room has a queen-sized bed and the other, a double bed. There's a large living room complete with piano and cable TV to enjoy. Children are welcome. A full breakfast is prepared and evening snacks are always on hand. Your hosts are Greg and Karen Curry. Rates Sun.-Thurs. are $40; Fri. and Sat., $50. Go straight east past Der Dutchman and, once you get beyond the hedge at the corner of SR 515 and Walnut St. (TR 444), you'll see the sign in their yard on Walnut St. Write P.O. Box 42, Walnut Creek, OH 44687, or call 330-893-3189.

Shaker furniture made by Mulheim's of Wilmot decorates the rooms of **The Inn at Walnut Creek**. Each of the 17 rooms has a color TV and A/C. Ten of the rooms have 2 extra-long double beds and the other seven rooms have queen-sized beds. The Inn purchased what was Troyer's Country View B&B when it was on the market last year and this now provides 4 suites for guests. They have an awfully complicated rate structure, dependent on days of the week and months of the year so, instead of trying to explain it all, my advice is just to call and ask. Located at 4869 Olde Pump St. in downtown Walnut Creek. For reservations, call 330-893-3599 or 1-800-262-7181.

The 52-room, Victorian-style **Carlisle Village Inn** is a delight to see. Each room is individually decorated and they have such enchanting names as Rose Trellis, Summerview, Peaceful Garden, Victorian Memories, and Afternoon Tea. There are facilities here for the physically challenged. Conference, meeting, and banquet rooms for groups of up to 475 people are located in the lower level. Rates for May 1-October 31 on Sun.-Thurs. begin at $76 for a room with one queen bed. The same room is $81 on Fri. and Sat. You can't possibly miss the inn because its impressive size dominates this small community. Located next to Der Dutchman Restaurant at 4949 SR 515, Walnut Creek, OH 44687.   PH: 330-893-3636 or FAX 330-893-2056.

TRAIL

Fridays and Saturdays are the days to visit the **Dutch Country Flea Market** in Trail on the corner of SR 515 and TR 414. Vendors sell such things as antiques and crafts, farm-fresh produce, baked goods, homemade ice cream, and the sorts of odds and ends you usually find at a flea market. Open 9 am-5 pm. For more information call 330-893-2062 or 330-339-5572.

If you've never tasted Trail Bologna, you've missed one of Amish country's most popular delicacies. **Troyer's Genuine Trail Bologna** is *the* home of the original bologna, created from a still-secret recipe in 1924. This ring-style, smoked bologna is available in most local cheese houses and grocery stores, or you can go right to the source to buy it. In addition, the same recipe is now made in large, sandwich-style and water-cooked deli chugs. At Troyer's Store you can sit down at the counter to enjoy a bologna sandwich or buy jams, jellies, and a variety of local cheeses. This company ships bologna and cheese everywhere. It's on the Christmas lists of many out-of-towners and displaced Holmes Countians. Find Troyer's in downtown Trail at 6530 SR 515, Dundee 44624. PH: 330-893-2407 or 893-2414. Store hours are Mon.-Sat. 7 am-5 pm; Wed. and Fri. until 8 pm.

You might find just about anything from antiques to motor oil, a box of corn flakes to an old tricycle at **Vogt General Store**. Handed down from father to daughter to daughter, this establishment has been in downtown Trail for decades. Antiques and collectibles offer lots of interesting things to browse through. Located at 6501 SR 515. PH: 330-893-2544. Hours are Mon.-Sat. 8 am-5 pm.

WALNUT CREEK TWP.

1. Roy E. Miller handcrafts **cedar chests** in his home-based shop. Nothing compares to the fresh, clean aroma of cedar. Mr. Miller makes two sizes of the large chests in walnut, cherry, oak, or cedar. Then he also crafts a small table-top chest and cute children's rockers. Find him at 3960 US 62, Dundee, OH 44624.

2. If you have a chair that needs the caning replaced or a rickety wicker piece needing repairs, you should talk to Mahlon and Betty Schmucker at **Cherry Ridge Caning and Wicker Repair**. They are located at 1565 Cherry Ridge Rd. (CR 140), Sugarcreek, OH 44681. Be sure to call them at 330-852-2310 for an appointment.

3. Springtime compels the gardener in us. You may find what you're looking for at **Cherry Ridge Greenhouse**. Owned by Floyd and Marlene Yoder, this business has gardening supplies and hanging baskets as well as bedding plants and vegetables. At 1855 CR 140, Sugarcreek, OH 44581. PH: 330-852-4302. Hours are Tues.-Sat. 10 am-5 pm. Closed Sun. and Mon.

4. **Chestnut Ridge Sewing** can sell you either a treadle or electric sewing machine. They will also rent them for $5 per day per machine, and have sergers, sewing notions, and locally made cabinets. Located at 3654 SR 39, Millersburg, OH 44654, on the corner of TR 401 west of Walnut Creek. Hours are Mon.-Sat. 7 am-5 pm.

5. Find **Country Lane Upholstery** at the William J. Troyer home at 4045 CR 168, Millersburg, OH 44654.

6. One of Amish country's most unusual businesses is **Dundee Donkeys**. These fuzzy-faced, adorable critters come in a wide array

of colors, including spotted. Their appeal is ageless. Raised by the John A. Mast family who also have emus, ostriches, and deer on their farm at 6370 TR 401, Dundee, OH 44624.

7. **Erb's Tarp Shop** can meet all your needs for canvas and vinyl boat covers, truck tarps, and the like at their business right on SR 515 just north of town.

8. Ervin Schrock makes wooden toys and crates at **Felza Bush Crafts**, 5200 TR 401, Millersburg, OH 44654. PH: 330-893-2053.

9. If you've never tried **goat milk fudge**, you owe it to yourself to discover this sweet, creamy treat. Located at the first home on the right on TR 422 just off SR 39 east of Walnut Creek.

10. **Heritage Wood** makes custom cabinets and will stain and finish the interior trim in your home. Contact owner Dan Borntrager at 5631 TR 419, Millersburg, OH 44654. Located 3 mi. northeast of Walnut Creek.

11. Swing sets, playhouses, and sandboxes for the kids are made by Aden E. Hershberger at **Hershberger Wood Shop**. He also builds lawn furniture and porch swings and makes pine crafts. Located next to Wendling's at 2495 CR 168, Dundee, OH 44624. Open Mon.-Sat. 9 am-6 pm.

12. **Hiland Wood Products** is a division of Schrock's. Here they make all types of decorative wooden moldings. They will give you a catalog of their designs and price list if you stop by and ask for one, write P.O. Box 138, Walnut Creek, OH 44687, call 330-893-2617, or FAX 330-893-3132. Located on TR 401 just south of SR 39.

13. **C.L. Karn** recently moved to this location on TR 401 north of SR 39. Mr. Karn is a maker of leather goods, specializing in customized English-style harness, saddlery, luggage, etc. He also makes historical reproductions and offers restoration and repair service. Or you might be interested in his 5-strand braided driving lines, carriage bags, backpacks, folded breast collar, breeching and belly bands, Bible covers, briefcases, or saddle bags.

14. It started out as a favor for a neighbor, but **Mrs. Kaufman's Jams & Jellies** has been in business since 1973. They now make 18 varieties of jams, jellies, pickles, butters, and relish. You can find these products in several local stores, or stop at 3483 SR 39, Millersburg, OH 44654. PH: 330-893-3278.

15. Owner Virginia Koucky moved **Land of Canaan Quilts** from its former location across from Walnut Creek Cheese to a new shop next door to Schrock's Cabinets. Wall hangings, crib quilts, baskets, dolls, rugs, and bed-sized quilts made by area Amish ladies are in stock. Custom quilting is also available. She will send you a free brochure of quilt designs if you write to her at 3340 SR 39, Millersburg, OH 44654. PH: 330-893-3028. Hours Mon.-Sat. 11 am-5:30 pm. Closed Dec.-Feb.

16. Here's one of the very few businesses in this book which doesn't hang out a sign. The *grapevine* gave me the tip, so I checked it out and thought many of you would like to seek out the services of **Log Cabin Crafts**. Lydiann, Rosie, and Carol Miller do wholesale, retail, and custom quilting. Eyeglass cases, placemats, toaster covers, wallhangings, quilts—anything you want quilted, they'll try it. Allow a minimum of 2 to 3 months for a bed-sized quilt. Now, the important part—how to find them. Take TR 401 north off SR 39 between Berlin and Walnut Creek, then turn left (west) onto TR 366. Log Cabin Crafts is at the first farm on the right. It's not difficult to find if you remember it's a farm you're looking for and not simply the first house. Their address is 3883 TR 366, Millersburg, OH 44654.

17. **The Marketplace of Walnut Creek** is now the name of a whole complex of businesses which includes the Amish Flea Market, a new strip mall, and three other businesses. Rather than clutter the map with numbers that wouldn't fit anyway, I'll list them all here:
    Open from April to mid-December, the **Amish Flea Market** is one of the area's most popular destinations. It's not exactly your tried-and-true flea market. It's a 58,000 sq.ft. mini-mall with the emphasis on crafts. Another building was added in 1995, so they have about 350 vendors selling products. The String-A-Longs band performs two Saturdays a month. Of course, there's food, too. No admission charge. Also in 1995, they began opening on Thursdays,

so shoppers can shop 'til they drop Thurs.-Sat. from 9 am-5 pm. Located ½ mi. west of Walnut Creek on SR 39.

The **Amish Country Peddlar** offers pine furniture, cedar lawn furniture, mail boxes, wooden crates, pottery, baskets, and all sorts of decorative wooden items. Address is 3239 SR 39, Walnut Creek, OH 44687. PH: 330-893-2701. Hours are Mon.-Fri. 9 am-8 pm and Sat. until 6 pm in the summer; 10 am-5 pm in the winter.

The **Carriage House** is filled with gift and decorative items for the home such as lamps and lampshades, wooden and upholstered furniture, prints, wallhangings, and a Christmas corner. PH: 330-893-3653. Hours are Mon.-Sat. 10 am-6 pm. Look for them to be open only on Fri. and Sat. 10 am-5 pm during Jan. and Feb.

Homespun Treasures has bird houses and feeders, a Christmas corner, and wooden furniture next to collectibles and antiques. Ashland's Linda McFarlin's fine pencil drawings of the Amish and their life are available here on cards and prints. Amish and folkart dolls and stuffed animals are plentiful in this interesting shop. PH: 330-893-2134. Summer hours are Mon.-Thurs. 10 am-5 pm; Fri. and Sat. 9 am-6 pm. In winter hours are 10 am-5 pm Mon.-Sat.

These are the shops in the new strip mall at this location:

Grandma's Ice Cream Shoppe will be glad to feed you a sweet, icy treat. They make their own ice cream and frozen yogurt, then create shakes, malts, floats, "buggy whips," sundaes, and cones. Yummy! PH: 330-893-3960. Open Mon.-Sat. 11 am-10 pm.

Kid's Collection is the perfect place to bring the kids or shop for them. In addition to all sorts of toys, they have a nature/science section, and a large assortment of puzzles and games. They specialize in play that's imagination-driven, not battery-powered. The staff also plans programs for families to enjoy together such as weekly reading nights. PH: 330-893-4122. Hours Mon.-Sat. 10 am-6 pm; Thurs. until 8 pm.

The Secret Garden stocks gifts from Mother Earth. Their inventory includes handmade silver and stone jewelry; all kinds of minerals and semi-precious stones such as crystals, geodes, soapstones, and onyx; carved wood; and fossils such as trilobites and ammonites. A percentage of all sales goes to Save the Rain Forest. PH: 330-893-3865. Open Mon.-Sat. 10 am-6 pm.

Spoonful of Sugar offers gourmet coffees and teas, fudge, nuts, and candy, candy, candy. They have 40+ flavors of jelly beans and

200+ kinds of candy, including sugar-free and chocolates. PH: 330-893-2220. Hours Mon.-Sat. 10 am-6 pm; Thurs. 'til 8 pm.

18. For more than 12 years **Miller's Farm Market** has been selling fresh fruits and vegetables in season. You'll find everything from home-grown cantaloupes to sweet corn, peaches, tomatoes, pumpkins, apples, squash, and cider. Located at 3460 SR 39, 1 mi. west of Walnut Creek., PH: 330-893-2235. Hours are Mon.-Fri. 8 am-5:30 pm; Sat. 'til 5 pm.

19. If you have a need for harness, you'll find **N&A Harness Shop** at 6005 TR 419, Dundee, OH 44624.

20. There are two businesses and lodging at this location:

If you're into creating your own floral decorations for your home, you'll want to stop at **Country Craft Outlet**. They have all sorts of Victorian prints, ready-made floral swags and garlands, and plenty of silk and dried flowers and greens for the do-it-yourselfer. Owners Darrell and Barb DeVore also have ready-cut mats and frames. Barb does personalized poems suitable for framing and giving as gifts. At 3824 SR 39, Millersburg, OH 44654. PH: 330-893-3854. Open Mon.-Sat. 10 am-6 pm.

Outlet in the Country offers shoppers an extensive array of merchandise. They have the largest selection of dolls in the area—vinyl, porcelain, and handmade. Locally made oak furniture is available such as glider rockers, loveseats, curio cabinets, and entertainment centers. With over 400 designs to choose from, their T- and sweatshirt transfers should include something for even the most finicky shirt lover, available in sizes 12 month to 7 extra large. Located halfway between Berlin and Walnut Creek at 3824 SR 39, Millersburg. PH: 330-893-3500. Hours are Mon.-Sat. 10 am-6 pm.

See lodging section for Little House in the Country.

21. Do you like to make crafts? Do you know someone who does? If so, you'll be intrigued by the variety of crafts supplies offered at **Quality Supply**. They have wooden cutouts and the brushes and paints necessary to create your own one-of-a-kind decorative item. There are kitchenware, towels, and baby items too. Find this crafter's delight just east of Walnut Creek off SR 39 at 4579 CR 114,

Sugarcreek, OH 44681. A further enticement is the homemade ice cream they sell here on Saturdays and holidays during the summer. Hours are Mon.-Sat. 8 am-5 pm.

This is also the location for Cottage on the Hill (see lodging section).

22. **Rockwood** is another division of Schrock's and makes interior and exterior doors in oak, cherry, birch, walnut, mahogany, maple, and poplar. Panel designs in many styles include glass windows and arched doors also. Located just north of SR 39 at 5264 TR 401, Millersburg, OH 44654. PH: 330-893-2392 or FAX 893-2212.

23. **Schrock's of Walnut Creek** has been known for years as a place to buy beautiful custom kitchen and bath cabinetry. They have a wide variety of styles available and their showroom is guaranteed to make you long to refurbish that old kitchen or drab bathroom. They also make wonderful grandfather clocks. Now they've added a line of Shaker-style furniture. Located at 3360 SR 39, Millersburg, OH 44654. PH: 330-893-2141. The showroom is open Mon.-Fri. 7 am-5 pm; Sat. 8 am-noon.

Beside Schrock's cabinet shop is **Schrock's Buggy Shop**. If you have a need for these services, be sure to stop by.

24. Gazebos, gliders, porch swings, flower boxes, rockers, wishing wells, and picnic tables are just some of the items you'll discover at **Swiss Country Lawn Furniture**. Their pieces are locally made by Krestview Woodcraft. PH: 330-852-2031. Located at 2293 SR 39, Sugarcreek, OH 44681. Open Mon.-Sat. 8:30 am-5 pm.

25. All types of fencing, including easy-care vinyl, are available at **Swiss Valley Fence**. Gardeners might be interested in a vinyl hot bed for getting an early jump on the growing season. Located 1 mi. east of Walnut Creek at 2407 SR 39, Sugarcreek, OH 44681. PH: 330-852-4460. Hours are Mon.-Fri. 8 am-5 pm; Sat. until noon.

26. **Swiss Valley Furniture and Crafts** opened in 1995 with locally made pine and oak furnishings. There're lots of unfinished pieces if you want to put your personal touch on something. They have some painted wood decorative items and shelving as well as rolltop desks,

chairs, wagon seat benches, etc. At 2433 SR 39, Sugarcreek, OH 44681. PH: 330-852-3702. Open Mon.-Sat. 10 am-6 pm.

27. Another one of those shops where you might find a bargain is **Trail Furniture & Appliances**. Owned by Paul and Esther Beachy, this store features a good selection of used glassware, household items, furniture, toys, and miscellaneous items. If you don't find what you want today, stop back next week. They offer a 30-day replacement warranty on appliances. Find this interesting store at 2328 TR 415, Dundee, OH 44624. Hours Mon.-Sat. 7:30 am-8 pm. Closed Thurs. and Sun.

28. They do custom work at **Troyer's Cabinet** at 2243 TR 444, Sugarcreek, OH 44681. PH: 330-893-3409. Take Walnut St. and it becomes TR 444 east of town.

29. More than cheese is available at **Walnut Creek Cheese**. They advertise "everything for your kitchen from eggs to the dinner bell" and they're not far wrong. If you like cookbooks, this store has the largest selection anywhere in the area. There are also ceramic tea sets, canisters, baskets, bulk foods and candies, iron skillets, graniteware, and a big variety of meats and cheeses, as you'd expect. At the rear of the store is the ice cream parlor and lunch counter where you can have a sandwich and a cold, luscious treat. Located just east of Walnut Creek at 2804 SR 39. PH: 330-852-2888. Hours are Mon.-Sat. 8 am-6 pm.

30. **Walnut Creek Furniture** has an excellent selection of locally made oak and cherry furnishings and upholstered sofas and chairs for your home. One room features children's furniture such as rockers, rocking horses, tables, chairs, and wooden toys. They also have linens and laces, pictures, dried wreaths and swags, and lamps to help complete your decor. Located right on SR 39, 1 mi. west of Walnut Creek. Mailing address is P.O. Box 24, Walnut Creek, OH 44687. PH: 330-893-3383. Hours are Mon.-Sat. 10 am-5 pm; Fri. 'til 6 pm.

31. Coffee and end tables, cedar chests, and tea carts are handmade at **Walnut Creek Woodworking**, 4930 CR 172, Sugarcreek, OH 44681.

32. If you want to scratch that itch in your green thumb, try **Walnut Valley Greenhouse**. Owners Robert and Mattie Yoder have bedding and vegetable plants, hanging baskets, and perennials. Located at 4054 TR 162, Sugarcreek, OH 44681.

33. Here's another one of those businesses where the craftsman can customize a kitchen, bath, or office for you. **Wendling's Custom Cabinets** is located on the northeast corner of CR 168 and SR 515. PH: 330-893-3446.

34. Find **Woodland Woodcrafts** just east of town at 2323 TR 444.

35. A 116-acre working farm is the setting of **Yoder's Amish Home**. Visitors flock here for guided tours of two authentic Amish homes. An 1866 house demonstrates how the Amish and Mennonites lived at that time. The other, a large, 10-room house, shows how the Amish live today. The tour concludes with a visit to the farm animals in the barn. Tickets are $3 for adults and $1.50 for children 12 and under. There are also buggy rides available at $2 for adults and $1 for children. Combination tour/ride tickets are $4.50 for adults and $2.25 for children. A gift shop features locally made crafts. Interested travelers might want to witness their old-fashioned apple butter stirring held on Saturdays in Sept. and Oct. or the hog butchering days held the last Fri. and Sat. of Oct. Located north of Walnut Creek at 6050 SR 515, Millersburg, OH 44654. PH: 330-893-2541. Open mid-April through October, hours are Mon.-Sat. 10 am-5 pm.

Dining

36. If you have a family or group of 15 or more looking for an interesting dining experience in Amish country, contact Maudie Raber of **Raber's Home Cookin'**. She serves reservation-only dinners of chicken and ham or chicken and steak with all the trimmings, including homemade pie, for $9.50 per adult and $6 per child with children free under age 3. Maudie also makes jams and jellies from apple to watermelon and has *Raber's Country Kitchen Cookbook* which she can mail to you. The jams and jellies are $3 per 8 oz. jar, plus $2 shipping. The cookbook is $5.95 postpaid. Contact her at 3497 CR 135, Millersburg, OH 44654.

Lodging

You'll need to bring your own food to cook on an open fire or the gas range if you stay at **Cottage on the Hill**. The one room includes a kitchen, full bed, and sofa bed and has no electricity. There is a gas refrigerator, battery or kerosene lighting, and a bath with shower. It is heated. Stop at Quality Supply (see #21 for their location) or call their answering service at 330-852-4994 to make reservations. Open April-Oct. Rates are $50 per couple with extra persons (including children) $10. You can see the cottage across the valley from Quality Supply's shop, so it's not far.

37. There are hiking trails and plenty of nature to enjoy on a 68-acre farm when you choose to stay at **Indiantree Farm Bed & Breakfast**. Guests can choose from a 2-room upstairs efficiency apartment or a 5-room downstairs suite with a kitchen. A complimentary breakfast is included. Rates for 1 or 2 persons upstairs are $60 with extra persons $15. The downstairs suite is $70 for one bedroom or $100 for both bedrooms. Weekends require a 2-night stay. Sorry, no pets, smoking, or children under 6. Located on SR 515 north of Walnut Creek. Write Larry and Carol Miller for more information at P.O. Box 103, Walnut Creek, OH 44687, or call 330-893-2497.

House in the Country offers "whole house comfort" next to Outlet in the Country (see map #20 for location). This would be a good place for a family to stay. A continental breakfast from Der **Little Dutchman** restaurant is served. The house has A/C. Rates are $50 per couple; $65 for a family with children; $75 for 2 couples. There's a trampoline in the backyard for the kids to enjoy. Owners are Junior and Iva Mast. PH: 330-893-3500 or, if no answer, 893-2618.

38. **Marbeyo Bed & Breakfast** offers guests private rooms with baths and air conditioning. You'll find pastries in the dining room and a coffee maker when you're ready for your continental breakfast. The Country and Victorian rooms have queen-sized beds and the Farmhouse room has two queens. Rates begin at $55. This is located on a working farm, so comes complete with cattle and probably a few other animals as well. Contact hosts Mark and Betty Yoder at 2370 CR 144, Sugarcreek, OH 44681, or PH: 330-852-4533.

39. Constructed to resemble a traditional Amish farmhouse, **Miller Haus Bed & Breakfast** offers rooms decorated with antiques. There are seven rooms with private baths and double or queen-sized beds and two new suites, one with double and single beds and the other with a queen and single. The quilts on the beds are hand-stitched, some of them by Amish relatives. There is a cathedral ceiling in the sitting-dining area and a fireplace. Since this B&B sits on a hill, the front porch offers a beautiful view of the countryside. A full family-style breakfast including pancakes, bacon, homefries, freshly ground coffee is served. Room rates begin at $85 and $105 for the suites. Located on CR 135 between Walnut Creek and Charm. For reservations or more information contact owners Daryl and Lee Ann Miller at P.O. Box 126, Charm, OH 44617, or call 330-893-3602.

40. Guests at **Peaceful Valley Bed & Breakfast** will be housed in a different apartment when Mr. and Mrs. Miller move into smaller quarters. It will have a private entrance and include a bedroom with two full-sized beds, bath, sitting room, and kitchen. A playpen is available, so children are welcome. Mrs. Miller's continental breakfast includes homemade bread with jams and jellies, coffee, tea, cereal, and usually one other baked goodie. This bed & breakfast is on a farm so you'll truly be able to get away from it all. Rates are $55 for a couple. Located on CR 144 1½ mi. east of Walnut Creek. Phone the Millers at 330-852-2388 for information or reservations.

41. If you want to stay on a genuine Amish farm in a genuine Amish home, contact Noah L. and Mary Troyer at **Sleep on the Farm**. They have two bedrooms with queen-sized beds in an addition to their home. There's a shared bath, kitchenette with refrigerator and stove, and *no electricity*. (I told you this was a genuine Amish home.) Mrs. Troyer serves her homemade sweet rolls with the continental breakfast. Guests can see the farm and maybe even help with the chores. Rates are $40 per couple or $45 for a family or if both bedrooms are used. What a unique experience this could be! They are closed Dec.-March. You can contact them by mail at 5950 TR 409, Millersburg, OH 44654.

Amanda Troyer is your hostess at **Tea Rose Bed & Breakfast**. She has two bedrooms in her home with queen-sized beds and a third room with a sofa sleeper. There is a shared bath. All rooms have A/C. Mrs. Troyer serves a continental breakfast with homemade bread and fresh coffee cake and fruits. Rates are $60 per couple. Extra persons $10. See map location #2 as this B&B is right down the road. Located at 1587 CR 140, Sugarcreek, OH 44681. PH: 330-852-4325.

Please Note: The Amish do not have telephones in their homes. If you want information on products, services, or prices, drop a letter into the mail. Enclose a self-addressed, stamped postcard or envelope for their convenience. They will reply.

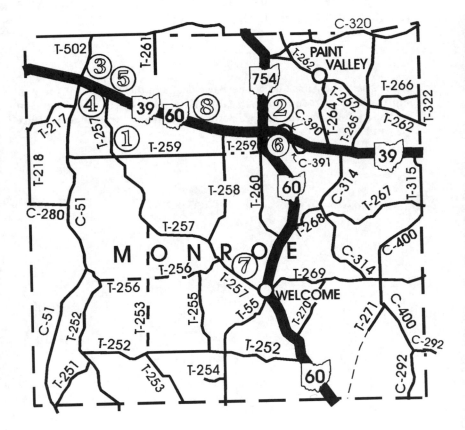

Monroe Twp.
Holmes County

Chapter 13
Welcome and Monroe Twp.

I doubt that either Welcome or Paint Valley will show up on your Ohio map. Paint Valley lies in a picturesque valley in the northeastern portion of Monroe Twp. at the intersection of TRs 262 and 264. Once upon a time, it boasted a post office, a photography studio, etc., but today it's just a small collection of residences.

Welcome owes its continued existence to the fact that SR 60 goes right through it. Located between SR 39 and Killbuck, Welcome is another crossroads community of homes.

MONROE TWP.

1. Enos A. Byler makes custom furniture at **Byler's Wood Shop**. He and his wife also make wooden toys such as a farm set with painted barn and animals, or horses pulling carts or wagons, and Mrs. Byler paints other wooden gift items. Ask about homemade jams or jellies she has in stock to buy. The Bylers sell grapes, apples, and cider in season, too. Located at 5772 TR 257, Millersburg, OH 44654.

2. It's just Finney's around here, but **Finney's Marathon** offers AAA road service, including towing, and is a full-service station with the two Finney 'boys' providing competent, general auto mechanics. In addition, there's a convenience store selling groceries, snacks, and ice cream cones. Located at 11061 SR 39, Millersburg, OH 44654, at the

Box 202, Winesburg, OH 44690. Open daily 8 am-5 pm; closed Wed. and Sun. PH: 330-359-5092.

Yoder's Variety Shoppe is now in that cute little shop where Unique Treasures was. Household decorations are a feature with Amish-made rugs, floral decorations, baskets, ceramics, and more. Owner Rosie Yoder also has baked goods such as breads, cookies, and rolls. Located at 2097 US 62. Hours Mon.-Sat. 10 am-5:30 pm.

Dining

What tastes better on a hot afternoon than a sweet, creamy, cold ice cream cone? **Winesburg Dari-ette** can satisfy those ice cream cravings. Of course, that's not all you can get here. If you're *really* hungry, have a sandwich or a chicken or fish dinner. Unlike most such small eateries, this one is open all year. Located southwest of Winesburg across from the SR 515 intersection at 2467 US 62. PH: 330-359-5715. Hours are Mon.-Sat. 10:30 am-8 pm.

Start your day off right with breakfast at **Winesburg Family Restaurant**. They serve the morning meal until 10:30 am. Trail Bologna and cheese, mushroom steak, and creamed chicken sandwiches are among the offerings on the lunch menu. You can have Amish fries, french fries, seasoned potato wedges, or any of the other side dishes with that. Sunday dinners are a great bargain with Swiss steak, baked ham, home-style fried chicken, and haddock the featured entrees. For about $6 these dinners come with a tossed salad, cole slaw, or jello; mashed potatoes or sweet potatoes; noodles or dressing; buttered corn or peas; and a roll with butter. Then you can top off your meal with a piece of their cream or fruit pies or some ice cream. Located at 2096 US 62, right downtown. PH: 330-359-5110. Hours are Tues.-Sat. 6 am-7 pm; Sun. 8:30 am-3 pm. Closed Mon.

Lodging

Eagle Song Bed and Breakfast is the first of our new lodging establishments in Winesburg. This is the home of William and Carol Kallberg, built in the mid-1800's. They have two upstairs guest rooms, one with a double bed and the other with a queen-sized bed. A continental breakfast is served with Carol's homemade bread. Guests can enjoy the view from a swing under a tree or stroll through the perennial and herb gardens. Adults only. Rate $60 single or double occupancy. Closed during the winter.

The Grapevine House has four bedrooms with queen-sized beds and private baths on the second floor of a renovated 1834 home. Two rooms also include double beds. A/C and TVs are provided. Children are welcome. The $65 charge per couple includes breakfast at either the Winesburg Family Restaurant or Boyd & Wurthmann Restaurant in Berlin. Relax on the wide back porch and enjoy the scenery and garden. Your hosts are Tim and Jean Hostetler. At 2140 Main St. P.O. Box 223, Winesburg, OH 44690. PH: 330-359-7922 or 330-893-2173.

PAINT TWP.

1. You can't have gotten this far into the book without realizing that cabinet shops are a very popular business in Amish country. Ready for another one? **Alpine Cabinets** will customize cabinets to fit your specifications for kitchen or bath. Owner Eli Wengerd has a showroom to display his handiwork. Find this shop at 7932 TR 662, Dundee, OH 44624. Or call their answering service during business hours at 330-877-5808.

2. Moses B. Raber operates **Alpine Clothing & Variety** where shoppers can buy kitchenware, gifts, children's clothing, mutza suits, and all sorts of things. About ½ mi. south of Alpine-Alpa at 8170 TR 662, Dundee, OH 44624. Open Mon.-Fri. 8 am-8 pm; Sat. 'til 5 pm.

3. **Alpine Structures** will construct a solid cedar gazebo on your site in sizes ranging from 8-14 feet. Note: you can also get that with screens, if desired. Or, maybe a storage barn is what you need. Several sizes of these are also available. Located 1½ mi. southwest of Winesburg at 2675 US 62, Dundee, OH 44624. PH: 330-359-5708.

4. For your spring planting needs from strawberries to potatoes and house plants try **Alpine Valley Greenhouse** at 1218 US 62.

5. Stop in and talk to Jonas A. Yoder if you need repairs or a replacement for that old buggy. **Ashery Buggy Shop** is at 4028 CR 200, Fredericksburg, OH 44627.

6. The "Grandma of the Bulk Food Stores" is **Ashery Country Store**. They advertise more than 500 items in stock. Among these are 70 spices, all sorts of bulk foods, meats and cheeses, and Goshen Dairy ice cream. They advise you to bring your own containers for such things as peanut butter, honey, corn syrup, and marshmallow creme. This is one of the largest bulk food stores around. Located at 8922 SR 241, Fredericksburg, OH 44627. PH: 330-359-5615. Hours are Mon.-Sat. 8 am-5 pm.

7. If you've a need for harness, stop at **Ashery Harness Shop**, 8959 TR 652, Fredericksburg, OH 44627.

8. **Ashery Woodworking** makes oak and cherry end tables. They also make mantle clocks. Located at 9247 SR 241, Fredericksburg, OH 44627.

9. **Handmade baskets** are made at this location on TR 652.

10. Handmade 100% beeswax candles in 13 colors, crafts, gifts, and baskets are made at **R&E Betterbee**, 8188-B TR 656, Fredericksburg, OH 44627.

11. Ever wonder what an Irish collar is? You can see all sorts of horse collars, even made into clocks and mirrors, at **Coblentz Collar Shop**, 3348 SR 62, Millersburg, OH 44654. Answering service at 330-893-3858. Hours are Mon.-Fri. 7 am-4 pm; Sat. until noon.

12. Remember when the epitome of technology was the wringer washer? You thought they quit making those 25 years ago, didn't you? Wrong! Mose and Arie Weaver will sell you a new Maytag wringer washing machine at **Country Washer Sales**. Or, how about a self-heating gasoline iron? See housewares, hardware, games, toys, books, and Bibles at 8781 TR 656, Fredericksburg, OH 44627. Hours Mon.-Thurs. 6 am-8 pm; Fri. 8am-8 pm; Sat. 8am-3 pm.

13. Joseph Miller is the **Countryside Blacksmith** at 9252 TR 659, Dundee, OH 44624.

14. Susan and Sara Miller run **Der Alte Quilt Shoppe**. They custom make quilts if you can't find one in stock which suits you. Look over their other quilted pieces and, if you get the urge to try your hand, there are fabrics and notions you can choose from. Lamps, tea carts, small rocking chairs, and cedar chests can also be seen here. Located at 3795 US 62, Dundee, OH 44624. Open Mon.-Sat. 8 am-5 pm.

15. If you're looking for one of those authentic Amish-run general stores, stop in at **Der Trail Duch Store**. (Pronounce like duke. It means fabric.) This shop has Coleman products, fabrics and sewing notions, school supplies, wedding supplies, handmade baby clothes, and lots more. Find it just north of Trail at 6815 SR 515, Dundee, OH 44624. Hours are Mon.-Sat. 8 am-5 pm.

16. **Fairview Country Acre Bulk Foods** has all those things our area's bulk food stores are famous for. Located at 7814 TR 654, Millersburg, OH 44654. PH: 330-359-5772. Open Mon.-Sat. 9 am-5 pm; Fri. 'til 7 pm.

17. Harness and tack are sold at **Fairview Country Sales** on CR 160.

18. In addition to the traditional rockers, **Fairview Hickory Rockers** also make hickory chairs, footstools and end tables. At 3370 CR 160, Millersburg, OH 44654.

19. **Fairview Tarp Shop** can meet your tarp needs but also sells stable blankets at their shop on CR 160.

20. **Hilltop Buggy Shop** may be able to meet your horse-drawn vehicle needs. Turn north onto N. Chestnut St. at Whitmer's Store in Winesburg. This becomes TR 671. The shop is located back the long lane at 8011 TR 671, Dundee, OH 44624.

21. Across SR 515 from Der Trail Duch Store is **Indian Trail Harness Shop**. They sell tack, blankets, lap robes, and even plants and shrubs in season. Located at 6830 SR 515, Dundee, OH 44624.

22. **M&H Woodcraft** makes outdoor furniture, including benches, trash bins, and bird houses, at 9252 SR 241, Fredericksburg, OH 44627. Right behind M&H is **Buckeye Wood** which makes oak swings, gliders, and other outdoor furniture items.

23. We can't spend all our time in craft and furniture stores. At some point the gas tank will register empty and you'll realize it's time to feed the car. One of the problems with being in an area you're unfamiliar with, especially one that runs on four-legged horsepower rather than the wheeled variety, is where to go before the motor coughs and dies. In the Winesburg area, you can get gas, oil, and even a snack for yourself at the **Marathon Food Mart**. Located just south of the Winesburg Dari-ette at 2595 US 62. Hours are Mon.-Sat. 6 am-10 pm; Sun. 7 am-10 pm.

24. If you haven't found the piece of lawn furniture which really suits you yet, this shop may have it. **Meadow View Wood Shop** specializes in over 20 different items of treated lawn furniture. Find this business just north of Der Alte Quilt Shoppe at 3731 US 62, Dundee, OH 44624.

25. **Miller Cabinet Shop** makes solid oak chairs mostly for children. They have bow-backed rockers, high chairs, regular chairs, and a style they call acorn in either high chairs or rockers. They also make children's tables and adult-sized glider rockers with matching ottomans. While most of their products are sold wholesale, they will do retail sales. Located at 9111 TR 659, Dundee, OH 44624.

26. For guns, hunting, or fishing supplies, try **Miller's Gun Shop**. Located at 2755 CR 160, Millersburg, OH 44654.

27. They build all kinds of surries, buggies, hacks, and carts at **Pleasant Hill Buggy Shop**. They also have used buggies in stock, accept trade-ins, and do repairs. Located at 8500 TR 656, Fredericksburg, OH 44627.

28. If you're not tired of looking at handmade furniture yet, stop by **Pleasant View Furniture**. Dining and bedroom suites of solid oak, gliders, and "icebox" furniture are just some of what's on display.

You'll also find quilts and craft items. Turn east off US 62 to 6782 TR 423, Dundee, OH 44624. Hours Mon.-Sat. 10 am-5 pm. PH: 1-800-893-3702, Ext. 805.

29. Picnic tables, gliders, windmills, wishing wells, and more are made at **Raber's Wood Shop**, 7410 TR 668, Millersburg, OH 44654. PH: 1-800-893-3702, Ext. 666.

30. **Ruby's Country Store** is one of those interesting variety stores where variety is the key word. Everything from housewares to gifts, toys, and school supplies are available. Located next to Winesburg Dair-ette on US 62. Open Mon.-Sat. 8 am-5 pm.

31. You can see playhouses, swing sets, lawn furniture, quilts, and crafts at **Stoltzfus Woodcrafts**. Sam and Sandi Stoltzfus are the owners at 3259 US 62, Dundee, OH 44624. PH: 330-893-3693. Open 9:30 am-5 pm Mon.-Sat.

32. Paul and Martha Yoder own **Stonehedge Fabrics**, featuring an array of dry goods, clothing, baby items, etc. At 7189 TR 664, Dundee, OH 44624. Hours 8:30 am-8 pm Mon., Wed., and Fri.; until 5 pm Tues. and Sat. Closed Thurs. and Sun.

33. Mary and Lovina Swartzentruber are a pair of busy sisters. In addition to the goodies they bake daily for **Swartzentruber Bakery**, they also offer quilts in queen and baby sizes and wallhangings for sale in the house. Cinnamon rolls and bread are their specialties, but don't overlook those pies. Located west of Winesburg off CR 160 at 7977 TR 654, Millersburg, OH 44654. The bakery is closed from Christmas to May, but the quilt shop is open.

34. The large display of lawn furniture, bird houses and feeders, playhouses, and storage barns at **Twin Oaks Barns** will catch your eye as you drive along US 62. Located at 3337 US 62, Dundee, OH 44624, across the road from Coblentz Collars. PH: 330-893-3126.

35. **Wendell August Forge** has a large, airy, timber-frame structure to showcase their line of hammered aluminum giftware. In addition, they have a workshop in the rear where you can watch the craftsmen

at work. A theater and museum area highlight the company's history, and there is a snack area serving ice cream, gourmet coffees, and fudge. Right on US 62 at 7007 Dutch Country Lane, Millersburg, OH 44654. PH: 330-893-3713. Open Mon.-Sat. 9 am-6 pm.

36. David A. Mast is the owner of **Woodside Furniture** where you can buy new and used furniture and household items such as a wood cookstove. Located at 7895 TR 652, Millersburg, OH 44654.

37. Joseph A. Yoder doesn't ply his trade under a spreading chestnut tree, but he is a real working blacksmith. If you stop at **Yoder's Blacksmith Shop** (or any blacksmith shop for that matter), be prepared for the strong odor of horse urine. Watch your step, too. Hey, nobody said it would be purty! Located at 8900 TR 652, Fredericksburg, OH 44627.

38. If harness shops hold no interest for you, you probably think there's one around every corner in Amish country. Well, here's another one—**Yoder's Nylon Halter Shop** at 7682 TR 652, Millersburg, OH 44654.

Dining

39. There is a viewing area where visitors can watch the making of cheese at **Alpine-Alpa**. Sometimes with all the hype about this attraction, it's easy to forget that Alpine-Alpa started as a small cheese factory in 1935. Fourteen varieties of cheese are made daily from milk supplied by Amish dairymen. You may have heard about the restaurant or the world's largest cuckoo clock.

Started by Swiss couple, Hans and Alice Grossniklaus, Alpine-Alpa's chalet-style building reminds visitors of the family's roots. The Swiss Market Place offers imported foods, meats and cheeses. Doesn't smoked Swiss sound yummy? The Black Forest Cuckoo Clock Shop is a showcase for cuckoo clocks of all sizes and styles, as well as bells, steins, glassware, etc. And the world's largest cuckoo clock is open to visitors from spring to Thanksgiving.

The restaurant features Alpine dioramas painted by Swiss artist Tom Miller. Watch the train wend its way through the mountains. From the menu you can enjoy "Der Deutscher," a spicy German wurst served with their warm Heidi potato salad or any of the other menu choices. Family-style meals are served every day except Sunday and you can choose from chicken, ham, roast beef, or Swiss steak. There is a salad bar and a children's menu. For dessert, choose from Black Forest cake, carrot cake, or hot apple pie served with mild Swiss, sharp cheddar, or ice cream. Or how about a creme de menthe sundae?

They've recently added a deli and bakery area so you can take some of that goodness with you. Located at 1504 US 62, Wilmot, OH 44689, Alpine-Alpa opens at 9 am in time for breakfast which is served until 10:45 am. It's open 7 days a week until 8 pm. PH: 330-359-5454.

Lodging

40. Each of the two cabins at **Blue Bird Hideaway Log Cabins** will sleep six, so you might want to try this if you're bringing the kids along. The cabins are furnished and include a microwave and small refrigerator. Showers are in the restrooms. Try a campfire at the outdoor fire ring. Rates start at $49. Located 1 mi. south of Wilmot at 1046 US 62, Wilmot, OH 44689. For reservations phone 330-359-5151.

41. If you'd enjoy staying in a Mennonite home, then Raymond and Mattie Wengerd's **Mattie's Tourist Rooms** is the place for you. They have three rooms, one a suite with sitting room and kitchenette. One room has two queen-sized beds and the other has one queen-sized bed. Private baths. Rates are $26-$35. North of Winesburg beside Amish Country Campsite at 1942 US 62, P.O. Box 137, Winesburg, OH 44690. Non-smoking. PH: 330-359-5069 or 359-5226.

42. There are now four rooms at **Raber's Tri-County View Bed & Breakfast**. The new addition is a 2-bedroom suite with shared bath, which would be ideal for a family. Of the other rooms, one is decorated in traditional Amish-style, complete with hardwood floor and hickory rockers. Another is country-style, and the third is Victorian with lace curtains and bedspread. Each room has queen-sized beds, private baths, refrigerators, microwaves, and coffee pots as well as individual temperature controls and ceiling fans. A full

breakfast is served. All rooms are smoke- and pet-free. Rates are $55-$85. Located 1 mi. south of Wilmot on US 62. Mailing address is P.O. Box 155, Wilmot, OH 44689. PH: 330-359-5189 for more information or reservations.

43. **Stonehedge Guest Cottage** is owned by Dave and Helen Schlabach. It offers whole-house privacy with two bedrooms, living room with sofa sleeper, kitchen, and bath. The cottage sleeps 6 and the Schlabach's rent to only one couple/family at a time. TV/VCR and A/C are available. No breakfast is served but coffee is available. Rate is $65 per couple and $5 per additional person. At 7438 TR 664 (Stonehedge Dr.), Winesburg, OH 44690. PH: 330-359-5460.

Camping

44. The last few years have seen the creation of a few campgrounds in the heart of Amish country. If you're one of those who own a camper and enjoys this popular method of travel, **Amish Country Campsite** offers 60 sites with water hookups and electricity. There is a dump station. Some of the lots are pull-through for your convenience. The shower house has hot showers and flush toilets, and there are picnic tables, fire rings, and free firewood. Rates are $13 per night. The gift shop here is home to **Ruth's Amish Dolls**, doll furniture, and wooden items. Located just north of Winesburg at 1930 US 62, P.O. Box 203, Winesburg, OH 44690. Office hours are Mon.-Sat. 9 am-9 pm; closed on Sun. For reservations phone 330-359-5226.

Please Note: The Amish do not have telephones in their homes. If you want information on products, services, or prices, drop a letter into the mail. Enclose a self-addressed, stamped postcard or envelope for their convenience. They will reply.

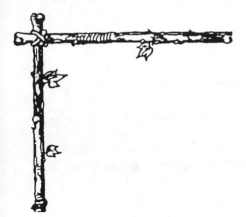

Section II
Wayne County

East Union Twp.
Wayne County

Chapter 15

Apple Creek and
East Union Twp.

Wayne County is billed as Ohio's foremost agricultural area. Evidence of its strong farming community is amply provided every September at the Wayne County Fair.

I was raised in the village of Overton northwest of Wooster and spent nearly my entire life in its vicinity before moving to Holmes County in 1981. Overton lies in the picturesque Killbuck Valley and I ice skated on Killbuck Creek's frozen surface in my youth. There is plenty of beautiful countryside to see in Wayne County but I'm partial, of course, to that lovely valley.

Visitors will find Amish country in the southern half of Wayne County. Kidron, Fredericksburg, and Apple Creek are well known areas, and Shreve is certainly becoming so.

Of course, there are other attractions in Wayne County to be savored if you have the time.

The Wayne County Historical Society complex at 546 E. Bowman St., Wooster, consists of four buildings and is well worth a visit.

Ohio's largest junior fair begins the first Saturday after Labor Day at the Wayne County fairgrounds. Raised on the Wayne County Fair, I've yet to find one which equals it. If you enjoy county fairs, this is an excellent one.

Summer's premier event in Wooster is the Ohio Light Opera. With performances at the Freedlander Theater on the College of

Wooster campus, the Ohio Light Opera has been delighting audiences for many years. The season runs mid-June through mid-August and in 1996 includes operettas by Gilbert & Sullivan, Offenbach, Millöcker, and others. For information and tickets call 330-263-2345.

The Ohio Agricultural Research and Development Center on the south edge of Wooster is the largest such research institute in the country. Visitors are welcome to tour beautiful Secrest Arboretum and the Rose Garden. Maps and information are available at the Visitor's Center in Fisher Auditorium, or by calling 330-263-3700.

See Chapter 1, Tips for Travelers, for where to write or call for more information about Wayne County.

Well, it's time to get out your map and crank up the car. Here we go again!

East Union Township was taken from the western portion of Sugar Creek Township and formed in 1814. Simon Chafin from Union, Maine, gave East Union its name, though he might have more accurately called it West Union.

The township is divided by a ridge that in places is 1200 feet high and runs northwest to southeast, separating the western land drained by Apple Creek from the eastern portion drained by Little Sugar Creek.

Indians had a maple sugar camp west of N. Carr Road and hunted in the area. They traveled the Great Trail which ran on the high ground from Paint Township to the southeast through land now owned by the Apple Creek Developmental Center to Wooster's Spruce Street and on to Sandusky on Lake Erie.

Local lore says that Beaver Hat, a Delaware Chief, built a cabin in an apple orchard overlooking Apple Creek. This orchard was stocked by John Chapman, better known to us as Johnny Appleseed, who had a nursery on the Little Sugar Creek.

The area where the Apple Creek crossed what is now US 250 was settled by Scotch-Irish Presbyterians who built a church there by 1817. In 1832 William Thomas and John Cheyney platted a town named Edinburg. The town grew eastward along what is now Apple Creek's Main Street to higher ground.

When the Cleveland, Akron, and Mt. Vernon Railroad began buying land for a proposed railway in 1852, John Hindman owned quite a sizable piece of land from Apple Creek Road to Hackett Road.

He laid the first plat for Apple Creek Station east of Main Street between High and Maple Streets.

In the 1860's the school and churches moved up from the "old town" to this fast-growing section. Since much of the area between the two towns was built up by 1877, the decision was made to incorporate them all as Apple Creek.

Today, Apple Creek owes most of its busy-ness to US 250 which funnels many cars and trucks through the town every day.

Summer's big event in Apple Creek occurs the last full weekend in July. Johnny Appleseed Days are held in the park on Mill St. The fun includes a parade on Saturday afternoon, contests, live entertainment, dancing under the stars, the Johnny Appleseed Classic finals, and at least one chicken barbeque.

APPLE CREEK

Lynn Teeples owns **Apple Creek Hearts & Flowers**, a full-service floral shop featuring fresh cut flowers and silk and dried arrangements. In addition, there's an array of hand-made Amish crafts, baskets, wooden decorative items, and gifts. Lynn notes that most of her inventory is made either by her or local craftspeople and cannot be found elsewhere. She will also custom-design floral pieces to match your decor. Located at 81 E. Main St., Apple Creek, OH 44606. Mailing address is P.O. Box 338. PH: 330-698-2323. Hours are Mon.-Sat. 10 am-5 pm or by appointment.

Books, gifts, music, and cards are some of what's available at **Choices Christian Resource Center** located in the new Village Square Shopping Center at 43 Maple St. PH: 330-698-5222. Open Mon.-Fri. 9 am-8 pm; Wed. and Sat. until 5 pm.

Den's Archery at 502 W. Main St. may be of interest to the sportsman. PH: 330-689-1266.

Elm House is another of the new businesses in downtown Apple Creek since the last edition. Specializing in cross-stitch, Elm House has all sorts of needlework supplies, patterns, fabric, and floss. Located at 126 W. Main St. PH: 330-698-4403. Open Mon.-Fri. 10 am-4 pm; Sat. until 2 pm.

If you've got an auto racing enthusiast in your family, take them to **Lehman Racing Collectables** at 19 W. Main St. They have diecast models of your favorite NHRA, NASCAR, IROC, and World of Outlaws sprint cars as well as sprint car models you can put together. In addition, there are T-shirts, hats, collectible cards, magazines, and books. Popular local driver, Kenny Jacobs of nearby Holmesville, is featured on some T-shirts. The only thing they don't have in race-car memorabilia is Indy cars. PH: 330-698-1900. Open Mon. & Fri. 10 am-8 pm; Tues.-Thurs. 'til 6 pm; Sat. and Sun. 'til 3 pm.

Red Barn Furniture has the largest selection of Cat's Meow pieces I've seen in one place. Owners Bill and Sue Page also have some lovely Fenton Glass. There are Amish-made lawn furniture and solid oak tables, chairs, cabinets, deacon's benches, etc. Red Barn also has upholstered pieces. Located 1 mi. east of Apple Creek on US 250 at 8522 Dover Road. PH: 330-698-2991. Hours are Mon., Tues., Wed. and Sat. 9 am-5:30 pm; Thurs. and Fri. until 8 pm.

In business since 1974 **Troyer's Home Pantry** doesn't quite qualify as a restaurant, but they do have a couple of tables where you can relax and enjoy their wonderful pastries or a slice of pie with a hot cup of coffee or cold glass of milk. Just walking through the door is a treat for the olfactory nerves. Located at 668 W. Main St. Hours are Mon.-Fri. 6 am-8 pm and Sat. 'til 5 pm. PH: 330-698-4182.

Dining

William and Mary Dettmer are the owners of the **Apple Creek Restaurant**, serving Pennsylvania Dutch-style cooking. Menu dinners range from ham and pork chops to roast beef, steaks and seafood. Or enjoy a sandwich. In addition to the usual array, they have Reubens and Philadelphia steak sandwiches. Then top off your meal with one of their hot apple dumplings. For those more conscious of their waistlines, there's a soup and salad bar and a "light" menu with smaller portions. Children's menu available for the 12-and-under crowd. Located at 80 E. Main St., restaurant hours are Mon.-Sat. 6 am-8 pm and Sun. 7 am-7 pm. PH: 330-698-2171.

The Dutch Heart Restaurant starts serving breakfast at 7 am in a smoke-free atmosphere. They have daily specials and all-you-can-eat fish on Fridays. The kids' menu has their favorites. Located on the north side of town at 690 W. Main St., this family restaurant offering home-style meals is open Mon.-Sat. until 8 pm. PH: 330-698-7400.

The **Golden Bear Dairette** is open seasonally. For those wondering where the name came from, Waynedale High School's athletes are the Golden Bears. They have the usual menu of sandwiches, ice cream treats, and drinks. Located at 546 W. Main St. PH: 330-698-1423.

Larry's Pizza Shop can satisfy those pizza cravings. Located at 72 E. Main St. Hours are Sun.-Wed. 4-9 pm; Thurs.-Sat. 11 am-10 pm. Call orders in to 330-698-9000.

Located in the Village Square Shopping Center is **Laurie's Ice Cream Parlor**. Rick and Laurie Blackburn, owners of Wooster's popular Hero House, are the owners. They have the same great sandwiches, but beware—the "small" size is a *huge* 7½-inch sub. Treats made with award-winning Goshen Dairy ice cream include cones, sundaes, milkshakes, banana splits, floats, and sodas. They also sell fudge, nuts, candy, and chips. At 45 Maple St. PH: 330-698-6111. Open Mon.-Sat. 10:30 am-9 pm; Sun. 4-9 pm.

EAST UNION TWP.

1. Joe Miller is the **Apple Creek Blacksmith** located at 5705 Criswell Road, Apple Creek, OH 44606.

2. A beautiful cherry bedstead was sitting in the crowded entry of **Carr Road Furniture** when I was there, along with many oak pieces. Find this furniture maker at 3926 Carr Rd., Apple Creek, OH 44606.

3. Vernon Tschiegg's hobby is making things out of wood. If he's home, he'll be happy to show you through **Cherry Hill Collections**, a museum of his creations. In it you'll discover Mr. Tschiegg's wooden automobiles; an octagonal table which, when lighted, offers a delightful optical illusion; a musical ferriswheel commissioned to advertise Hershey's M&Ms; and a magnificent ship that took him 1½ years to make. Find Mr. Tschiegg at 10716 Hackett Rd.

4. **Country Bedding Co.** makes mattresses and box springs and specializes in odd sizes. Crist D.A. Miller is the owner. If you want a customized set in an unusual size, bring your measurements to 2696 S. Carr Rd., Apple Creek, OH 44606. Shop hours are Mon. and Sat. 8 am-5 pm; Tues., Wed. & Fri. 'til 7 pm. Closed Thurs. and Sun.

5. Stop at **Crossroads Chair & Craft**, 1816 S. Carr Rd., Orrville, OH 44667, to see what's on sale today.

6. Aaron R. Yoder is the **Kansas Road Blacksmith** at 2890 S. Kansas Rd., Apple Creek, OH 44606.

7. There's a nice little bulk food store at **Kansas Road Bulk Foods**, 2626 S. Kansas Rd., Apple Creek, OH 44606.

8. Find Amos Miller of **Kansas Road Tarp Shop** at 2275 S. Kansas Rd., Orrville, OH 44667, for your tarp needs.

9. **Kidron Woodcraft** is tucked in an out-of-the-way spot at 5373 S. Kansas Rd., Apple Creek, OH 44606. Oak, cherry, and walnut furniture is made here with dovetailed drawers and fine finishes. Much of what they do is sold wholesale, but they will do some custom work. However, expect to wait several months because they're busy.

10. Variety is the key word at **Miller's Variety Store**, 1922 S. Carr Rd., Orrville, OH 44667.

11. Andy A. Yoder is justly proud of the custom-made sleeping bags he makes at **The Nylon Nook**. He'll make one for you in the colors and weight of your choice or choose from those on display. Mr. Yoder also does tent repairs. Hours by chance when he's home. Go up the driveway and around to the right to his shop. Located at 10651 Lautenschlager Rd., Apple Creek, OH 44606.

12. **Weaver's Shoe Shop** at 11962 Emerson Rd., Apple Creek, OH 44606, specializes in shoes for the whole family, including Herman and LaCrosse rubber footwear. The shop is permeated by the wonderfully clean scent of leather. Mr. Weaver also does shoe repairs and offers all sorts of shoe-care products.

13. **Y & M Chair Co.** makes oak and cherry dining room and desk chairs in a variety of styles with either high or low backs. Although most of their business is wholesale, they will do retail sales. Located at 6569 S. Kansas Rd., Apple Creek, OH 44606.

14. Find everything to meet your gardening and landscaping needs at **Yoder's Greenhouse & Nursery**. They'll stay open until dark if there are customers. Visit them at 6341 S. Kansas Rd., Apple Creek, OH 44606. PH: 330-698-7644. Closed Sundays.

Please Note: The Amish do not have telephones in their homes. If you want information on products, services, or prices, drop a letter into the mail. Enclose a self-addressed, stamped postcard or envelope for their convenience. They will reply.

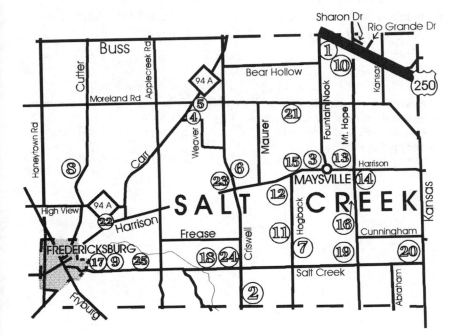

Salt Creek Twp.
Wayne County

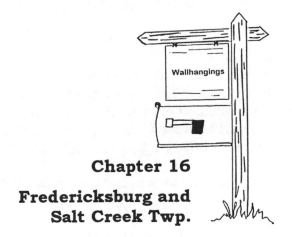

Chapter 16

Fredericksburg and
Salt Creek Twp.

Salt Creek Township was named after three salt licks found in the southwestern part of the township. These salt licks also gave names to the two branches of the Salt Creek which drain most of the township and join just south of Fredericksburg. This township was organized in 1816.

The quiet village of Fredericksburg lies in a lovely valley between the branches of the Salt Creek. Jacob Frederick platted the first lots south of the creek along Mill Street in 1825. The first house here was built by blacksmith James Russell. Then in 1831 William Searight platted lots north of the creek and called them Searightsburgh. Today it's all known as Fredericksburg and is frequented by many of its Amish neighbors.

FREDERICKSBURG

Amish Heritage Meats does custom butchering of beef and hogs. They make their own bologna and weiners. The small retail room has a variety of fresh and frozen meats and cheeses. At 4906 Harrison Rd., Fredericksburg, OH 44627. PH: 330-695-5383. Hours Mon.-Fri. 8 am-4:30 pm; Sat. 8-11:30 am.

Right on the square in town is **Fredericksburg General Store**. Antiques and collectibles are sold here. This is a good place to spend time browsing through all sorts of interesting things in several rooms. General hours are Tues.-Sat. noon-6 pm. Open Sundays by chance.

SALT CREEK TWP.

1. **C & J Mattress** has custom-sized mattresses, handmade to order for regular and antique beds, trucks, and RV's. These are produced by Rainbow Bedding Company. (See their listing in the Holmes County section, Charm and Clark Twp. chapter.) Located 3 mi. east of Apple Creek on US 250 at the corner of Fountain Nook Rd.

2. If custom kitchen cabinets are your dream, talk to **Cabinet Specialties** at 10622 Criswell Rd., Fredericksburg, OH 44627. Oak and cherry cabinetry is their specialty and just walking into their showroom is enough to fire the imagination about the possibilities for your home. PH: 330-695-3463.

3. **Country Cupboard Bulk Foods** is now in Maysville on the corner of Fountain Nook and Harrison Roads at 8381 Fountain Nook Rd.

4. Katie E. Byler's **Country Dry Goods** is full of the plain fabrics Amish women sew into clothing. But there is enough here to make interesting browsing, including handmade infant sleepers and a good selection of books. At 7304 Carr Rd., Fredericksburg, OH 44627.

5. If you're a fisherman, you'll enjoy the large selection of lures, tackle, etc., at **Country Sports**. They have some hunting supplies also at 7879 E. Moreland Rd., Fredericksburg, OH 44627. At the corner of Moreland and Carr Roads. Open evenings. Do you know what a rattletrap is?

6. **Criswell Harness Shop** stocks collars as well as harness, does oiling and repair of harness, and makes shoe repairs. Also in the shop you'll find hickory furnishings such as rockers, end tables, foot stools, chairs and tables. Find this shop at 8438 Criswell Rd., Fredericksburg, OH 44627.

7. Eli S. Hershberger does furniture stripping and refinishing, but he doesn't do those pesky painted pieces. You may have to wait 6

months, but he'll put you on his list if you contact him at **E.S. Refinishing**, 9894 Hogback Rd., Fredericksburg, OH 44627.

8. **Fredericksburg Greenhouse** is open year 'round to meet your indoor and outdoor gardening needs. Find it 1 mi. north of Fredericksburg at 8645 Cutter Rd., Fredericksburg, OH 44627. Closed Sun.

9. **Fredericksburg Harness & Shoe** carries a variety of Redwing and LaCrosse footwear, plus harness and horse supplies. At 6910 Salt Creek Rd., Fredericksburg, OH 44627. Open Mon.-Sat. 7 am-5 pm; Fri. 'til 7 pm. Closed Wednesday.

10. On Mt. Hope Rd. you can find two Gingerich families who make **baskets**. Just ¼ mi. south of US 250 at the first farm on the right is Miss Lydia Gingerich at 6491 Mt. Hope Rd., Apple Creek, OH 44606. Lydia fashions five different sizes of tulip and egg baskets, and one with a flat back she calls a "wallhanger." Just tell her what shape and color you want and Lydia will give it a try. A little farther down the road on the left at 9556 Mt. Hope Rd. Mahlon Gingerich gets some assistance from his brothers to make square, handled casserole baskets and large, sturdy, laundry baskets with wooden bottoms. He too makes egg baskets. Both of these craftspersons are busy, so be prepared to place your order and allow them time to complete it.

11. **Keim Buggy Shop** specializes in buggies, of course. Find Leroy A. Keim at 9821 Hogback Rd., Fredericksburg, OH 44627.

12. **Master Woodcraft** is the new name for Hogback Woodworking. I've not yet talked to the new owner, but they still advertise custom work, specializing in bedroom suites and hutches. Solid oak and cherry furniture is made on the premises. Located at 9334 Hogback Rd., Apple Creek, OH 44606. PH: 330-695-2551.

13. **Maysville Fabrics** is full of dry goods and carries locally made Flying Eagle hats. At 10476 Harrison Rd., Apple Creek, OH 44606 (in Maysville). Hours Mon.-Wed. and Sat. 8 am-5 pm; Fri. 'til 8 pm. Closed Thurs. and Sun.

14. Atlee E. Yoder carries a complete line of horse supplies and even footwear for the family at his **Maysville Harness Shop**. If you're into horses, you'll enjoy browsing. Located at 8572 Mt. Hope Rd., Apple Creek, OH 44606.

15. See the handmade oak and cherry dining tables and chairs at **Miller Woodcraft**, 9656 Harrison Rd., Apple Creek, OH 44606. Closed Sat. and Sun.

16. Eli Raber specializes in rolltop desks at **Raber's Woodcraft**, 8673 Mt. Hope Rd., Apple Creek, OH 44606.

17. **Ruth's Kitchen** makes donuts and creamsticks and takes orders for pastries at 6568 Salt Creek Rd., Fredericksburg, OH 44627.

18. If you want to see how a blacksmith makes his living, stop at **Salt Creek Blacksmith**, beside the lane to Yoder's Bargain Store, 7792 Salt Creek Rd., Fredericksburg, OH 44627.

19. Mattie and Ida Kaufman can repair that worn piece of furniture and make it look good as new at **Salt Creek Upholstery**, 10458 Salt Creek Rd., Fredericksburg, OH 44627.

20. Nylon harness and backholds are made at **Stutzman's Nylon Shop**, 11958 Salt Creek Rd., Fredericksburg, OH 44627.

21. Another place to buy dry goods of all types is **Summit Valley Fabrics** at 9367 E. Moreland Rd., Apple Creek, OH 44606. Owners Clara and Lizzie Troyer also have baby items, children's clothes, and much more. Open Mon.-Fri. 8 am-5 pm; Sat. 'til 4 pm. Closed Thurs. and Sun.

22. The art of the smithy hasn't changed much in the past hundred years. **Valley Blacksmith Shop** shoes horses Wednesday through Saturday and repairs buggy wheels just east of Fredericksburg on Harrison Rd.

23. **Weaver Woodshop** makes octagon picnic tables at their shop on the corner of Harrison and Criswell Roads.

24. **Yoder Bargain Store** is a true variety store. Their sign is painted on a large rock at the end of the driveway. The lane is a long one, but at the end you'll find a store chockful of housewares, including a large array of glassware. They also have a nice catalog available for $2. Find the store at 7806 Salt Creek Rd., Fredericksburg, OH 44627. Stop in Mon.-Fri. during daylight hours; Sat. 8 am-5 pm.

25. Get fruits and vegetables in season at **Yoder's Produce**, 7000 Salt Creek Rd., Fredericksburg, OH 44627.

Restaurants

Technically speaking, the **Horse n Harness Pub** is not in Salt Creek Twp. but in Prairie Twp., Holmes Co. That's why it doesn't show up on this chapter's map. However, it is only about 3/4 mile southwest of Fredericksburg and the locals consider it a part of the community, so I'm breaking my own rules in the interest of easier locating. "The Pub," as it is known, has an English pub decor and a bar area. They serve homemade soups and specialty sandwiches, as well as dinners. If you like to eat where the natives do, The Pub is one of those places. In Fredericksburg take Crawford St. west. This quickly becomes Wayne CR 438 which, as soon as you hit the county line, becomes Holmes CR 192. Located at 9260 CR 192, Fredericksburg, OH 44627. PH: 330-695-3431. Hours are Mon. 11 am-9 pm; Tues., Wed., Thurs. 11 am-10 pm; Fri. 9 am-1 am; Sat. 9 am-midnight.

Please Note: The Amish do not have telephones in their homes. If you want information on products, services, or prices, drop a letter into the mail. Enclose a self-addressed, stamped postcard or envelope for their convenience. They will reply.

Sugar Creek Twp.
Wayne County

Chapter 17
Kidron and
Sugar Creek Twp.

The first settlers came to Sugar Creek Twp. in 1809. Organized on April 11, 1812, this was one of four townships that comprised Wayne County at that time.

The area known as Sonnenberg (meaning sun mountain) was established by Swiss Mennonites who first arrived in 1819. It included the spot where the village of Kidron now stands. Kidron got its name after a post office was established in the early 1890's and the government required it to have a name. It is said that George W. Rose, a Christian gentleman, suggested the town be named after the stream which flowed through the village. So it was.

Of today's 600+ residents, 80 percent are either Amish or Mennonite. Notice that l-o-n-g hitching rail at the Kidron Auction.

The Kidron-Sonnenberg Heritage Center opened in 1994 in time for the community's 175th anniversary celebration. The building is on the grounds of the Kidron Auction, across the street from Lehman's Hardware and Olde Millstream Plaza. The two-story, stucco building resembles the style of homes in the Bern region of Switzerland.

The majority of the displays, which tell of the area's history, were given or donated by local families. An early 1800's home now resides on the main floor, showing how settlers lived. The second floor houses genealogical materials. Operated by volunteers of the Kidron Community Historical Society, the museum is open Tues.-Thurs. and Sat. from noon-4 pm. No entry fee, but donations are accepted.

A major Wayne County attraction on Friday and Saturday of the first weekend in August is the Ohio Mennonite Relief Sale & Auction. Held at Central Christian High School, 3970 Kidron Rd., north of Kidron, this is a fund-raising event of the Mennonite Central Committee. It is the Committee's mission to help relieve human suffering in the world. To that end, it now serves in 54 countries around the world, doing everything from feeding the hungry and healing the sick to planting crops and rebuilding homes. *Money* magazine ranked the MCC as the second best relief and development agency in America.

This sale sells only what is donated by church groups, businesses, and individuals. All labor and services are also donated and all proceeds go to the MCC. Beginning Friday at 4 pm, the sale includes craft demonstrations, chorale singing, SELF-HELP crafts from around the world, a large Swiss Pantry which never has enough baked goods despite at least 200 donated pies, and Saturday's 5K "Run and Walk for Relief." Sausage, pancakes, and omelets are served beginning at 6 am Saturday. The highlight of this 2-day event are Saturday's Quilt Auction at 9 am, with more than 125 quilts plus afghans and wall hangings, and the Wood Item Auction at 10 am. This is one of 26 such sales across the U.S. and Canada. 1996 will be the 31st year for the sale, a very large event for a worthy cause.

KIDRON

Mrs. Ruth E. Hershberger offers custom-designed quilts at **Cozy Corner Quilts**, across the street from Lehman's Hardware in downtown Kidron. Ruth has forty years' quilting experience and can supply patterns and prices upon request. She also has quilts and other quilted items, hand-crocheted tablecloths, and rag rugs in the shop. Send your request to P.O. Box 37, Kidron, OH 44636. Catch her in the shop Wed.-Sat. 10 am-5 pm,. or set an appointment by calling her at the shop, 330-857-0441, or at home, 330-359-5365.

Lawn furniture, storage buildings, upholstered pieces, and oak and cherry furnishings as well as a book store attract shoppers to **Eastwood Furniture**. There are a lot of interesting things to see here. Across the road from Lehman's Hardware at 4722 Kidron Rd. Open Mon.-Sat. 9:30 am-5 pm; Thurs. 8 am-8 pm. Closed Sun.

Gerber's Poultry, Inc. has a retail store where customers can buy fresh-dressed chicken. However, if you're unable to rush home and refrigerate it, you might rather purchase a dinner, box, or individual pieces of this tasty treat with either spicy or mild breading. Ask to see their carryout menu, then try to decide just what you're hungry for. Located at 5889 Kidron Rd., Kidron, OH 44636. PH: 330-857-2731 or 1-800-362-7381. Open Mon.-Fri. 8 am-7 pm and Sat. until 5 pm.

If you love quilts, you'll enjoy **Hearthside Quilt Shoppe** in the Olde Millstream Plaza behind Lehman's Hardware. But bed quilts aren't all they have. Wallhangings, lap quilts, pillows, placemats, potholders, jackets and vests, aprons, and handbags—if someone can quilt it, they've got it. For those who'd rather quilt their own, they have a big selection of fabrics and supplies. A catalog is available by sending $2.00 to P.O. Box 222, Kidron, OH 44636. PH: 330-857-4004. Store hours are Mon.-Sat. 9:30 am-5 pm.

If you want to see one of our colorful weekly auctions in action, the **Kidron Auction** claims to be Ohio's oldest, in business since 1923. The regular livestock auctions are held every Thursday, beginning at 11 am. This is an excellent time to mingle with the local Amish participants. You can sit in the arena and watch the bidding, or wander the grounds and see what's available in produce or flea market items. Flea markets are held every Sat., April through October, from 8 am-4 pm. The Kidron Auction is located in the heart of town. PH: 330-857-2641 if you'd like information on the special sale days scheduled here.

See the tables, hutches, desks, chairs, benches, bedroom furniture, and TV stands at **The Kidron Oak Connection**. Their solid oak and cherry pieces are made by craftsmen in Holmes and Wayne Counties. I'm particularly taken with the graceful lines of their garden bench which comes with a natural finish or in white or green paint. They also have a good selection of decorating accessories. Send for a free copy of their furniture catalog to P.O. Box 203, Kidron, OH 44636, or stop at the store in the Olde Millstream Plaza. PH: 330-857-2909. Hours are Mon.-Sat. from 9:30 am-5 pm; Thurs. 'til 8 pm.

Christmas ornaments and nativity sets in the Christmas Room, hand-woven linens and clothing, and much more are offered here. Gifts bought here for friends and loved ones won't be duplicated and you'll be contributing to a worthy cause. Visit this store any Mon.-Sat. from 9:30 am-5 pm. PH: 330-857-0590. P.O. Box 78, Kidron, OH 44636.

SUGAR CREEK TWP.

1. **Baskets** are handmade at the Swartzentruber farm, 3929 Fahrni Road, Dalton, OH 44618.

2. **E&B Cheese Corner** is a tiny store filled with meats, cheeses, and grocery items. See this thriving cottage business at 4548 S. Wenger Road, Dalton, OH 44618.

3. At **Hickory Acres** you'll see a yardful of lawn furniture, gazebos, barns, and playsets for the kids. All styles are available in oak, redwood, cedar, and pressure-treated lumber. The folks here say that if they don't have it, they'll try to get it or they'll make it! Located 3 miles east of Kidron at 4724 S. Mt. Eaton Rd. (SR 94), Dalton, OH 44618. PH: 330-857-2595. Open Mon.-Fri. 9 am-7 pm, and Sat. 'til 5 pm.

4. Sandra Boulet serves her customers with "warm Wayne County hospitality" at **Meadow Lane Country Store**. The emphasis here is on bulk food items of all sorts, but there is also a gift shop with Shaker furniture and baskets. Amish baked goods are available Thurs. through Sat. There's no charge for a list of the items they handle, but prices are impossible to quote because they constantly change. Located east of Kidron at 18274 Jericho Road, Dalton, OH 44618. PH: 330-832-1087. Hours are Mon.-Sat. 8 am-5 pm.

5. Ronald and Florence Smith are proud of the quality and value they offer at **Smith's Bulk Foods**. Shoppers can find a large assortment of bulk foods here, including a wide selection of different types of grain flours. If you have an allergy to wheat gluten, stop in and see if they have what you've been looking for. They also have fresh-baked Amish treats. Send for a copy of their price list or visit the store at 5413 S. Mt. Eaton Rd., Dalton, OH 44618. They're at the corner of

Mt. Eaton and Jericho Rds. PH: 330-857-1132. Hours are Mon.-Sat. 8 am-5 pm.

Lodging

6. **Mary's Place Bed & Breakfast** at 4179 S. Mt. Eaton Rd. (SR 94), Dalton, OH 44618, promises "whole-house privacy" to overnight guests. There are 3 bedrooms and a bath with shower upstairs; a living room, kitchen with dining room, laundry room, and small bedroom with bath downstairs. Owner Wanda Gerber serves a continental breakfast. Rates are $35 per couple. Located about 3 miles east of Kidron at the corner of Baumgartner and S. Mt. Eaton Roads. Call 330-857-3611 for reservations.

Please Note: The Amish do not have telephones in their homes. If you want information on products, services, or prices, drop a letter into the mail. Enclose a self-addressed, stamped postcard or envelope for their convenience. They will reply.

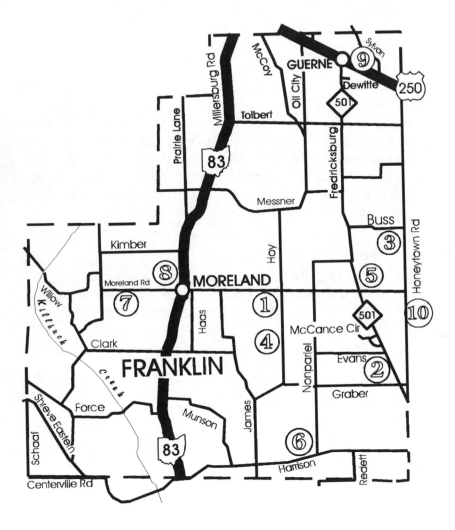

Franklin Twp.
Wayne County

Chapter 18

Moreland and Franklin Twp.

Franklin Twp. is composed mainly of farms and small family businesses. It was named after Benjamin Franklin and organized in 1820. Several farms here are owned by the Ohio Agricultural Research and Development Center of Wooster.

Much of the township's western half lies in the Killbuck watershed and has been bought up by the State of Ohio as part of the Killbuck Marsh Wildlife Area. For a first-hand look at this intriguing marsh habitat from the seat of your car, I suggest taking Moreland Road (CR 77) west of Moreland. It wends its way down through the valley and comes out on SR 226 just north of Shreve.

If you venture off on the township or county roads in this area, be aware that most are marked as high-water areas, meaning they may be too dangerous to travel if the area's had heavy or prolonged rains.

On a trip from Millersburg to Shreve one autumn day a couple of years ago, I daydreamed my way right past the county-line road (Centerville Rd. on the Wayne Co. end and CR 1 on the Holmes Co. end). In an attempt to find a short cut I turned onto Clark Rd. Well, the road just got worse and worse, rutted and bumpy. I passed the "High Water Area" sign without giving it much thought. Imagine my surprise when I spotted water across the road ahead. Needless to say, I backed up and turned around.

· I later read in the newspaper that the ODNR was going to help the county raise a mile-long stretch of Clark Rd.to keep it above water. I thought I'd be able to report by now that this was a *fait accompli*, but the sign says the road's closed, so I guess plans fell through.

Force Rd., between Clark and Centerville Rds., is also *not* vehicle negotiable because there's no longer a bridge across Killbuck Creek. If curiosity's got the better of you, park the car and use shank's mare. But please exercise common sense and caution when traveling in this lovely, valuable wetlands area. (See the Shreve and Clinton Twp. chapter for further information on the Killbuck Marsh Wildlife Area.)

Moreland is one of two villages in Franklin Twp. The other is Guerne in the northeast corner along US 250. We will touch upon it, too, in our travels. However, since the township is traversed north to south by SR 83, I chose Moreland as the touchstone for our visit.

The first building in Moreland was a blacksmith shop. Jonathon Butler and George Morr laid out the community on January 17, 1829.

There are a few small businesses in Moreland today and nice residential areas. SR 83 means there's a lot of traffic through this community.

MORELAND

You will see the sign for **Goldstein's Antiques and Tole** because it's right on SR 83 (6724 Millersburg Rd., Wooster, OH 44691) in Moreland. However, Eve Goldstein warns that, since she and her husband are retired, they don't keep regular shop hours. She advises anyone who wants to assure they can see the shop to call ahead—330-264-1724. Mrs. Goldstein holds tole painting classes and has a good selection of unfinished wooden items and painting supplies on hand. The shop offers an array of interesting ceramics and glassware, several trunks which are Leonard Goldstein's specialty, antique lamps, quilts, and furniture. They don't sell anything "in the rough" and do all their own refinishing. Advertised shop hours are Mon., Tues., Wed., and Fri. noon-5 pm; Thurs., Sat., and Sun. by chance or appointment.

Machine-made quilts are the specialty of **Log Cabin Quilts**. Bob and Phyllis Pavlovicz do the designing and quilting and offer custom work so customers can pick out the fabric, pattern, and backing they want. Phyllis does the actual machine quilting and can turn out three to four quilts a week. She says she's not trying to compete with the handmade quilts, but hers are available for those who want the beauty of a quilt and cannot afford the pieced variety. Located at 910 Kimber Rd, Wooster, OH 44691. PH: 330-264-6690. Open Tues.-Sat. 10 am-5 pm and Thurs. until 8 pm. Closed Sun. and Mon.

FRANKLIN TWP.

1. Finishing, refinishing, and repair of furniture are available at **Furniture Fixers**. They do their stripping by hand. At 7489 Hoy Rd., Fredericksburg, OH 44627. PH: 330-695-6904.

2. Ray and Katie Hochstetler do custom furniture and auto upholstering at **Graber Road Sales**, 3920 Graber Rd., Fredericksburg, OH 44627.

3. **Janet's Upholstery** is located at 4711 Buss Rd., Wooster, OH 44691. Phone Janet Marcum at 330-698-2564.

4. Archery supplies and more are available at **Jerry's Archery**. Also at this location are Minute-Men muzzleloading supplies. At 7785 Hoy Rd., Fredericksburg, OH 44627. PH: 330-695-2910. Open 7 days.

5. If you're looking for registered Haflinger horses, contact Raymond Besancon at **Luray Acres**, 6710 Fredericksburg Rd., Wooster, OH 44691. PH: 330-262-3896.

6. The southern part of Franklin Twp. is noticeably more Amish, especially as you approach Fredericksburg, lying on the township's southeastern line. One of the most popular Amish modes of transportation is bicycles. At 2980 Harrison Rd. near the intersection of Nonpariel Rd. (TR 202) you'll find **Miller's Bike Repair**. You can buy a new BCA, Head, or Gold Eagle bicycle or get your old one repaired. The shop is open evenings after 5 pm and Saturdays.

7. You can pick your own fresh fruit to eat right away or to freeze and can at **Moreland Fruit Farm**. Their season starts with sweet, juicy strawberries and includes raspberries, cherries, blueberries, and peaches, ending with tantalizing apples. They have a farm market here for those who'd rather leave the picking to someone else. Located 1 mile west of Moreland at 1558 W. Moreland Rd., Wooster, OH 44691. Hours are Mon.-Fri. 9 am-7 pm; Sat. 9 am-4 pm; Sun. 1-5 pm. PH: 330-264-8735.

8. If you're in the area at Christmastime, be sure to drive west on Moreland Rd. off SR 83 until you get to **Strock's Christmas light display**. It's worth the visit.

9. Kathy Franks operates **Willow Lane Nursery & Greenhouse** in the Village of Guerne. Here you'll find lots of annuals, herbs, perennials, flowering shrubs, and trees for your yard and garden. Kathy says that since hers is a small, family-owned business she can give you some individual help with gardening questions and problems. At 3738 Dover Rd., Wooster, OH 44691, right on US 250, Willow Lane is open 7 days a week from 10 am until dark during the growing season.

10. Dennis and Sharon Mays own **Windsong Acres** at 7376 S. Honeytown Rd., Fredericksburg, OH 44627. They breed registered Percheron draft horses. PH: 330-695-2691.

Please Note: The Amish do not have telephones in their homes. If you want information on products, services, or prices, drop a letter into the mail. Enclose a self-addressed stamped postcard or envelope for their convenience. They will reply.

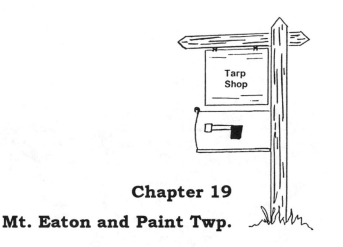

Chapter 19

Mt. Eaton and Paint Twp.

Named for a spring whose water stained the area red, Paint Twp. was organized in 1816. But, in 1825 the southern 40 percent of the township was ceded to Holmes County when that county was formed.

Also in 1825 a wave of French-Swiss immigration began into the area. When Germans from Switzerland started arriving, local lore has it that rivalries sprang up between the two groups.

Mt. Eaton is the oldest village in Wayne County and has the highest altitude (1,320 feet). Platted in 1813 as Paintville, it was renamed in 1829. The old part of the present cemetery grounds was the site of the first church, a log structure erected in 1818.

In the very early days of the community the town square was one block west of its present site where Paint Street intersects US 250.

The Amish began migrating into Paint Twp. in the 1920's. Today most of the land is occupied by their farms. Mt. Eaton is a busy village at the crossroads of two well-traveled highways—US 250 and SR 241.

If a visitor to Amish country wanted to travel one road and see a broad spectrum of the Amish cottage industries that flourish here, there could be none better than Salt Creek Road. I'd recommend a drive on this road to anyone interested in capturing the flavor of the countryside and discovering first-hand the industriousness of our Amish community. Notice all the businesses in this chapter and the Fredericksburg chapter which have Salt Creek Rd. addresses.

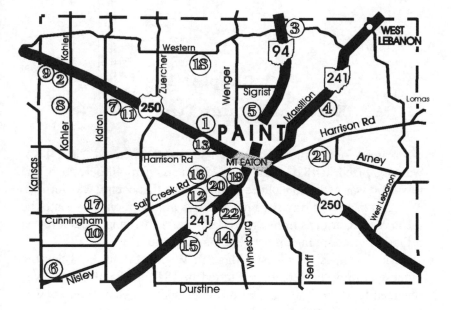

Paint Twp.
Wayne County

Whether you stop to investigate these small businesses and chat with the amiable owners or just drive by, I think you'll be impressed by the number and variety of family enterprises.

Salt Creek Rd. (CR 109) begins on the western edge of Mt. Eaton and makes a fairly straight shot across Paint and Salt Creek Twps. to end about 10 miles away at Fredericksburg. To find it from Mt. Eaton, take either Paint St. south off US 250 or Berry St. west off SR 241, turning left onto Paint St. at the stop sign. Paint St. becomes Salt Creek Rd. just outside of town.

MT. EATON

If your interest is beekeeping, stop in at the **Amish Hills Bee Farm** located right on US 250 in downtown Mt. Eaton. They not only sell honey, honey candy, and bee supplies but also hunting equipment and have video tape rentals which see them through those long winter hours. Contact Amish Hills Bee Farm at P.O. Box 54, Mt. Eaton, OH 44659. PH: 330-359-5061. Hours are Mon.-Thurs. 4-8 pm; Fri. 4-9 pm; and Sat. 1-9 pm.

Clara's House of Crafts at 8626 S. Market St. is on the corner of SR 241 and US 250. Here Clara Schlabach sells unfinished, decorative pine pieces and all sorts of crafts and candles. She has some beautiful, collectible dolls too. This is *the* craft shop in Mt. Eaton. P.O. Box 39, Mt. Eaton, OH 44659. PH: 330-359-5566. Summer hours are Mon.-Fri. 10 am-5 pm; Sat. 'til 4 pm. Winter hours are Tues.-Sat. 10-5.

As its name implies, **Mt. Eaton Bulk Food & Country Store** has plenty of those popular bulk food items, meats and cheeses, brown eggs, dried fruits and nuts, crafts, and Amish baked goods on Fridays and Saturdays. On other days orders are taken for these home-baked goodies. Located at 16044 W. Main St., right on US 250. PH: 330-359-5605. Hours are Mon.-Sat. 8 am-5 pm.

Mt. Eaton Sports Shop offers a complete selection of sporting goods for hunting, fishing, and archery. Roy Yoder will even custom-make arrows. Located at 15966 E. Main St. PH: 330-359-5955. Hours are Mon. and Tues. 9 am-6 pm; Thurs. and Fri. until 8 pm; Sat. until 9 pm. Closed Wed. and Sun.

Spector's has been in business for over 50 years, catering mainly to the Amish. It's actually a small chain of dry goods stores with other shops in Sugarcreek and Berlin. In Mt. Eaton it's at the intersection of US 250 and SR 241. Stop in and browse a while. P.O. Box 275, Mt. Eaton, OH 44659. Hours are Mon.-Fri. 8 am-5 pm and Sat. until 3 pm.

Dining

Ruby's Family Restaurant is on the southeastern edge of Mt. Eaton right on US 250. Owner Ruby Lehman offers a 30-item salad bar with everything from pickled eggs to potato salad and fresh greens. Homemade soups, including German Spaetzle, are a specialty. Germany is also represented on the dinner menu with bratwurst and knockwurst and sauerkraut. Like those all-you-can-eat specials? Wednesdays it's chicken; Thursdays it's spaghetti; and Fridays it's fish. Top off your meal with a piece of chocolate peanut butter cream pie. A breakfast buffet is served every Sat. (7 am-noon) and Sun. (8-11:15 am). The Sunday lunch buffet is served 11:30 am-2 pm. There's also a children's menu for the under-10 crowd. For 25 cents times the child's age, kids can enjoy the salad bar, too. Open in the summer Mon.-Sat. from 6 am-9:30 pm; Sun. 6 am-8 pm. Winter hours are 6 am-8 pm Sun.-Thurs. and 6 am-9 pm Fri.-Sat. For reservations call 330-857-5521 or 330-359-5626.

PAINT TWP.

1. Mary C. Miller owns the **Bulk Food Country Store** which stocks all the baking supplies, spices, nuts, chocolates, and candies you could want as well as bulk cake, cookie, and brownie mixes. She also has Forever Living Aloe Vera products and Tupperware specials. Located 1 mi. west of Mt. Eaton on US 250 at 14396 Dover Rd., Dalton, OH 44618.

2. **Coblentz Furniture** has been in business since 1975. In addition to upholstered furniture, their showroom contains many pieces which owner Ray Coblentz's son and sons-in-law make in the shop next door. They use solid oak and cherry to create bedroom and dining room furniture, desks, and custom pieces. The Coblentzes say if they

don't have it, they'll make it! Located on the corner of Kohler Rd. and US 250 between Apple Creek and Mt. Eaton, their address is 12573 Dover Rd., Apple Creek, OH 44606. No phone. Hours are Mon. and Fri. 8:30 am-8:00 pm; Tues.-Thurs., and Sat. until 5 pm.

3. **Colonial Clocks** has 27 years' experience with clocks, clock movements, and watches. Find them just east of SR 94 at 16458 Western Rd., Dalton, OH 44618. Hours are Mon., Tues., and Thurs. 8:30 am-5:30 pm; Fri. until 8 pm; Sat. until 5 pm. Closed Wed.

4. Another business where you can see plenty of locally handmade furniture is Paul and Naomi Swartzentruber's **Green Acres Furniture**. Oak and cherry bedroom suites are their specialty, although they carry a complete line, including upholstered living room pieces. Find them 1½ miles north of Mt. Eaton on SR 241 at 7412 Massillon Rd., Navarre, OH 44662. Hours are Mon. 9 am-8 pm; Tues.-Sat. until 5 pm.

5. **Handmade baskets and fresh produce** are available at the home of Dan E. Schlabach, 7691 S. Mt. Eaton Rd.

6. Ben B. Kauffman makes **hickory rockers** in his shop at 4131 Nisley Rd., Fredericksburg, OH 44627.

7. **Kidron Road Greenhouse** sells bedding and vegetable plants, a few perennials, and produce such as green beans, beets, peas, and cucumbers in season. Just off US 250 at 7478 Kidron Rd., Apple Creek, OH 44606.

8. Lawn furniture is available at **Kohler Woodworking** here on Kohler Rd.

9. **Lone Pine Quilts-N-Crafts** has lots of decorative items, among them handmade quilts and quilted wallhangings, plush animals, dolls, feedsack jumpers, quilt fabrics, and craft supplies. They also do custom quilting. On US 250 at 12324 Dover Rd., Apple Creek, OH 44606, their hours are Mon.-Sat. 9 am-5 pm.

10. The out-of-the-way stores which cater to our Amish neighbors probably seem pretty unusual to folks used to shopping downtown or in malls. They are scattered throughout the area and one of them is **Marie's Variety Store**. Like all such stores in Amish country, they carry a little bit of everything to meet all sorts of needs. At 2760 Salt Creek Rd., Fredericksburg, OH 44627.

11. Marvin and Anna Burkholder sell most of their woodcrafts at the Amish Flea Market (see the Walnut Creek chapter for details). However, they will do some retail at their home, **MarvAnn Woodcrafts**, 13943 Dover Rd., Apple Creek, OH 44606. They make oak breadboxes, shelving, lazy susans, etc., and offer custom matting and framing. PH: 330-857-0525.

12. Even on snowy winter days the Amish can be seen riding their bicycles to or from work and school. Brrrrr! As incredible as it seems, the alternative—walking—is not all that appealing. **Mt. Eaton Bike Shop** is a complete bicycle store selling new bikes and parts and offering repair service. Find this shop on Salt Creek Rd. about a mile west of Mt. Eaton. Open Mon.-Fri. 8 am-8 pm; Sat. until 5 pm. Closed Thurs. and Sun.

13. **Mt. Eaton Greenhouse** at 15172 Harrison Rd., Apple Creek, OH 44606, is a good place for gardeners to catch a powerful dose of temptation to buy hanging baskets, bedding plants, seeds, and all those garden embellishments that capture our imagination as regularly as spring fever. Located ½ mile west of Mt. Eaton. Hours are Mon.-Fri. 8 am-8 pm; Sat. until 5 pm.

14. Saddles, tack, and footwear for the whole family can be found at **Mt. Eaton Harness & Shoe Repair**. Hours are Mon.-Fri. 7:30 am-6 pm and until 5 pm on Sat. Take SR 241 south of Mt. Eaton and turn left onto Winesburg Rd. (CR 37) to 10265 Winesburg Rd., Dundee, OH 44624.

15. **Mt. Eaton Solid Oak** makes deacon benches to order and cedar chests. Michael J. Miller is the owner and you can find him at 9880 Massillon Rd. (SR 241), Dundee, OH 44624.

16. Across from the bike shop on Salt Creek Rd. is the **Mt. Eaton Tarp Shop**. You'll find many tarp shops in Amish country, so if you have a need for a boat or truck cover, tent repair, etc., stop in and talk to the owners.

17. Joe A. Miller operates **Preferred Wood Products**. Pedestal and end tables of solid oak, crafts, and lamps are sold wholesale and retail. Find this business at 12758 Cunningham Rd., Apple Creek, OH 44606, first place on the right west of Kidron Rd.

18. Raymond Burkholder specializes in kitchen cabinets with raised-panel doors at **Ray's Woodworking**. He also makes chairs, does custom furniture, and general woodworking. 14993 Western Rd., Dalton, OH 44618. PH: 330-857-7571.

19. Mary Shetler has a year's waiting list for her furniture finishing and refinishing skills at **The Renusit Shop**. The one thing Mary doesn't handle, however, is painted finishes. Talk to her about your heirlooms at 15039 Salt Creek Rd., Apple Creek, OH 44606, 1 mile west of Mt. Eaton, on Mon., Wed., or Fri. from 9 am-7 pm. Closed in January and February.

20. **Upholstery A New** can help you revitalize those tired upholstered pieces which have seen better days. Right next door to Mary Shetler's shop is this one run by her sister-in-law, Anna Shetler. Between these two ladies they can make your old furniture sparkle like new. Find Anna at 14955 Salt Creek Rd., Apple Creek, OH 44606. She also has a telephone: 330-359-5334.

21. Open Tues.-Sat. from 10 am-5 pm, by chance or appointment, Pauline and Orion Miller's **Whittlers & Weavers** offers handmade dulcimers, baskets, and woodcarvings. They are 1 mile east of Mt. Eaton at 17247 Harrison Rd., Navarre, OH 44662. PH: 330-359-5206.

Lodging

22. Ed and Linda Pattin are the hosts at **Lakeview Bed & Breakfast**. There are four rooms with double beds and a tennis court where you

can play. A continental breakfast is served. Rates are $60 per couple. Located just south of Mt. Eaton at 9193 Winesburg Rd., Dundee, OH 44624. PH: 330-359-7174.

Please Note: The Amish do not have telephones in their homes. If you want information on products, services, or prices, drop a letter into the mail. Enclose a self-addressed, stamped postcard or envelope for their convenience. They will reply.

Chapter 20

Shreve and Clinton Twp.

Clinton Twp. is named for DeWitt Clinton, Governor of the State of New York in the early 1800's. It was organized in 1825 and is in the extreme southwestern corner of Wayne County.

The original settlement in the Shreve area was not at the site of this present-day village and it was not called Shreve. Located at Centerville, the crossroads of SR 226, SR 514, and CR 1 about a mile south of Shreve, was a village named Stuckeytown.

When the Pennsylvania Railroad was laid out in 1853, the abundance of fresh water and fuel led to the construction of a depot at the future site of Shreve. Originally called Clinton Station, the name was changed because of confusion with a second community of the same name. The name, Shreve, honors Thomas Shreve, a local landholder who was president of the convention which placed Wayne County's influence behind the railroad project. Freight trains still run regularly through the village.

In 1993 part of the character of Shreve was destroyed when all the large trees shading SR 226, the main thoroughfare, were cut down. Why village council made such a decision seems beyond understanding. It did not appear the trees were unsound since the logs I saw were solid. I'll concede some might have been in dangerous condition, but every one? Some type of pear trees were replanted and may bloom prettily, but they'll never equal the beauty of those mature trees which were probably here before the village was founded.

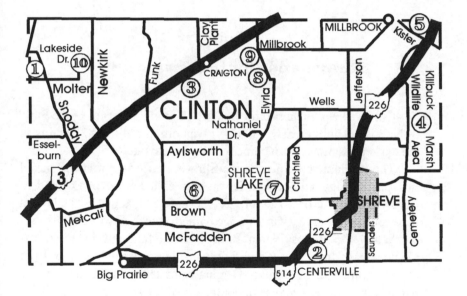

Clinton Twp.
Wayne County

Though I still haven't forgotten this travesty against nature, I'll get off my soapbox and say this had no effect on the business district of Shreve which is south of the scene of destruction. So, take time for a visit to this rural community. It's fast becoming a popular stop for visitors to Amish country.

SHREVE

Country Tots and Antiques and Collectibles has used baby and maternity clothing in like-new condition at reasonable prices. Judy Carmony, Carla Redick, and Sara Speicher are the proprietors and invite you to come in and browse through these and their miscellaneous collectibles, quilts, and antiques. They have a chair caning service and supplies available. At 240 N. Market St., their mailing address is P.O. Box 64, Shreve, OH 44676. PH: 330-567-3036. Hours are Thurs., Fri., and Sat. 11 am-5 pm.

If you like Cat's Meow and other collectibles, stop in and take a look around **The Goose Nest** at 114 N. Market St. in the center of Shreve. They have gourmet foods, meats and cheeses, candles, lovely prints,, and lots more. Hours are Mon.-Fri. 9 am-6 pm; Sat. 9 am-7 pm. PH: 330-567-2776.

James Guns & Ammo, Inc., has hunting, fishing, archery supplies, live bait, and licenses. At 236 N. Main St., Shreve, OH 44676. PH: 330-567-2484. Hours are Mon.-Fri. 9 am-6 pm; Sat. until 5 pm.

A restored 1830 log cabin is the working art studio of Linda Scheck's **Log Cabin Treasures**. Originally located on the Old Portage Trail (now SR 585) in Smithville, the house was painstakingly dismantled and moved to this location next to Scheck's IGA on the edge of town at 395 W. South St. (SR 226). Be sure to look at the series of photos which document the restoration process. Also enjoy Linda's original artwork in paintings and many other interesting forms. She paints Amish scenes and wildlife and has included salt-glazed pottery, dried flowers, bird houses, and rugs among the crafts she offers for sale. There is no phone in the studio but Linda can be contacted at P.O. Box 526, Shreve, OH 44676. Business hours are 10 am-5 pm Mon. and Wed.-Sat. Closed Tues. and Sun. Also closed Jan.-Feb.

The Lollipop Tree Boutique is Shreve's only boutique, offering the latest misses' fashions. Located next to The Goose Nest. Open Mon.-Fri. 9 am-5 pm; Sat. until 7 pm.

The newest store in town is the **Market Street Country Store** operated by Stephanie Geib and Renée Spencer. They sell bulk foods, meats and cheeses, candies, teas and coffees, and are expanding their handcrafted items. At 202 S. Market St. PH: 330-567-3735. Hours are Mon.-Sat. 9 am-5:30 pm.

If you enjoy the current Victorian revival and love the look, you'll certainly want to browse through Anne Foster's **Queen Anne's Lace** shop at 157 N. Market St. in downtown Shreve. This is a Victorian gift shop from start to finish with lace curtains, doilies, tablecloths, and lamp shades. There are plenty of reproduction antique picture frames to choose from. And for m'lady? How about a bottle of Nuit d'Amour bath oil or a delicate glass perfume bottle? Heavenly! Anne has a brochure and price list available for anyone who wants to mail order the Heritage Lace. Write for a free copy to P.O. Box 505, Shreve, OH 44676, or call 330-567-9706. The shop is open Mon.-Thurs. 10 am-5 pm; Fri. and Sat. until 8 pm.

Quilts 'n Things at 193 S. Market St. has Amish-made quilts, a roomful of calicos and quilting supplies, and local handcrafts, including a big selection of unfinished wooden pieces. They take special orders for quilts too. This shop is owned by the Nelson brothers of Des Dutch Essenhaus. Open Mon.-Thurs. 11 am-6 pm; Fri. and Sat. 10 am-8 pm. PH: 330-567-2212.

If you like to poke around in old-fashioned hardware stores, **Shreve Hardware** is for you. It's crowded with all sorts of hardware items, many in those tiny wooden drawers which have probably been here since the store opened. Upstairs is a selection of furniture. Located next to Des Essenhaus. PH: 330-567-2121. Open Mon.-Fri. 7 am-6 pm; Sat. until 8 pm.

For want of a better name, this store is called **Shreve Used Furniture**; however, there's no sign to announce this. It's where the Ford dealership used to be, so there's plenty of space to display the myriad collection of used home furnishings that crowd it. This is an interesting place to browse if you're looking for something to fill that empty niche at home. They have a whole roomful of odds and ends of glass from the collectible to the useful. Right on Market St. PH: 330-567-3115. Hours are Mon.-Fri. 11:30 am-5 pm, Sat. 10 am-5 pm, and Sun. 1-5 pm.

Silly Goose Emporium sells crafts, collectibles, and antique glassware at their shop at 227 W. McConkey St. Go one block west at the traffic light. You'll see the sign. Open Mon.-Fri. 10 am-5 pm.

If you're in the area and need a fresh Christmas tree or some greenery to decorate your home at that time of year, stop by **Twinsberry Tree Farm** on SR 226 on the north edge of town. They make wreaths and swags and have balled and burlapped trees as well as cut ones. PH: 330-567-3902. In season they're open Sun.-Fri. noon-6 pm; Sat. 9 am-6 pm.

Teddy bears from the huggable to the collectible can be seen at **Village Bears & More** located in the first 2-story house built in Shreve, a circa 1853 brick. Owners Carol and Bill Heller have a whole houseful of stuffed delights. Muffy Vanderbear and Steiff bears are here for collectors as well as Paddington, Beatrix Potter, and Gund and bears by artists such as Debbie Altman, Linda Fulmer, and Vicki Stephenson. They've recently expanded into their upstairs rooms, so take your time and enjoy! PH: 330-567-2211. Open Mon.-Thurs. 10 am-6 pm; Fri. until 8 pm; Sat. 9 am-8 pm.

Fresh flowers, houseplants, and dried/silk arrangements are the specialties of **Village Floral**, 240 N. Market St. They also have gift items and a full-service floral shop. Plant and flower lovers particularly will enjoy this one. P.O. Box 152, Shreve, OH 44676. PH: 330-567-2425. Hours are Mon.-Fri. 9 am-5 pm; Sat. until 3 pm.

Dining

Des Dutch Essenhaus is undoubtedly one of the reasons so many people *discovered* Shreve. Owners Jim and Bill Nelson have spent the past 17 years developing a restaurant known far and wide for its

Amish cooking and family-style dining. My daughter's favorite menu item is homefries with gravy. In the winter there's a kettle of soup simmering over the fire. Don't be surprised if there's someone sitting at the quilt frame applying needle and thread to a quilt-in-the-making. They have a salad bar in a wagon and a modified Amish buggy where 4-6 diners can sit to enjoy a meal. A breakfast buffet is served on Saturdays from 7-11 am. Before you leave the restaurant, be sure to look at the handmade crafts, large selection of quilts, and bakery items. Open 7 am-8 pm Mon.-Thurs.; Fri. and Sat. until 9 pm. At 176 N. Market St. in the heart of Shreve. PH: 330-567-2212.

The Quick Chek, a convenience store at 275 N. Market St., now houses the **Quick Chek Subway**. Breakfast is served 6-11 am. Subway's assorted sandwiches are offered on freshly baked wheat or Italian bread and they also have salads. PH: 330-567-3846. Open Mon.-Fri. 6 am-11:30 pm; Sat. 7 am-11:30; Sun. 7 am-11 pm.

Shreve Dari-Bar is a good place to grab a quick sandwich or an ice cream cone. They serve daily specials. But the specialty here is frozen yogurt—not the chemically flavored kind but the *real* kind in 41 flavors! How about fresh strawberry 'n coconut or banana walnut or black cherry or peanut butter oreo? Mmmmmm! Check it out! There's always room for yogurt. At 136 W. South St. (SR 226). PH: 330-567-2429. Open 10:30 am-9 pm Mon.-Sat.; 1-9 pm on Sun. Closed in winter.

Hungry for pizza? **Top Dawg Pizzeria** is now where Dough-Licious used to be at 195 Jones St., just ½ block east of Market St. (SR 226). Their specialties are Hawaiian, supreme, and taco pizzas but they have all the toppings we love. In addition, they have daily lunch specials and serve spaghetti, tacos or burritos, subs, salads, wings, stuffed baked potatoes, and cheesecake. They have a tiny dining area if you want to eat in. Call 330-567-2700. Open Mon. and Thurs. 10 am-1 pm and 4-9 pm; Fri. 'til 11 pm; Sat. 4-11 pm only; Sun. 3-9 pm only. Closed Tues. and Weds.

CLINTON TWP.

1. **Backyard Crafts** has small, handpainted, decorative wooden items

here at their shop near the entrance to Lake Wapusun. During the winter they also have space in Millersburg's Gallery of Crafts (see that chapter) if you don't happen to be in this area. At 11119 Molter Rd., Shreve, OH 44676. PH: 330-496-3145. Hours April through mid-October are 10 am-6 pm. Closed Tues. and Weds.

2. **Cow-nty Line Crafts** is on what the locals call the county-line road (CR 1), but on your map it's 5491 Centerville Rd., Shreve, OH 44676. Evelyn Martin makes ceramics here and has a wide variety of greenware, bisque, supplies, and painted pieces. Southwest designs are popular and Evelyn has a good assortment. There is also a collection of Father Christmases—Bavarian, Italian, Mexican, Irish, Ukranian, Greek, an oriental design, and Black Peter with a basket of apples in one hand, a sack of coal in the other and a bundle of switches on his back for the bad children. Summer hours Tues.-Thurs. 11 am-6 pm; Sat. 12-4 pm. Winter hours the same, plus Wed. until 9 pm. PH: 330-567-2509.

3. If you're looking for kitchen collectibles, primitives, old advertising art, and tinware, stop at **Heichel's Antiques & By-Gones**. Steve and Linda have an ever-changing variety of things. Open daily by chance or appointment. Located on SR 3 just south of Craigton at 7050 Columbus Rd., Shreve, OH 44676. PH: 330-264-3587.

4. Between SR 226 and SR 83 flows Killbuck Creek. Since 1969, the State of Ohio has bought 5,492 acres between Wooster and Holmesville for the **Killbuck Marsh Wildlife Area**. This marsh is the largest remaining wetland in Ohio away from Lake Erie. Thousands of trees and shrubs have been planted for permanent wildlife cover. Wright's Marsh is a 350-acre diked wetland off SR 226. In January 1991 river otter, an Ohio endangered species, were released in the wildlife area on the Killbuck. The 5-mile, walking-only trail for wildlife observation passes through a variety of habitats. It runs along an abandoned railroad bed but I haven't hiked it yet. Mom and I'll give it a try in the spring and see what birds we can spot. Several roads offer access to the area and there are small parking lots scattered throughout. For more information, contact the Area Manager, Killbuck Marsh Wildlife Area, 1691 Centerville Rd.,

Shreve, OH 44676. PH: 330-567-3390. A tip if you're in the area: They built a "map box" at the end of the driveway on Centerville Rd. (CR 1), so you can stop anytime to get information on the marsh without worrying about whether there's someone in the office.

5. I'm delighted to announce that Jim and Jean Milligan have reopened a National Historic Landmark, **Kister Water Mill**. The grist mill originated at this spot in 1816, was converted into a woolen mill in 1845, and was purchased by John Kister in 1881. Mr. Kister turned it back into a grist mill and added a woodworking shop. He added a cider press in 1896 and a saw mill in 1910. A new, wooden, overshot water wheel was built in 1967 by 83-year-old Guy Kister, the third generation of Kisters to run the mill. He used the same pattern his father used. That water wheel still powers the grist mill, cider press, woodworking shop, and saw mill. This is a fascinating slice of history come back to life. Tours are available Tues.-Fri. at 1 pm and Sat. and Sun. at 1 and 3 pm. Admission is $3 for adults, $1.50 for ages 7-18, and 6 and under are free. Across the road is The Mill Store where you can buy organic corn meal, whole wheat flour and spelt ground in the mill, food items, candles, stone bakeware, and much more. A blacksmith operates a forge and gives demonstrations on Sundays. Located at 3936 Kister Rd., Shreve, OH 44676. Turn west off SR 226. PH: 330-567-3500. Since it has no heat, the mill is closed Jan.-March. Hours are Tues.-Sat. 10 am-5 pm; Sun. noon-5 pm. Closed Mon.

6. For your gardening needs you'll want to check out the bedding and vegetable plants at **Moore's Greenhouse**. They also have hanging baskets, herbs, and everything your garden needs. Find them at 8073 Brown Rd., Shreve, OH 44676. PH: 330-496-2291.

We're reaching just outside of Clinton Twp. (and off the map) to point out **The Pine Tree Barn**. Located on SR 226 about 3 miles north of Shreve, The Pine Tree Barn is truly a feast for the eyes for anyone who enjoys fine furniture in room-like settings. This circa 1868 Dutch bank barn housed farm animals for more than 100 years. When it opened in 1980, the total business was Christmas trees and a tiny Christmas shop. Through the years, the Christmas trees have endured. Beginning in November, you can ride in horse-drawn wagons through the fields and tag your own tree which will be cut in December. The Pine Tree Barn itself has grown into a year-round home furnishings center. The Christmas shop is still here, though, and the whole Barn is marvelously decorated at holiday time. Hungry visitors can enjoy a gourmet luncheon in The Granary. There is a lot to see and you may want to linger over the delightful gifts and home accessories, so allow plenty of time. Lunch is served Tues.-Sun. from 11:30 am-2 pm. Shop hours are 10 am-5 pm. Closed Mon. They do have a calendar of events available. Located at 4374 Shreve Rd., Wooster, OH 44691. PH: 330-264-1014.

7. **Shreve Lake Wildlife Area** on Brown Road is a 228-acre wildlife area where public hunting and fishing are allowed. There are parking lots, latrines, and a boat launch (restricted to electric motors only). No swimming, camping, or fires are allowed. There is a sign announcing Shreve Lake on SR 226 in Shreve. However, that one sign does not properly instruct the interested in how to find the lake. So, from SR 226 turn west on Robinson St., then south on Main St., then west again on Liberty St. Shreve Lake is about a mile down the road. South of Shreve, take Elyria Rd. (CR 149) north off SR 226, then turn west on Brown Rd. Contact the Area Manager, Killbuck Marsh Wildlife Area, 1691 Centerville Rd., Shreve, OH 44676, for more information. PH: 330-567-3390.

8. Handmade baskets are crafted by Fannie and Maryann Yoder at **Yoder's Baskets**, 7515 S. Elyria Rd., Shreve, OH 44676. The sign says "wicker baskets and cradles" and they have a nice woven wicker cradle with a wooden base and rockers which can be painted in your choice of colors. They also make tulip, egg, and fruit baskets in all sizes. Open daylight hours Mon.-Sat. Closed Sun.

9. **Yoder's Canvas Shop** is located next to Yoder's Baskets at 7483 S. Elyria Rd., Shreve, OH 44676. Daniel S. Yoder makes boat covers and truck tarps to order and does repair work. Ask to see their lawn furniture while you're there. Open daylight hours Mon.-Sat. Closed Sun.

Camping

10. **Lake Wapusun Campground** is at 10787 Molter Rd., Shreve, OH 44676, on the western side of the township, off of SR 3. Open mid-April to mid-October, this family campground has 400 mostly wooded sites, each with a fire ring and picnic table. Rates of $15 per couple with additional persons $2 (child) and $5 (adult) include electric and water. Full-hookup sites are available. There is a 23-acre swimming and fishing lake and 5 smaller lakes. The activity schedule has family entertainment almost every weekend, including an annual Indian pow wow, a bluegrass festival, and fireworks on the 4th of July. Have no tent or camper? How would you like to rent a camper ($70 with 2-night minimum), or a cottage ($175 per week up to 4), or an A-frame with full bath ($280 per week up to 5), or even a teepee ($20-$25 per night per couple)? You can at Lake Wapusun. PH: 330-496-2355. Office hours are 8 am-11 pm, April-October, 7 days a week.

Whispering Hills Recreation, Inc., operates a large campground 3½ miles south of Shreve on SR 514. Although it's closely associated with Shreve, it's in Holmes County. See the Holmes County section, Big Prairie and Ripley Twp. chapter, for more information on the campground and its **Ol' Smokehouse Restaurant**.

Please Note: The Amish do not have telephones in their homes. If you want information on products, services, or prices, drop a letter into the mail. Enclose a self-addressed, stamped postcard or envelope for their convenience. They will reply.

Chapter 21
Wilmot

Somebody's going to get technical with me, so I'll explain why I decided to put the Village of Wilmot here.

True, Wilmot is not even in Wayne County. For the benefit of you map-watchers, it's in Stark County. *However,* I'm not doing a section on Stark County. And, since it's right down US 250 from Mt. Eaton and right up US 62 from Winesburg in Holmes County, and since it has some intriguing places I thought you'd all like to know about, it just seemed best to include it here.

Since interesting sights in the general area that comprises Ohio's Amish country don't always adhere to my self-imposed rules, it's necessary to toss out the rules occasionally and pray that you, dear reader, will not only forgive my lapses but also be able to make sense of them.

So...let's discover Wilmot!

As many small communities in their early days, Wilmot sprang to life under another name. In this case it was the Village of Milton, founded in 1836, and not renamed Wilmot until 1866. The first pioneers here were hardy souls on the ever-westward migration and hailed from Pennsylvania.

Today, Wilmot is a busy crossroads for two major thoroughfares. A lot of people drive through each day on their way to somewhere else. They might be pleasantly surprised if they could be persuaded to stop and peruse the village's several very nice businesses.

WILMOT

The Wilmot School building on US 250 has been sold and will once again be a school, though a private one. So, the Schul Haus Kompleks is no more. **Alpenstock** has new quarters next to Vintage Collectibles on US 62. Alpenstock (Swiss for walking stick) is a place to celebrate the Earth. T- and sweatshirts boast nature's creatures. Jewelry, artwork, windsocks, and various gift items can be found here. They can also outfit you for light hiking. And that background music? It's available on tapes or CD's. PH: 330-359-5540. They'll be open Mon.-Sat. but I don't have hours confirmed yet. Should be at least 10 am-5 pm.

The same folks who bring you the Amish Door Restaurant own **Amish Door Furniture** in the heart of the village. They've expanded to include kitchen and bath cabinets in oak or cherry and do custom cabinetry as well as furniture. They offer dining room and bedroom furnishings and pieces for infants and children. At 102 E. Main St., Wilmot, OH 44689 (right on US 250), their hours are Mon.-Thurs. 10 am-6 pm; Fri. and Sat. 10 am-8 pm. PH: 330-359-7121.

The **Amish Door Shoppes** are located in what used to be the Amish Door Restaurant. Now, instead of meals, they sell bulk food items, meats and cheeses, candy, and a variety of kitchenware in Grandma's Pantry. The Country Loft occupies the barn section and is filled with country-style accessories for the home. They have a large selection of Precious Moments collectibles. It's my understanding The Wooden Toy Shop was to find a home here after the sale of the school house. There is a lot to see here, so take plenty of time to enjoy! Located on US 62 on the southern edge of town, P.O. Box 214, Wilmot, OH 44689. PH: 330-359-5700. Hours are Mon.-Sat. 9 am-8 pm. Until 9 pm Fri. and Sat. from June-October.

Brad and Fran Hamric have opened **The Art Shop** where Ma & Pa's Oak Furniture used to be. Brad specializes in oils, particularly portraits, and also teaches and does custom work. Fran and family members make the craft items. Watercolors by Don Weisgarber are also available. At 407 Massillon St. (US 62 north of US 250). PH: 330-359-5031. Hours Mon.-Sat. 10:30 am-5 pm.

Handmade baskets are made at the Weaver farm. Turn south on Lawnford St. at Alpenstock and travel about a mile. The farm is located at the intersection of Lawnford and Lawnfield Streets.

Sally O'Connor opens **The Corner Shops** on Saturdays from 11 am-5 pm. Here you'll find antiques on consignment and some very interesting and unusual folk art dolls, rag rugs, collectibles, and tinware. She also has Amish ladies making quilts in the traditional, conservative Amish colors and fabrics. If you don't know the difference between these and other quilts, stop in and find out. Located at 107 Main St. E at the intersection of US 250 and 62.

The Gateway House is located just outside of Wilmot, south on US 62, in an early 1900's farmhouse. Offering oak and antique furniture, collectibles, jewelry, candles, rugs, pottery—well, a houseful of all kinds of things—this is an interesting mix of old and new that's constantly changing. They've also expanded into the barn so, for folks who like to poke around, it's heaven! In addition, they're an outlet for those good Breitenbach wines made near Sugarcreek. Mailing address is P.O. Box 201, Wilmot, OH 44689. PH: 330-359-5884. Hours are Mon.-Sat. 10 am-6 pm; Sun. 1-6 pm.

At **Harvest Blessings** you'll find a wide variety of painted decorative wooden items. They also have a general inventory of locally made oak pieces. Be sure to take a peek in the basement of this circa 1860's building and read about its early history as "The Mud Palace Saloon." Located on the left one block north of US 250 on US 62 at 303 Massillon St., Wilmot, OH 44689. PH: 330-359-7111. Open Mon.-Thurs. 10 am-5 pm; Fri. and Sat. until 6 pm.

When you walk into **Mulheim & Son Furniture**, you know immediately you've happened upon a rare jewel because what greets the eye is the tranquility and simplicity of the Shakers. Among the country and Shaker-styled pieces you catch only a rare glimpse of oak. My favorite, cherry, is featured and, instead of poplar, they're now using maple. A piesafe with pierced tin or raised panel doors will house your TV and VCR. They have huntboards, Welsh cupboards, tables for every room of the house, ladderback chairs, beds, and more. Everything is made on the premises by the Mulheim family. Open the drawers to discover that even the dovetailed inner surfaces are satin smooth to the touch. At 112 Main St. W, the showroom is open Mon.-Sat. 10 am-5 pm. Closed on Mon. from January-May. Write to P.O. Box 191, Wilmot, OH 44689, or PH: 330-359-5755.

With the sale of the school house, **Ohio Star Quilt Shop** has returned to its former location on Main St. next door to Mulheim & Son Furniture. They have a selection of handmade quilts, fabrics and quilting supplies, and craft books. Expect them to be open Mon.-Sat. 10 am-5 pm, although I've not gotten the final word on that yet.

The 1880 Longenecker House is home to **Vintage Collectibles,** a Victorian gift shop. This is part of the Amish Door Shoppes and is right next door. However, it's distinctive enough to deserve its own listing. From the white wicker which invites you to enjoy the front porch to the stained glass lamps, English china tea sets, array of lovely linens, and reproduction Victorian-style jewelry, Vintage Collectibles is a turn-of-the-century delight. One room upstairs is filled with things for infants' and children's rooms. Every nook and cranny holds something of interest, so enjoy. Open Mon.-Thurs. 9 am-8 pm; Fri. and Sat. until 9 pm.

The Wilderness Center, Inc. is a nonprofit nature center whose 573 acres of forests, prairies, and marshes encompass parts of Holmes, Wayne, and Stark Counties. There are seven nature trails here, totaling over 10 miles. The Sigrist Woods Trail, which wanders among some of the oldest trees in Ohio, has been designated an Ohio Natural Landmark. The trails are open all year from dawn to dusk and are wonderful for hiking, birding, and photography. In the winter some are popular for cross-country skiing. An Interpretive Building offers an exhibit room, bookstore and gift shop, a planetarium, a wildlife observation room, and an auditorium. Closed on Mondays, the Interpretive Building is open Tues.-Sat. 9 am-5 pm and Sun. 1-5 pm. Muscles cramped from a too-long drive? The Wilderness Center is a great place to get out, stretch your legs, and enjoy some peaceful moments with Mother Nature. Contact the Center at P.O. Box 202, Wilmot, OH 44689 or by PH: 330-359-5235 for more information on their wide variety of special events, courses, and workshops. Located about a mile west of Wilmot just off US 250.

Dining

The Amish Door Restaurant is styled like a v-e-r-y large Amish home. In addition to the restaurant which can seat 450, there is a 400-seat banquet facility, a second-floor gift shop, and a bakery which opens at 6 am for donuts and coffee. They've also got plans to construct a 50-room hotel behind the restaurant. This may be up and running by the time I update information for the next edition, so keep a look out. The popular family-style dinners are served here with your choice of broasted chicken, ham, or roast beef. If you'd rather, order soup, a sandwich, or dinner from the menu. Dinners include the extensive salad/dessert bar loaded with enough items for a meal in itself. A children's menu is available. Just outside the front door there are carriage rides available. If you're interested, it's $2 for adults, $1 for children 3-12, and under 2 are free. The Amish Door is located on the south edge of Wilmot on US 62. PH: 330-359-5464. They are open Mon.-Sat. 7 am-8 pm; until 9 pm in the summer season.

If your tastebuds happen to be craving pizza the day you visit, try **Wilmot Pizza**. They have a pleasant dining room with booths and tables and serve pizza with all your favorite toppings, subs, fish dinners, and broasted chicken. Hours are Mon.-Thurs. 4-9 pm; Fri. 9 am-10 pm; Sat. 2-10 pm; and Sun. noon-8 pm. PH: 330-359-5551.

Lodging

The A. Grafe Mercantile Building housed a successful hardware business from 1866 until 1908 when Abraham Grafe died. This circa 1840 building with 14" thick brick walls has been nominated to the National Register of Historic Places. Today it is owned by Sally O'Connor who has opened **The Corner Brick Bed and Breakfast** at 107 Main St. E. Sally had one suite downstairs open for guests. However, it's currently being used as an apartment. If you want to know whether the B&B has reopened for guests, contact Sally at P.O. Box 128, Wilmot, OH 44689, or PH: 330-359-5658.

The **Hasseman House Inn** occupies a circa 1900 farmhouse just west of Wilmot on US 62. It's a gorgeous house with oak woodwork, hardwood floors, and stained glass windows, furnished with period antiques. The three guest rooms are on the second floor and each has a private bath. The attic is the honeymoon suite with bedroom, bath, and sitting area. Guests enjoy the Hasseman House Special for breakfast at the Amish Door Restaurant Mon.-Sat. On Sundays a continental breakfast is served because the restaurant is closed. Rates are $79-$95 and $110 for the attic suite. Reservations can be made by calling the Amish Door Restaurant at 330-359-5464 or 330-359-7904.

The Herb Nest Bed and Breakfast is operated by Walt and Sue Helline. They have two guest rooms with double beds and shared bath. The rooms are furnished with antique and reproduction Victorian or country-style pieces. A continental breakfast is served. Rates are $45-$55. Located at 13642 Navarre Rd. SW, Beach City, OH 44608, one mile north of Wilmot off SR 62. Take the second road to the right. Look for the farm lane with a group of mailboxes. The Herb Nest is in the yellow farmhouse. PH: 330-359-5087 for reservations.

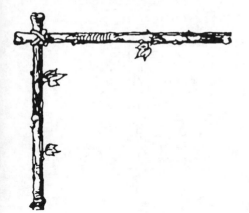

Section III
Tuscarawas
County

Chapter 22
Baltic

Our visit to Tuscarawas County as part of Ohio's Amish country is limited to the small community of Baltic and Sugarcreek Township which contains the decidedly Swiss-flavored town of Sugarcreek.

There is a large Amish population in residence in the county and you may want to explore other areas which aren't included here.

Ragersville, just south of Sugarcreek in Auburn Twp., boasts a cheese factory. At the Old Store and Cafe you can get a pizza or a sandwich, ice cream, groceries, and rent a movie. The building, constructed in 1846, features an abundance of antiques and the bar from a saloon which was located next door.

The Good House Restaurant has developed quite a reputation as a gourmet restaurant even in out-of-the-way Ragersville. They serve lunch Wed.-Sat. and dinner Tues.-Sat. Make reservations by calling 330-897-4000.

Atwood Lake with its resort and lovely scenery is in the far eastern part of the county.

Dover has the J.E. Reeves Victorian Home and Museum and the Warther Museum with its intricate carvings.

Neighboring New Philadelphia, the county seat, has New Towne Mall, the closest you'll find to Amish country.

Kids of all ages love carousels and Tuscora Park boasts a 1928 antique carousel which will give you the world's longest ride for 25 cents. There are also kiddie rides, an 18-hole miniature golf course, a swimming pool, concession stands, and picnic grounds. For more information write or call Tuscora Park, New Philadelphia Park & Recreation Dept., 166 E. High Ave., New Philadelphia, OH 44663; PH: 330-343-4644.

Both cities feature plenty of places to get a bite to eat and find a bed for the night.

Nearby is historic Schoenbrunn Village, a State Memorial. Founded in 1772 by Moravian missionary David Zeisberger, it was the first settlement in Ohio. Today, visitors can see 17 reconstructed log buildings, the original mission cemetery, and more than two acres of planted fields. The outdoor drama, *Trumpet in the Land*, tells the dramatic story of Schoenbrunn Mondays through Sundays from mid-June to late August. If you haven't experienced this kind of entertainment, it's a wonderful way to spend a summer evening.

Another Tuscarawas County delight is Zoar Village, founded in 1817 by German immigrants who prospered in a self-contained community until the turn of the century. If you enjoy historic sites, this is a must-see for its lovely buildings and gardens. Visitors might also want to partake of one of the many special events going on here during the year.

Did you know Ohio had a Revolutionary War fort? Fort Laurens near Bolivar was built in 1778. The fort is no longer standing, although you can still see its outline, but there is a museum containing artifacts taken from excavations. A recreation of a Revolutionary War encampment is held here during the summer.

To find out more about all the places of interest get in touch with the Tuscarawas County Convention & Visitors Bureau, P.O. Box 349, New Philadelphia, OH 44663 or call them at 1-800-527-3387.

Visitors are just beginning to discover Baltic. Of course, this has its good and bad points as far as natives are concerned. But, we can't stop progress and Baltic is one of those little-known spots where you don't have to fight the traffic and crowds—so far anyway.

This small town within spitting distance of Holmes and Coshocton Counties is on the extreme west edge of Tuscarawas County where the county line makes a little jog.

First named Rowville in 1848 for founder Lewis Row, Baltic once also carried the name Buena Vista. However, it's been Baltic at least since its incorporation in 1903.

The Conotton Valley Railroad which gave birth to Sugarcreek also meant a boom to Baltic in the 1880's when it was the railroad's southern terminus. Later, the tracks were extended to Coshocton and Baltic's station was removed. It was not, however, the death knell for the little community and Baltic has persevered.

These days it's one of the best-kept secrets in Amish country. However, if you expect to find lots of craft shops, you'll be disappointed. Those will probably move in as this area's popularity increases. Right now there are some things in Baltic you won't find elsewhere, so let's discover what there is to see and do here.

BALTIC

Want to grab a cold drink or quick snack? Stop in at **Baltic IGA**. They have a deli and a bakery and all those grocery-store goodies. Located on SR 93 on the north edge of town. PH: 330-897-7361. Hours are Mon.-Sat. 7 am-9 pm; Sun 11 am-5 pm.

The wood-fire smokehouses of **Baltic Meats** produce succulent hams, and smoked turkeys, ribs, and hocks. Throw a couple of those smoked hocks in your pot of bean soup and you'll have a winter taste treat that's hard to beat. Baltic Meats also has freezer beef and pork as well as lunch meats and cheeses. Located on S. Ray St. (SR 93) south of the intersection of SR 651. PH: 330-897-7025. Hours are Mon.-Fri. 8 am-5 pm; Sat. until 4 pm.

Alvin and Esther Miller have lovingly restored one of downtown Baltic's historic treasures and one of Ohio's oldest flour and feed mills. As a lover of old buildings who hates to see them destroyed, I applaud the Millers' efforts to breathe life into this circa 1908 brick mill which once manufactured "Little Daisy" flour. One of the amazing things about the building is that most of the machinery was left in the mill when it was abandoned. That's made the Millers' job somewhat easier and they do plan to open the top two floors at some point in the future. **Baltic Mills** opened in 1993 and Mr. Miller conducts guided tours for $3.00. Children under 8 get in free. The tour takes about 20-30 minutes. They have a corn sheller and grind corn and several kinds of flours. There is also a gift shop where you can buy all sorts of baking mixes and flours, a nice selection of handcrafted items, including souvenir T-shirts and heavy paper bags with reproductions of the "Daisy Flour" advertisement on them. Because there's no heat in the mill, it's open only April-October, depending on weather. The gift shop is open until just after Christmas. Find Baltic Mills at 111 Main St., P.O. Box 213, Baltic, OH 43804. PH: 330-897-0522. Hours are Mon.-Thurs. 9:30 am-5:30 pm; Fri. and Sat. until 8:30 pm.

Right next door to Baltic IGA is **Erb's Shoe and Variety**. Owner Lizzie Ann Erb carries all sorts of merchandise from dry goods, straw hats, and housewares to shoes and boots. PH: 330-897-3301. Hours are 9 am-5 pm Mon., Tues., and Thurs.; until 8 pm Wed. and Fri.; and until 4 pm on Sat.

Henery A. Hershberger makes cedar bird and squirrel feeders, bluebird and wren houses, mailboxes, and butterfly houses in his shop at **Long View Wood Products**. Go east at the 4-way stop on SR 93, past the school house to the first place on the right. You'll immediately realize why it's called Long View. What a view!

If you love flowers and gardening, you're about to discover one of Baltic's best-kept secrets. **Meitzler's Iris Garden** sits on a mere 1/10th acre but grows nearly 200 varieties of irises, 45 varieties of peonies, and more than 150 varieties of daylilies. Gertrude and Louis Meitzler are the gardeners extraordinaire and their plants are for sale. You're invited to visit during bloom time and pick out what you'd like. Then, after the plants are dug, the Meitzlers contact you to pick up your selections. There is a free price list available by writing them at P.O. Box 69, Baltic, OH 43804. The number of plants available for sale is governed by what can be safely harvested each year. Located at 215 W. Main St. PH: 330-897-6733. They are open most days when the flowers are blooming.

Schumaker Hardware is one of those old-fashioned hardware stores stocking a little bit of everything. Stop in and see for yourself at this store on W. Main St. PH: 330-897-2771. Open Wed. and Fri. until 8 pm.

Dining

Management changed recently at **Baltic Bar & Grill** and they now have all-you-can-eat fish or a ribeye dinner on Fri. and Sat. These and other dinners are served 5-9 pm. On Main St. PH: 330-897-0507.

Der Bachen Haus opens at 6 am with fresh donuts, creamsticks, and other pastries, breads, rolls, cakes, muffins, pies, and cookies. By lunchtime (11 am) they're making pizzas with all those good toppings. At 117 E. Main St. PH: 330-897-1003. Open Mon.-Thurs. until 8 pm; Fri. & Sat. 'til 11 pm.

For that taste of Amish cooking in Baltic, it's **Miller's Dutch Kitch'n**. They start serving breakfast here at 5:30 am. The children's menu contains more than just sandwiches and chicken nuggets. At Miller's the kids can have a real meal such as roast beef or ham with 2 side dishes. Yes, they do have those family-style dinners. Choose from Swiss steak, ham, and chicken. There are daily specials from liver and onions to broasted chicken to baked ham beginning at 3 pm. Angel food cake is a favorite among our Amish neighbors and you can have a piece of it for dessert or choose from among their cream and fruit pies. Located at 114 W. Main St. PH: 330-897-5481. Open Mon.-Sat. 5:30 am-8 pm. Closed Sun.

Please Note: The Amish do not have telephones in their homes. If you want information on products, services, or prices, drop a letter into the mail. Enclose a self-addressed, stamped postcard or envelope for their convenience. They will reply.

Chapter 23

Sugarcreek and Sugarcreek Twp.

Frederick Domer came to the lands that would be Sugarcreek Twp. in 1807. Mr. Domer was a Dunkard or German Baptist from Somerset, PA, and was probably the first pioneer into the area.

Depending on which story you believe, Sugarcreek village got its name either from Sugar Creek, named for the many sugar maples which grew in the area, or from a Ragersville farmer who, after having too much to drink, failed to negotiate a bridge over the creek and ended up with part of his wagonload, including two sacks of sugar, in the creek.

However, everyone agrees that Sugarcreek owes its existence to the Conotton Valley Railroad which was built through the Sugar Creek Valley in 1882.

About a mile west, on higher ground, was the village of Shanesville, founded by Abraham Shane in 1814. It was the commercial center of the area until the advent of the railroad, and you will still see the name Shanesville well used in the vicinity.

More and more citizens and businesses drifted toward the railroad through the years, but it was not until a post office application was granted in 1888 that Sugarcreek became a reality.

Today the village of Sugarcreek has grown to encompass the ridges where Shanesville once carried on its separate existence.

It was the influence of the Ohio Swiss Festival, created to promote Ohio Swiss cheese and first held in 1953, which eventually

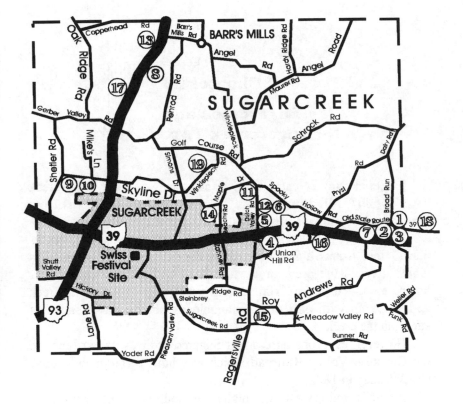

Sugarcreek Twp.
Tuscarawas County

led to Sugarcreek's transformation into the "Little Switzerland of Ohio." As that event, still held the fourth Friday and Saturday after Labor Day, became more and more popular, a building was purchased and transformed into an information center. It was given Swiss styling in 1973. One by one other downtown buildings have followed suit and now the appearance of a Swiss village prevails.

1996 will celebrate the Ohio Swiss Festival's 44th year. Polka bands, a parade, steinstossen (stone throwing), a 5-mile run, and schwingfest (Swiss wrestling) are part of the highlights.

Another festival which will celebrate its fifth year in 1996 is the Tom Miller Arts Festival. Held in May, this one-day event is a fine arts celebration begun to honor Swiss artist, Tom Miller. At 85, Mr. Miller is still painting. It is his murals which decorate the downtown stores and several other businesses in Amish country. Art exhibits, free entertainment, and food are parts of this festival.

One of the biggest events in Sugarcreek in 1995 was the moving of what is believed to be the first home built on the site of the town. The 1869 John S. Yoder home was saved from destruction by the efforts of the nonprofit Amish Heritage Foundation. The home was moved to a site off East Main St. on the edge of town. Plans are to restore and refurnish it with period pieces, then open it to visitors for tours. Eventually, they hope to create an Amish farm at the site. You can see the home, looking rather forlorn but hopeful, if you drive east across the railroad tracks. We'll anticipate developments at this historic house and look forward to seeing the Foundation's efforts come to fruition.

In the interest of facilitating a better flow of traffic through what is often a crowded area, the State constructed a wider, straighter SR 39. It begins west of I-77 and makes a beeline toward Sugarcreek where it reattaches itself to the original highway east of town.

This means the new highway bypasses many of the attractions on the twists and turns of the old road. It caused a lot of controversy and upset most of the business owners. But, the good news is those businesses are still there and so is old SR 39, although now it's CR 139. I admit I like the change because I can drive the old route without someone threatening to run over me.

You can pick up CR 139 about 4 mi. west of Dover and follow it to just past the Dutch Valley complex where you have to get on the new road, like it or not. And be sure to take time to see the businesses along the way. They have a lot to offer.

I'm pleased to say that new maps are now out, reflecting the naming of all the county's roads as well as the change in SR 39. Contact the Tuscarawas County Convention & Visitors Bureau, P.O. Box 926, New Philadelphia, OH 44663 (1-800-527-3387).

For more information about Sugarcreek contact the Sugarcreek Tourist Bureau and Information Center, 106 W. Main St., P.O. Box 158, Sugarcreek, OH 44681. PH: 330-852-4113 or 852-2223.

SUGARCREEK

If you're interested in gift items with a Swiss or European flavor, **The Alphorn** is the place for you. Located at 115 E. Main St. in Sugarcreek's first Swiss-styled building, this store has imports from Switzerland, Austria, and Germany. Among them are cuckoo clocks, Hummel plates, and solid pewter Christmas ornaments. PH: 330-852-2131. Hours are Mon.-Sat. 9 am-5 pm.

With three floors of displays, including many audio-visual, the **Alpine Hills Museum** is just the place to get a taste for the German, Swiss, and Amish history of the Sugarcreek area. This museum includes an 1800's cheese house and Amish kitchen, and a printshop, gunshop, and woodworking shop among others. Reportedly, over 50,000 visitors go through the museum during its April-November season. Alpine Hills Museum hosts an annual quilt show the last Fri. and Sat. of July. Free admission but donations are appreciated. Located on Main St. in downtown Sugarcreek. Talk to the folks manning the Tourist Information Center in the museum's lobby about area attractions. Hours are Mon.-Sat. 10 am-4:30 pm. Through the busy months of July-Sept. the museum opens at 9 am.

Alpine Hills Shuttle offers tours and sells tickets for them from a booth on the corner of Broadway and Main Streets. 1¼-hour tours are given Mon.-Sat., May-Oct., from 10 am-6 pm. Ages 11 and older, $5; children 3-10, $3; under 3 free. See Chapter 1 for more information on area tours.

Plants and gardening have been a passion of mine for many years. If they're also one of yours, stop at **Alpine Meadows Floral & Garden**. In addition to a full-service florist, you'll find houseplants and bedding and vegetable plants, hanging baskets, seeds, trees, shrubs, and bulbs. They also have silk arrangements. Located on TR 348 just east of Beachy's Country Chalet. PH: 330-852-4821. Hours are 9 am-6 pm Mon.-Sat.

Wall-to-wall crafts make for intriguing browsing at **Amish Collection**. They have other shops in Berlin and Hartville and you'll find a bit of everything here from folk art stuffed animals to wreaths of all kinds, baskets, hand-painted mailboxes, crocks, and dolls. Located right downtown at 102 W. Main St. PH: 330-852-3323. Hours are Mon.-Fri. 10 am-5 pm; Sat. until 6 pm.

The Amish Country T-Shirt Factory at 111 E. Main St. has lots of T-shirts and sweatshirts, particularly if you're interested in one as a souvenir of your visit to Sugarcreek. In addition, they feature gift items, hex signs, framed prints, and an assortment of stamps to thrill any child—or maybe even a grownup. PH: 330-852-4598. Hours are Mon.-Sat. 10 am-5 pm.

Started in the spring of 1948, **Andreas Furniture** has grown through the years into one of the largest furniture dealers in the area. They have a fine selection of quality upholstered sofas and chairs in room-like settings, and lovely accessories. If you're in the mood for a new living room or bedroom suite, stop by and take a look. People from all over the state shop here. Located at the corner of Factory St. and SR 39. PH: 330-852-2494. Hours are Mon.-Sat. 9 am-9 pm.

Harry and Claudia Arnold opened **Artisans Mercantile** in 1993 after 25 years in the hardware business. With a 10,000 sq.ft. store, there's room for almost 200 craftsmen to display their wares. I've seen artwork by Steve Polomchak and Diana Glanco, carved decoys, eye-catching quilts, finished and unfinished wooden furniture, raku pottery, and much more. Be sure to allow plenty of time to look over everything in this interesting craft mall. This is also the home of Amish Country Bike Rentals. (See Chapter 1 for more information about renting a bike while you're here.) Located at 110 Andreas Dr., across from Beachy's Country Chalet. PH: 330-852-2456. Hours are Mon.-Wed. 10 am-6 pm; Thurs.-Sat. until 8 pm. Closed Sun.

Since 1890, **The Budget** has become known far and wide for "Serving the Amish-Mennonite Communities Throughout the Americas." Anyone who would like to get a feel for how active, widespread, and close-knit these communities are will find an issue of this weekly paper very interesting. News comes in to the Budget from as far away as Missouri, Delaware, the Carolinas, Wisconsin, Tennessee, and even Romania, Canada, or Belize. Of course, there's plenty of news from Ohio also and the ads are fascinating. Published on Wednesdays. Price is 60 cents. The office is located at 134 N. Factory St., Sugarcreek, and open Mon.-Fri. 8 am-5 pm.; Sat. until 11 am. PH: 330-852-4634 or FAX 330-852-4421.

Lots of locally made, unfinished wooden items can be found at **Der Hammer Und Nagel**. There are also country-style decorations and some antique collectibles. Find this interesting gift shop at 112 N. Broadway. PH: 330-852-2831. Open 11 am-5 pm Mon.-Sat.

Der Village Pantry is a convenience store which is part of a complex with two eateries. You can buy a sandwich or snack, rent a video, get a cup of hot coffee or a cold soda, as well as buy gasoline. Located right on SR 39 on the east side of town. Hours are Mon.-Sat. 6 am-11 pm; Sun. 8 am-10 pm.

The **Goshen Dairy** at the corner of Main and Factory Streets is a convenience store. For more than 75 years Goshen's been dishing up award-winning ice cream in cones, sundaes, and shakes. Sandwiches, snacks, and sodas are also available. Open 7 days a week from 6 am-11 pm.

Originally selling gospel music in their home, David and Erma Stutzman's business has grown into **The Gospel Shop**. Located at 112 E. Main St., this store still sells a wide variety of gospel music, but now also sells Bibles and books, cards, gift items, and supplies for churches and weddings. They have a good selection of Precious Moments collectibles, too. PH: 330-852-4223. Hours are Mon.-Sat. 8:30 am-5 pm; Fri. until 8 pm.

Heritage Collection features oak and cherry furniture, wooden signs, flower boxes, and paintings by local artist Mary Ellen Yoder. They now have a small room of antiques in the back of the shop. Located at 124 E. Main St. Hours are Mon.-Fri. 10 am-5 pm; Fri. until 8 pm; Sat. until 6 pm.

The closest you'll get to a mall in Sugarcreek is **Huprich's Mini Mall** at 108 W. Main St., next to the Alpine Hills Museum. There are six businesses in this one location: **Sugarcreek Candles** specializes in wedding candles and centerpieces, but offers handmade candles in all sorts of shapes from ice cream sodas to Crayola crayons. There are lots of scented ones smelling of spiced apple, gingerbread, mulberry, and more. (PH: 330-852-3131.) In the **Hamas Haus** shoppers will find T-shirts, quilts, coverlets, a good selection of cards, and bulk teas among the gift items. The **Ice Cream Parlor** will feed you conies and krautdogs, hamburgers, and sloppy joes, as well as any of their 32 flavors of ice cream. **Global Crafts** is one of several shops in the area sponsored by the Mennonite Central Committee. Here you'll find one-of-a-kind crafts from third-world countries. This is a non-profit shop to benefit the world's struggling poor and the help in these shops is strictly volunteer. The **Music Box Chalet** has a thousand of these tinkling treasures. If you're a lover of the music box or know someone who is, this is the perfect place to find an appropriate selection. (PH: 330-852-3232.) **The Swiss Hobby Shop** is an excellent place to shop for the lover of model railroads. They also have model cars and airplanes to build, magazines, rockets, and souvenirs. (PH: 330-852-4299.) Hours in Huprich's Mini Mall are Mon.-Sat. 10 am-5 pm.

On SR 93 on the southwest edge of town the **J.C. Yoder Bicycle Shop** has been in business more than 25 years. They sell Nishiki, Raleigh, and Murray bikes and accessories, used bikes, and do repair work. PH: 330-852-4603.

Keith Travis says he keeps no *advertised* hours but is generally working at **Keith's Shoe & Saddle Repair** from 8 am-5 pm during the week. He has a selection of shoes and boots for sale but Keith's primary business is repairing saddles and all sorts of leather goods. He also makes one or two saddles a year. Find him at 130 S. Factory St. PH: 330-852-4665.

Two floors of crafts, gifts, and decorative items mean fun browsing at **Kuntry Korner**. Located at the intersection of SRs 93 and 39 at 993 W. Main St., this shop has a large selection of baskets, framed prints, dried and silk flowers, colorful cotton comforters, Cat's Meow, and dolls. Their Christmas room is open all year and has many collectibles such as lighted Christmas village pieces from Dept. 56. Summer and autumn hours (June-Nov.) are Mon.-Sat. 10 am-7 pm; Sunday 12:30-5 pm. Winter hours (Nov.-June) are Mon.-Sat. 10 am-5:30 pm. Closed Sun. in winter. Mailing address is P.O. Box 190, Sugarcreek, OH 44681. PH: 330-852-2555.

Mahlon's Art & Signs at 217 N. Broadway is operated by self-taught artist Mahlon Troyer. He's done a lot of commercial work such as signs and fancy lettering and pinstriping on vehicles. Mahlon also paints landscapes and wildlife with acrylics. In addition, he's started an "Amish Farm Series" of buildings and prints which you can see in several area shops.

In the middle of an area like Sugarcreek, which is so strongly Swiss in character, visitors expect to find a cheese house. Well, you won't be disappointed. Cheese was first made in town in 1885 and, although the business at 116 N. Factory St. has gone through several buildings and owners, cheese has been made here since 1918. Present owner, Paul J. Mueller, has operated **Mueller's Cheese** since 1972. The best time to watch the cheese-making process through the large windows in the back of the showroom wall is between 11-11:30 am every day. Mild, medium, and sharp Swiss cheeses are made here and you can select from an array of other cheeses and also meats. PH: 330-852-2311. Hours are Mon.-Sat. 9 am-5 pm.

Ever take a ride on a train pulled by a steam engine? Might want to give it a try on the **Ohio Central Railroad**. Located right in downtown Sugarcreek on Factory St., the depot was built in 1915 after fire destroyed the original one. These 1-hour, 12-mile journeys allow passengers a glimpse of the farms, fields, and hills of Amish country. Open May through the last Saturday in October, the train runs at 11 am, 12:30, 2, and 3:30 pm Mon.-Sat. Fares for adults 13 and older are $7; ages 3-12 are $4; under 3 free. It's suggested you arrive a half hour before departure time to purchase your tickets.

Ticket office opens at 10 am. There's a nice gift shop adjacent and many of the items, of course, have a railroad theme. Mailing address is P.O. Box 427, Sugarcreek, OH 44681. PH: 330-852-4676.

One of a chain of three local dry goods stores designed to serve the Amish community, **Spector's** is located right on Main St. If you're looking for fabrics, sewing notions, and quilting or craft supplies, stop in. Hours are Mon.-Sat. 8:30 am-5 pm; until 8 pm on Fri.

You can see the village smithy, Dale Schlabach, at work on S. Factory St. at the **Sugarcreek Blacksmith Shop**. PH: 330-852-4283.

The **Sugarcreek Livestock Auction** holds a cattle and livestock sale on Mondays and a horse sale on Fridays at the sale barn on S. Broadway St. As we've noted elsewhere in this book, farmers' auctions are a great place to rub elbows with those who live here. For more information call the sale barn at 330-852-2832.

Anyone out there who doesn't like fresh bread, pastries, or cookies? **Swiss Village Bakery** has a fresh assortment. They also carry bulk candies, nuts, cereals, dried fruits, jams and jellies, and apple butter. At 119 E. Main St. Hours are Mon.-Sat. 7 am-5 pm; Fri. 'til 8 pm.

Shoppers can find a little bit of everything in the way of bulk foods at **Swiss Village Bulk Foods**. With products from Union Salve and White Liniment to Watkins extracts to dried pear halves and papaya chunks to an extensive array of spices, toasted coconut, dried corn, and Jake & Amos pickled Brussels sprouts, it's no wonder this is a popular store. The in-store Dair-ette also serves sandwiches, cold drinks, and ice cream treats. There are two booths where you can relax with a quick snack. At 309 S. Broadway St. PH: 330-852-2896. Hours are Mon.-Sat. 8 am-5 pm; Fri. until 8 pm.

There are few things that make the mouth water like the sublime fragrance of chocolate. If you're even an occasional chocoholic, you'll want to stop in and see the selection of this sweet confection at **Swiss Village Chocolates**. In addition to the London candies and chocolates, including some sugar-free ones, they have teas and gourmet coffees. For 50 cents you can enjoy a cup of their daily coffee special—freshly brewed. At 104 Main St. PH: 330-852-4957. Open Mon.-Sat. 10 am-6 pm.

Swiss Village Country Store is one of two stores in town which bring you Christmas every day. Shoppers can browse through their roomful of Christmas trees decorated for the holidays. There's something here for anyone who loves this special season of the year. Elsewhere in the shop are comforters, place mats, teas, kitchen items, and Cat's Meow pieces. At 124 N. Factory St. PH: 330-852-4414. Hours are Mon.-Sat. 10 am-5 pm. Open until 6 pm in the summer.

Looking for quilts? They have a rainbow of colors and patterns to choose from at **Swiss Village Quilts & Crafts** at 113 S. Broadway St. Custom orders are accepted. There are also quilted wallhangings, potholders, and pillows, bolts of calico and sewing notions, woven rugs, and an array of unfinished wooden items. A sign suggests you ask about locally made oak and cherry furniture. PH: 330-852-4855. Hours are Mon.-Sat. 9 am-5 pm.

If you've been looking for a grandfather clock to grace your home, see the display at the **Swiss Village Time Shop**. They had absolutely gorgeous cherry Harrington House Ltd. clocks, several in oak, and one stunner in mahogany when I stopped by. All sorts of other time pieces such as mantle, wall, regulator, and cuckoo clocks as well as watches are also here. They specialize in watch and clock repairs. At 126 S. Factory St., P.O. Box 363, Sugarcreek, OH 44681. PH: 330-852-4041. Hours are Mon.-Sat. 9 am-5 pm; Fri. until 8 pm.

The **Tom Miller Gallery** now has reign over what was Gerber's. In addition to Mr. Miller's limited edition, numbered and hand-signed prints, shoppers can look over an assortment of fine collectibles that includes Mahlon Troyer's Amish Farm Series, Lizzie High dolls, stained glass items, furniture pieces, and more. At 100 E. Main St. PH: 330-852-2474. Open Mon.-Sat. 10 am-6 pm.

Troyer's Furniture has a good selection of upholstered and wooden pieces. Located next to Kuntry Korner at 985 W. Main St., Sugarcreek, OH 44681. Visit the store Mon.-Thurs. 9:30 am-5 pm; Fri. until 8 pm; Sat. until 6 pm. PH: 330-852-4752.

The second of two shops to entice us with Christmas all year 'round is **Victoria's Country Store and Christmas Shoppe**. I don't know about you, but I enjoy the special aura of Christmas even in the middle of July. There is a good selection of Santas and Christmas decorations and collectibles. In addition, there are country accessories for your home and a large variety of decorative flags. At 118 S. Factory St. PH: 330-852-3109. Hours are Mon.-Fri. 10 am-5 pm; Sat. until 6 pm; Sun. (June-Nov.) 11 am-5 pm.

The Wooden Craft & Toy Shop is owned by J.R. Schrock, who learned the art of working with wood from his father. His shop at 116B Mill St. features shelving, candle holders, trash bins, bread boxes, jewelry chests, wooden baskets, benches, and more for the grown-ups in the family. For the children there are wooden pull toys, doll furniture, and piggy banks. Turn south at the light onto SR 93 and it's ½ block on your right. PH: 330-852-3006. Open Mon.-Sat. 10 am-5 pm.

Eric Yoder opened **Yoder's Valley Pottery** on N. Factory St. across from Ohio Central Railroad. Eric throws his functional stoneware right in the shop where visitors can watch. Bowls, mugs, teapots, candle holders, and canisters are some of the pieces he makes. Open 10 am-5 pm Mon.-Sat.

Dining

For a good, rib-sticking meal of Amish cooking, try **Beachy's Country Chalet**. Yes, those family-style dinners are here with a choice of chicken, turkey, ham, or roast beef. But you'll also find such dishes as wienerschnitzel and bratwurst with sauerkraut. They offer daily specials. If you've still got room, enjoy a piece of egg custard, key lime, or rhubarb pie, an apple dumpling, or some date pudding. Don't forget to take a peek in their gift shop before you leave. Find this restaurant just east of the downtown area on Andreas Dr. PH: 330-852-4644. Hours are Mon.-Sat. 11 am-10 pm.

Crossroads Pizza occupies the former Zifer's Pizza spot. They have all those great pizza toppings, subs, salads, chicken tenders and wings, etc. There's a dining area so you can eat in. At 119 S.

Broadway. PH: 330-852-2993. Open Mon.-Wed. 4-10 pm; Thurs. 11 am-10 pm; Fri. and Sat. 11 am-11 pm; Sun. 3-10 pm.

Edelweiss Inn on the corner of Main and Factory Sts. used to be a bar but is now a family restaurant owned by John and Mary Hochstetler. The bar is still there, so grab a seat and enjoy one of the soda fountain goodies they make. The inn serves 3 squares a day with breakfast probably beginning at 6 am during the summer. There are daily dinner specials and homemade pies to top them off. You might enjoy dining outdoors in their garden area. PH: 330-852-3663. Open Mon.-Wed. until 8 pm; Thurs.-Sat. 'til 10 pm.

McDonald's has established three restaurants across the area—in Sugarcreek, Millersburg, and Loudonville. This one is located right on SR 39 on the east side of town. This is the only McDonald's which serves the Swissburger, a quarter pounder with Swiss cheese, onions, green peppers, and mushrooms. You know the rest of the menu and kids generally love it. Hours are Mon.-Thurs. 5:30 am-11 pm; open Fri. and Sat. until midnight; opens Sun. morning at 6:00 am.

The Pizza Parlor & Family Restaurant has undergone some changes beyond the name. It's now a combination of two entities. The Family Restaurant begins serving breakfast at 5:30 am with the usual breakfast menu. (No breakfast served on Sun.) Then, they serve homemade soup, sandwiches, and chicken dinners for lunch. The Pizza Parlor entity, well known in the area, begins making pizzas at 4 pm. There is a dining area. Find the restaurant in the complex with Der Village Pantry and Subway on SR 39 just west of McDonald's. Hours Mon. 5:30 am-2 pm (no pizzas served this day); Tues.-Sat. 'til 11 pm; Sun. 11 am-10 pm.

At the opposite end of the complex with the Pizza Parlor is a **Subway Shop**. This chain is noted for their freshly made subs and they bake their own rolls. PH: 330-852-4118. Hours are Mon.-Sat. 10:30 am-11 pm; Sun. 11 am-10 pm.

The **Swiss Hat Restaurant** reopened in mid-1994 after fire destroyed the original restaurant. Owners Pat and Sally Patterson have recreated the old restaurant, right down to their popular Swiss steak.

A breakfast buffet is served every day until 10:30 am, or diners can order off the menu. Currently, they serve a German buffet on Mon. evening, a Family Night Chicken Buffet Tues.-Thurs., an all-you-can-eat, beer-batter fish special or their Four-Meat Buffet on Fri. Dinner specials are also served beginning at 4 pm. If you want a plate dinner, choices include roast beef, meat loaf, and wienerschnitzel. Homemade pies top the dessert menu. There is no separate children's menu. Open 7 days a week, Mon.-Sat. 7 am-8 pm; Sun. 8 am-4 pm.

Lodging

Originally a cheese house whose cornerstone reads "Yoder 1858," the **Bed & Breakfast Barn** offers 12 guest rooms with private baths and A/C. Some also have TVs and each has a sliding glass door onto the 265 feet of deck built around the building. Downstairs there's a large, rustic living room and every guest can enjoy a full breakfast in the dining room. Room rates about $59.95-$69.95. Four cabins were open when I visited, with five more planned. Each has a bedroom with 2 queen-sized beds, bath, TV, stereo, A/C. Rates for the cabins are $79.95 for two. A country breakfast buffet is served to guests. Murder Mystery Weekends are held during the winter. Also on their agenda are plans for a full restaurant downstairs in the barn. Located on the east edge of Sugarcreek on CR 70. Contact owner Thomas Agler at P.O. Box 454, Sugarcreek, OH 44681, or call 330-852-2337.

The Breitenbach Bed & Breakfast is now open. There are four guest rooms decorated with antiques. Cable TV, A/C, and private baths are part of their accommodations. Owner Cynthia Bear Bixler's father built the home at 307 Dover Rd. (SR 39). Cynthia and her husband, Dalton, remodeled it into the B&B. Deanna Arthurs, Cynthia's sister, is the hostess. An expanded continental breakfast is served. Rates are $65-$85. PH: 330-343-3603 or 1-800-843-9463.

Dutch Host Motor Inn has 12 country-decorated units with A/C, C/TVs, radios, and phones. AAA rated. Rates for 2 persons, one bed, are $45-$50. Located on SR 39 ½ mi. east of town. PH: 330-852-2468 or 1-800-428-0075 for reservations.

Edelweiss Inn should have three rooms above the restaurant open by Memorial Day, 1996. The guest rooms will be decorated with vintage antiques and a continental breakfast will be served. If you want more information, stop by the Inn, write to P.O. Box 733, Sugarcreek, OH 44681, or call 330-852-3663.

SUGARCREEK TWP.

1. They've been making cheese since 1933 at **Broad Run Cheese House** and visitors can take a tour—during limited hours—for $1.50 or view the cheesemaking process through the windows in the mornings. They still make their Swiss the old-fashioned way in copper kettles. In 1995 Broad Run won reserve champion in the state's Swiss cheese contest. In addition, they feature a Victorian Shop full of beautiful things for your home. Ruffled and tailored curtains are available and there are pictures, laces, great period lamps, and decorative items. At the back of the building is a wide selection of outdoor ornamental statuary and pots. Find Broad Run on old SR 39 (now CR 139) just west of Der Marketplatz. PH: 330-343-4108 or 1-800-332-3358. Hours are Mon.-Sat. 9 am-7 pm; Sun. noon-5 pm.

2. Lots of wooden decorative items are made at **Broad Run Valley Crafts**. How about a dog or cat dish-holder with 2 bowls for your pet? Owner Mose Erb makes an unusual 3-in-1 combination rocking horse/high chair/desk any tot would enjoy. He also designs several Southwestern-styled pieces such as quilt/blanket racks, stools, cupboards, and benches. On CR 139 between Der Marketplatz and Little Switzerland Shoppe. P.O. Box 439, Sugarcreek, OH 44681. PH: 330-364-7580. Hours Mon.-Sat. 9 am-6 pm.

3. **Der Marketplatz** is the home of **Breitenbach Wine Cellars**, one of Ohio's award-winning wineries. That big purple barn is where the wines are made and they range from grape wines with such names as Old Dusty Miller and Charming Nancy to fruit wines like spiced apple, elderberry, and dandelion. I'm no wine connoisseur, but a taste of their most popular grape wine, a sweet white called Frost Fire, was nearly enough to convince me I ought to develop a palate. The wines here are produced as naturally as possible with little or no

preservatives. Der Marketplatz is where you can enjoy a taste of any of the wines they offer before you buy them. Then you can look through the shop which sells meats and cheeses, Amish hats, cuckoo clocks, hex signs, souvenirs, and crafts. A Dandelion May Fest features dandelion food, a national dandelion cookoff, entertainment for the whole family, and dandelion wine, of course. Located on old SR 39 just east of Broad Run Cheese. PH: 330-343-3603. Hours are Mon.-Sat. 9 am-6 pm and Sunday afternoons by chance—but no wine sales on Sun.

4. All the businesses which are part of the Dutch Valley complex are found at this location. During the summer they are open from 9 am-8 pm. In Jan. and Feb. they are open until 6 pm Mon.-Thurs. and until 8 pm Fri. and Sat. Find them just off new SR 39 on CR 139 east of town. Take time for the fun of discovering the variety that's here.

The first is **Dutch Valley Furniture and Antique Mall.** The Antique Mall is on the first floor and features 5,000 sq.ft. of antique furniture, collectibles, and books. I once discovered among their treasures a Victorian fainting couch that I'd have loved to own. The second floor is devoted to locally made oak and cherry pieces such as pedestal and drop-leaf tables, deacon's benches, chairs, and beds. They also have mattress sets and accessories for your home. PH: 330-852-4026.

With three floors of gift items, the **Dutch Valley Gift Market** is one of those stores just bursting at the seams with all sorts of beautiful things. There's Victorian wicker and country pine, lamps, and lots of artwork, scents of all kinds, candy, books, and plenty of things for the kids. PH: 330-852-4926.

David Warther Carvings is nothing short of fascinating. And, if the name Warther sounds familiar, it's no surprise. David's grandfather was Ernest "Mooney" Warther whose wonderful carvings of steam engines can be seen at the museum in Dover. David carved his first ship at age 6. Today, he has a converted brick home full of museum-quality ships carved of ebony and antique ivory from historic blueprints at a scale of 1/16 inch to 1 foot. The intricate details of such ships as Columbus' Santa Maria or the Brigantine yacht, Carnegie, are enhanced with scrimshaw and stippling. David continues to carve in a workshop where visitors can watch and ask questions. Some of his ships take 6 to 9 months to complete and contain over 3,000 pieces. They aren't sold and David Warther Carvings operates as a museum for the enjoyment of all who visit. Guided tours take about 20-30 min. Admission is $2.50 per adult and children under 18 are free with an accompanying adult. PH: 330-852-3455. Summer hours here are Mon.-Sat. 9 am-7 pm.

Fresh and frozen meats of all kinds, peppered hams and other smoked meats, cheeses, bulk foods and baking items, fruits, nuts, and candies are just some of what you'll find at **Yoder's Country Meat**. How about some hot pepper mustard or some locally made Tripp's potato chips? You're bound to find something that interests your taste buds. PH: 330-852-2631.

See the Dining section for information on Dutch Valley Restaurant.

5. **Dutch Valley Woodworking** can custom-design the elegant oak or cherry kitchen of your dreams. Step into their showroom and see if you can resist the temptation to transform that dreary old kitchen at home into a modern showplace. They also feature Corian countertops and fine appliances from Weaver Appliances. Hours are Mon.-Fri. 8 am-5 pm; Sat. until noon. Located at the corner of SR 39 and Dutch Valley Dr. east of Sugarcreek. P.O. Box 416, Sugarcreek, OH 44681. PH: 330-852-4319.

6. Belgians are a breed of draft horses much loved and worked by the Amish of the area. These handsome, golden horses with the blonde manes and tails can be found at **Hillside Acres Registered Belgians**. **Erb's Blacksmith Shop** is also located here at 7490 Spooky Hollow Rd. NW, Sugarcreek, OH 44681.

7. Interested in antiques and collectibles? Try the **Little Switzerland Shoppe**. This is another one of those businesses on the *old* state route (now CR 139), just west of Broad Run Cheese. They have a little shop mostly filled with small collectibles, particularly glass. Hours are Mon.-Sat. 10 am-5 pm. PH: 330-364-5362.

8. If you want to see a *real* Amish grocery store, stop at **Maple Valley Market**. As with many Amish businesses, be prepared for how dark the interior of the store may be. We're so used to electricity we take it for granted. It's rather disconcerting to walk into a dark

building. If you're like me, you keep wanting to ask them to turn on the lights. Notice the gas lighting hanging from the ceiling. At Maple Valley Market you'll find a lot of bulk foods, grocery items, and a variety of things to accommodate one-stop shopping. Take SR 93 north of Sugarcreek about 2½ miles. Hours are Mon., Thurs., and Sat. 8 am-5 pm; Tues. and Fri. until 8 pm; Wed. until noon.

9. Find hunting paraphernalia at **Miller's Gun & Supply**, on Skyline Rd. at the corner of Shetler Rd. Hours are Mon.-Fri. 12-8 pm; Sat. 11 am-4 pm. Closed Thurs. and Sun.

10. Fresh fruits and vegetables from strawberries to squash are available at **Miller's Produce**, 10434 Skyline Rd.

11. Leroy Stutzman runs **Stony Point Belgians** at 8116 Maple Dr.

12. **Sugar Valley Meats** offers custom slaughtering and processing. Freezer beef, smoked meats, and deer processing are specialties here. Anyone know what Krepples are? Well, they've got them and you can find it at Sugar Valley Meats. Located on Dutch Valley Dr., 1 mi. north of SR 39. PH: 330-852-4423. Hours are Mon.-Thurs. 7:30 am-5 pm; Fri. until 6 pm; Sat. 8 am-5 pm.

13. Third-generation antique dealer Claire Fath operates **Sugarcreek Antiques**. There's plenty to interest any antique hunter in this interesting shop. I saw Indian pounding stones, old clay pipes, bottles, glassware, lanterns, primitive and other furniture, crocks, and many collectibles. Claire's husband, Jeff, also does some furniture refinishing. Take SR 93 north and you'll find the shop almost across from the intersection with Barrs Mills Rd. Hours are Mon.-Sat. 9 am-5 pm. PH: 330-852-2231.

14. **Sugarcreek Storage Barns** will customize one of these in any size. They also make lawn furniture at their shop on Maple Dr. Follow the signs off SR 39.

15. Does the thought of hot, fresh potato chips make your mouth water? Then be sure to stop at **Tripp's Chips**, 513-3 Ragersville Rd. NW. This family-owned business makes regular and barbequed chips

and never has more than a 3-day supply on hand to keep 'em fresh. If the plant is in operation, they'll be glad to give you a tour and a sample of their product. They sell 12 oz. bags and 2 lb. decorative tins full of fresh, crispy chips. Tours available Mon.-Wed. 8 am-4 pm and Thurs.-Sat. only if they're working. Groups should call ahead to make arrangements. PH: 330-852-2827 or 852-2739.

16. **Weavers of Sugarcreek** has greatly expanded the scope of its business by building a new furniture store to go along with its complete line of wooden outdoor furnishings. This means you can choose from storage barns, gazebos, and playhouses or upholstered pieces for the living room, occasional tables, and bedroom and dining room suites. Located just beyond the Dutch Valley complex. Open Mon.-Sat. 9 am-9 pm. Contact them at P.O. Box 559, Sugarcreek, OH 44681. PH: 330-852-2103 or 852-2701.

Dining

One of the most popular restaurants in the area is the **Dutch Valley Restaurant**. Diners can enjoy their breakfast buffet Mon.-Sat. from 7-11 am, or you can pick something lighter from their morning menu. A 25-item salad bar might sound good for lunch, or a family-style dinner with chicken, ham, roast beef, turkey, or meat loaf which includes dessert and beverage. There's a children's menu for the under 10 crowd. If you can't eat dessert now, get it to go from their bakery. How about a German chocolate pie? Yum! Located at map #4, it's the crown jewel in the Dutch Valley complex. PH: 330-852-4627. Hours are 7 am-8 pm Mon.-Sat. Closed Sun.

Lodging

17. **Down on the Farm Bed 'n Breakfast** is on the Schlabach family's 140-acre farm. They have 2 bedrooms with queen-sized beds which share a bath with tub and shower. In addition, there's a living room with sofa sleeper, dining area, and outdoor patio with grill. They're also opening a basement room with queen and double beds and private bath. Mae Schlabach serves a full, home-cooked breakfast every morning except Sunday when a continental breakfast is available. Rates are $40 for a single, $70 for a couple, and $10 for

extra persons. North of Sugarcreek at 3360 SR 93. Please call 330-763-2013 for reservations and more information.

Camping

18. Located on 140 scenic acres is **Alpine Hills Resort**. Open spring through fall, they have RV and tent camping available. Plans call for the addition of chalets to rent but no word on when they will be built. Alpine Hills Resort also schedules gospel and country music concerts in their outdoor amphitheater. Rates for primitive sites $6 and for motor homes, $12 (not including hookups). Located just outside Sugarcreek Twp. on CR 139 east of Der Marketplatz. For more information on camping or their calendar of events, call 330-364-3244 or 1-800-241-7493.

19. Camping is available at **Winklepleck Grove** but I'm told this is much more a picnic area than a campground. There are no sites marked, although electric hookups are available, put in by the Airstream owners who take over the grounds during Swiss Festival time. There are outdoor restrooms but no dump station and no showers. This pleasant grove is owned by the village and, if you're interested in staying here, you need to call or stop in at the Village Hall, 202 N. Broadway, beside the fire station. Rate is $10 per night. Tents and RVs are allowed. Call 330-852-4112 between 9 am and 4 pm Mon.-Fri. for more information.

Please Note: The Amish do not have telephones in their homes. If you want information on products, services, or prices, drop a letter into the mail. Enclose a self-addressed, stamped postcard or envelope for their convenience. They will reply.

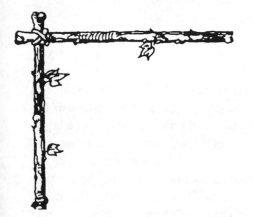

Section IV
Coshocton
County

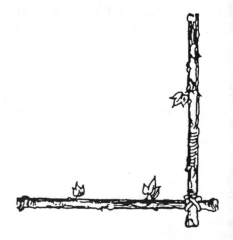

Chapter 24

New Bedford and Crawford Twp.

Ahhhh, Coshocton—land of rugged hillsides and deep green woodlands where deer, wild turkeys, and intrepid raccoons live undisturbed by the press of civilization. It's beautiful, wild countryside with widely scattered farms off quiet, tree-lined roadways.

In 1981 I moved from Wayne County to Holmes County and found it reminiscent of my growing-up years in Overton in the late 50's. The pace seemed slower and traffic less congested. But I've often thought if I ever decided to really "get away from it all," I could hardly do better than a move to the next county south—Coshocton.

For a driving tour take SR 206 south off US 62 through Tiverton Center. You'll eventually come out on SR 715 near Walhonding. The Kokosing and Mohican Rivers join to form the Walhonding River just west of town. Turn east on SR 715 and discover Mohawk Dam. Did you remember to bring a picnic lunch? Good! There's a lovely picnic grounds at the Dam where you can enjoy your meal.

At the little community of Nellie pick up US 36 east and continue driving through the broad, lovely valley of the Walhonding. This route will take you through Warsaw and on toward Coshocton. Of course, the closer you get to the county seat, the more civilized the land becomes. But it's beautiful and the highway is good, so relax and enjoy the sights.

Crawford Twp.
Coshocton County

If you need to head back to wherever you're resting your head tonight, SR 60 joins US 36 in Warsaw and, when it turns north just a short distance east of town, you can follow it back to Killbuck.

Not the least of SR 60's charms is a glimpse of Killbuck Creek in its original, serpentine course. You're near the southern terminus where it empties into the Walhonding east of Warsaw. This section south of the Holmes County line is probably the only portion of the creek that hasn't been channeled and straightened to accommodate man. Here, in its lazy, gentle way the stream is allowed to run free.

Thanks to local writer MaryLee and her article in *The Bargain Hunter*, I discovered something I didn't know existed. If you're interested in things historical, you might want to see it.

Traveling north on SR 60, you come to the village of Blissfield. Turn east on CR 25 toward what is left of the village of Helmick. At the junction of CR 343, you'll find the Helmick Covered Bridge. It was built across Killbuck Creek during the Civil War in 1863 and was placed on the National Register of Historic Places in 1975.

The Helmick Covered Bridge Restoration Committee, formed in 1991, is raising funds to restore this landmark. If you're interested in finding out more about the bridge or would like to send them a check, contact Committee President Evangelene Croft, 26962 CR 1, Box 631, Keene, OH 43828, or call her at 614-622-0549. The committee would appreciate any assistance, I'm sure.

So, what does Coshocton County have to offer visitors besides gorgeous scenery?

The most-sought destination is probably Roscoe Village which owes its historical significance to the fact it was once a thriving port on the Ohio-Erie Canal. The canal was built in the 1830's to connect Cleveland and Lake Erie with the Ohio River. When the canal closed in 1913, Roscoe Village began a decline from which it was saved by restoration efforts begun in 1968.

Visitors can walk around this lovely village and enjoy its restaurants, shops, gardens, and festivals, but they'd be wise to also see the 9 museums scattered among the various buildings. Cost of admission to all museums is $6 for adults; ages 8-18 get in for $3. More information about Roscoe Village and its variety of annual festivals is available by calling 1-800-877-1830.

Our tour of Coshocton County is limited to New Bedford and Crawford Twp.

If you enter Coshocton County via scenic SR 83, I'd urge you jaunt off on one of the side roads. CR 12 would be good and will take you north into New Bedford, as will SR 643 north. Such drives are worth it for the scenery alone and you'll enjoy glimpses of the scattered Amish farms nestled among the bright hills.

To discover Coshocton County, call 1-800-338-4724 for a free brochure pack, including a calendar of Roscoe Village events.

NEW BEDFORD

Sandwiches and crispy chicken dinners are available at the **New Bedford Country Store** if you find your tummy growling. They also have a variety of bulk foods and groceries. PH: 330-897-1021. Hours are Mon.-Sat. 7:30 am-5:30 pm; Fri. until 8:30 pm.

One drive through New Bedford will convince visitors this is a real Amish-centered village. You might conclude that New Bedford is way out of the mainstream, almost untouched by modern society. Not so! Incongruous as it may seem to outsiders, some trappings of modern life have been embraced even here. Among the hardware and horse medicines, live bait, soda pop, and myriad merchandise, **New Bedford Elevator & Supplies** offers its customers the convenience of a FAX service (330-897-1214). Located in the heart of town at 33906 SR 643, Baltic, OH 43804. PH: 330-897-6492.

You can watch a harness maker ply his trade at **New Bedford Harness Shop**. An array of shoes and rubber footwear, new and used saddles, riding tack, buggy and work harness, oil and repair services are available. Located at 33897 SR 643, Baltic, OH 43804.

Hunting is popular among our Amish neighbors and they're as likely to want up-to-date equipment as anyone else. All the hunting and fishing supplies they need are at **New Bedford Sportsmen Supply**. In addition there's a selection of outdoor games. At the intersection of SRs 643 and 651. Hours Mon. 5-8 pm; Tues.-Wed. 1-8 pm; Fri. 9 am-9 pm; Sat. 9 am-4 pm. Closed Thurs. and Sun.

If you have a piece of furniture or a truck, car, or van in need of new upholstery, talk to Aden M.C. Yoder, owner of **New Bedford**

Upholstery at 52597 SR 651, Baltic, OH 43804.

Schlabach Wood Design creates custom cabinetry for kitchens and baths as well as hutches, desks, bookcases, and entertainment centers. They offer free estimates. Located at 52567 SR 651, Baltic, OH 43804. PH: 330-897-2600.

Close enough to New Bedford to be considered part of the community is **Schlabach's Greenhouse**. They have trees, shrubs, bulbs, and perennials as well as strawberries, grapevines, blueberry plants, asparagus roots, garden seeds, and everything to meet your gardening needs. The Schlabachs have turned the production of greenhouse-grown bedding plants over to Hillside Greenhouse (see #7). Find Schlabach's less than ¼ mi. south off SR 651 at 33779 CR 10, Fresno, OH 43824. Spring hours are 7:30 am-8 pm on Mon., Wed., and Fri.; until 5 pm Tues., Thurs., and Sat. Open only until 5 pm as summer approaches, with Fri. hours until 8 pm.

CRAWFORD TWP.

1. Tucked back among the hills is **Brookside Carriage** at 32303 TR 272, Fresno, OH 43824.

2. To say Norman Stutzman handcrafts two-wheeled carts at **Buckeye Cart & Supply** is like saying Picasso was merely a painter. If you have a need for any type of cart to be pulled by regular or miniature horses, a pony, mule, llama, or draft horse, he can fix you up. Several models and options are available so you can get one custom-made to your specifications. Get a copy of their catalog by writing to 33698 CR 12, Baltic, OH 43804. PH: 330-897-9361. Located about 1 mi. west of New Bedford. Hours are Mon.-Sat. 8 am-5 pm with lunch from 11:30-12:30. Closed Sun.

3. **Cedar and oak chests** are made by the Masts at 33204 and 33208 SR 643.

4. We're going just across the Crawford Twp. line into Mill Creek Twp. to tell you about an unusual business in a picturesque setting.

Fender's Fish Hatchery is in the business of raising fish to stock farm ponds and lakes and you might want to stop, go in, ask some questions, and take a look around. But, even if you just want to drive by and see their operation from your car window, you'll discover that Fender's is also a great place to see llamas. There are no warning signs, but I'd think twice before sticking my hands through the fence. Located at the intersection of CR 12 and TR 220 barely west of the township line.

5. Want to eat a meal in an Amish home? You can do exactly that by making reservations with **Hershberger's Country Cookin'**. Lunch or dinner meals for 15-50 are served Tues.-Sat. from April-December at the home of Valentine and Sarah Hershberger, 53933 SR 651, Baltic, OH 43804. For $9 a plate diners enjoy two meats, mashed potatoes and gravy, stuffing, noodles or vegetables, salad, homemade bread, pie, and coffee, tea, or lemonade. Ages 4-12 are half price and under 4 are free. Remember, it's reservations only!

6. Although owner Melvin Hershberger has a thriving wholesale business, **Hershberger Country Store** is full of kitchenware, home, and farm supplies. A catalog is available for $2. Located south of New Bedford at 50940 TR 220, Baltic, OH 43804. Hours are Mon.-Sat. 7:30 am-5 pm; Wed. and Fri. until 8 pm.

Also at location #5 on the map is **Hillside Bulk Foods and Country Crafts** which stocks a full line of bulk foods for all your baking needs, plus jams, jellies, homemade bread, and candies. Their handmade crafts include quilts, wallhangings, potholders, bird houses, and bird feeders. Located between Baltic and New Bedford at 53933 SR 651, Baltic, OH 43804. Hours are Mon.-Fri. 8 am-8 pm; Sat. until 5 pm. Closed Sun.

7. **Hillside Greenhouse** is open from early spring to about the first of July. Find them on TR 235 for all your flower and vegetable plant needs.

8. Melvin A. Stutzman owns **Stutzman's Buggy Shaft & Wheel Works** just southwest of Buckeye Cart & Supply at 33650 CR 12, Baltic, OH 43804.

9. **Valley Bulk Foods** opened in June 1995. Find them on TR 231, ½ mi. north of CR 10, in the small house across the road from the Crist Raber farm.

10. **Wren and bluebird houses and squirrel feeders** are made at the Barkman farm, 33419 SR 643, Fresno, OH 43824.

11. For buggy robes or any tarp needs you have, see the folks at **Yoder's Tarp Shop**, 53302 SR 651, Baltic, OH 43804.

Lodging

12. The most southerly lodging establishment covered in our review, **Valley View Inn Bed & Breakfast** has 10 rooms, each named after the quilt design you'll find decorating the bed. One room boasts two double beds while the others each have queen beds. There is also a wheelchair-accessible room. This inn sits back off the road at the edge of a very steep hillside. The view is spectacular in any season and twilight might well allow you a glimpse of deer wandering out of the woodlands. A full family-style breakfast is served in the dining room every morning except Sunday. Only a continental breakfast is served on this day of rest. There are no accommodations for children under 13 and you're encouraged to call ahead if you have children. The living room on the first floor has a fireplace and offers a quiet retreat for reading a good book or magazine. Downstairs is a large family room with another fireplace, a player piano, and a game room where you can enjoy playing ping pong. Room rates are based on size, accommodations, and view and range from $75 to $105 for the room with two beds. Each also has its own bath and shower. Located 3 mi. south of New Bedford at 32327 SR 643, Fresno, OH 43824. PH: 330-897-3232 or 1-800-331-8439.

Please Note: The Amish do not have telephones in their homes. If you want information on products, services, or prices, drop a letter into the mail. Enclose a self-addressed, stamped postcard or envelope for their convenience. They will reply.

Chapter 25

What's Open on Sunday?

If you're from an urban area with malls, shops, and restaurants which are *always* open on Sunday, you may come to Amish country expecting to find things the same here. It ain't necessarily so!

Our Amish and Mennonite neighbors believe that Sunday is a day of rest and a time for spiritual renewal. They spend it at church services, sit around a dinner table in the afternoon, maybe nap, take a walk, do some reading, and play games with their families and friends. It is a day *not* to think about business and moneymaking. I remember when Sundays were like that everywhere, when life was more mellow—or at least I recall it that way.

This reverence for the seventh day is one of the things that makes Amish country the special place it is.

Some business people who *are* open on Sundays have mentioned hosting irate shoppers who vented their spleen because of what was, to them, a disappointing state of affairs. Pity the poor shopkeeper.

In the interest of promoting better public relations and in the hope of forestalling such disappointment, this chapter is dedicated to informing you about which businesses are open on this day. Whatever you're looking for, this will help you find it on Sunday.

I'm not going to go into great detail about each business since that information is available elsewhere in this volume. This chapter is divided into the same sections, hopefully making it easy for you to locate and read more about the areas and businesses that interest you.

If you plan to do some sightseeing, Sunday's a great day to discover some of Amish country's wonderful scenery. Traffic is light and in many areas Amish buggies are almost the only competition for the roads. Take a picnic lunch of Swiss cheese and Trail Bologna, some crackers, fresh fruit, and something to drink, or end your tour in an area which has a restaurant open. Relax and enjoy the sights.

One reminder: Winter hours may be different or find some craft shops closed, so keep that in mind and be prepared if you're visiting at that time of year.

HOLMES COUNTY

Beck's Mills and Mechanic Twp.

This is a terrific area to explore for the scenery alone and that's all you'll find open here on Sunday. It'll be real quiet on this day of rest—a perfect time to do some wandering about on wheels.

Berlin and Berlin Twp.

All the craft shops are closed in Berlin. However, the Berlin Sweet Shoppe does business spring-autumn. And, if you need gas or something for a picnic, The Dutch Cupboard has Sunday hours.

Not what you're looking for? Go to Bunker Hill and visit Heini's Cheese Chalet & Country Mall, and don't forget to walk across the road to Kauffman's Country Bakery for one of their sweets.

Two other restaurants which are open in Berlin Twp.—and both are very popular—are Chalet in the Valley and Dutch Harvest. Hey, if you're in this area, at least you aren't going to go hungry. Don't miss Guggisberg Cheese across SR 557 from Chalet in the Valley.

Big Prairie and Ripley Twp.

Prairie Station is open if you happen to be traveling in the vicinity of Big Prairie. Kow Kuntry Station on SR 514 north of Nashville is also open. Both are good prospects for some browsing.

The Ol' Smokehaus Restaurant should be serving up barbeque and other tasty foods. During the Christmas season be sure to see the light displays at Spring Walk Farm and Don and Mabel Plant's home.

Charm and Clark Twp.

You're deep in the heart of Amish country in this area, so there's nothing open. However, one business on the east side of the township offers fun for all ages. Cabin Creek Golf and has two challenging miniature golf courses, a driving range, putting green, and sand volleyball just waiting to entertain you. Get thee hence and enjoy!

Holmesville and Prairie Twp.

The Holmesville Market is open and can fix you up with snacks and cold drinks, or you can get a pizza or sandwich to go at Main Street Pizza.

If you like antiques, stop by Croco House Antiques. They're open only by chance, so take a chance and find out.

The deer, elk, buffalo, horses, and ponies carry on business as usual even on Sundays at Pioneer Acres.

Killbuck

What can you do in the Killbuck vicinity besides see gorgeous scenery? Browse Bittersweet Farm; play a game of miniature golf or try your swing in either the batting or driving cages at Country Greens; see a movie at the Duncan Theater; spend some time in the Killbuck Valley Natural History Museum; see if George and Caroline Smith are open at Palladium Antiques; or eat! Gallion's Front Street Restaurant is open and Pizza Parlor II is making great pizzas.

Loudonville

If there's one place in this book that's definitely open on Sunday, this is it! What's open in Loudonville? What's *not*? Canoe liveries and all the other outdoor entertainments are booming as long as the weather's good. This is a great place to take the kids. The downtown businesses are open if you want to shop. Mohican State Park awaits your visit. The restaurants are serving meals, and don't forget the Ohio Theater has a Sunday matinee and an evening showing.

There's too much to list separately, so turn to this chapter and try to decide if you can see and do everything you want to in one day.

Millersburg and Hardy Twp.

Millersburg has its share of Sunday delights. The Antique Emporium, Gallery of Crafts, Goodwill Thrift Shoppe, The Grocery Bag, Shell Food Mart, Thoughts That Count, and Wal-Mart are all open. The world of the Victorians awaits you at The Victorian House.

Then, of course, there are the restaurants. Almost all of them are open, so one of them is bound to serve what you're hungry for. Check this chapter to learn more.

Mt. Hope and Salt Creek Twp.

Sorry but in this bastion of Amish country you're not going to find anything open. If the shopping bug's bitten you, you'll have to go elsewhere.

Nashville and Washington Twp.

In Nashville the Buckeye Deli and Grocery is open and the guys will be glad to fix you up with a tasty pizza.

Lake Fork Canoe Livery can put you in a canoe for a paddle down the Lake Fork Branch of the Mohican River. Hey, this could be fun! Out On A Limb Wood and Gift Shoppe could have just the antique you've been looking for. Richardson's Greenhouse can scratch your green thumb during spring planting time. Charlotte's Cozy Corners will serve you a meal after you've spent the afternoon swimming at Long Lake Park.

Walnut Creek and Walnut Creek Twp.

You can see those cute critters at Dundee Donkeys but there's nothing else open in this area on Sunday.

Welcome and Monroe Twp.

Sunny Slope General Store will sell you gas or something to snack on, or you can get dinner at the Korner Kitchen Restaurant.

Winesburg and Paint Twp.

Winesburg Collectables is the only shop open, but you can enjoy Sunday dinner at the Winesburg Family Restaurant. The Marathon Food Mart will sell you gas or a snack.

Just outside of Winesburg is Alpine-Alpa where you can shop, enjoy a meal, or see the world's largest cuckoo clock.

WAYNE COUNTY

Apple Creek and East Union Twp.

Lehman Racing Collectables awaits the auto racing enthusiast and Apple Creek Restaurant, the Golden Bear Dariette, Larry's Pizza Shop, and Laurie's Ice Cream Parlor will feed hungry travelers.

Fredericksburg and Salt Creek Twp.

The Fredericksburg General Store may be open (by chance) for some great browsing among several rooms of antiques.

Kidron and Sugar Creek Twp.

Sorry, nothing's open except Mother Nature's scenery.

Moreland and Franklin Twp.

Goldstein's Antiques is open by chance and Moreland Fruit Farm will sell you homegrown fruits in season. If it's Christmastime and after dark, be sure to visit Strock's lovely light display. During the growing season Willow Lane Nursery & Greenhouse offers plants galore.

Mt. Eaton and Paint Twp.

Ruby's Family Restaurant offers good cookin'. Other shops in this area are closed.

Shreve and Clinton Twp.

Shreve Used Furniture is a good place to browse and you can always eat at Top Dawg Pizzeria, the Shreve Dari-Bar, or Quick Chek Subway.

Heichel's Antiques & By-Gones and Backyard Crafts are open. This would be a good day to take a tour of Kister Water Mill. Of course, nature does business 24 hours a day and is especially on view for you at Killbuck Marsh Wildlife Area. Moore's Greenhouse may be open during peak gardening season. The Pine Tree Barn beckons. You could plan to do some fishing at Shreve Lake Wildlife Area or enjoy one of the many events going on at Lake Wapusun.

Wilmot

The Wilderness Center, Inc. is open for those who want to stretch their legs and savor Mother Nature—not a bad idea for a Sunday afternoon. Don't forget the interpretive building while you're there.

TUSCARAWAS COUNTY

Baltic

You'll have to go elsewhere in Tuscarawas County to shop or enjoy a meal.

Sugarcreek and Sugarcreek Twp.

The convenience store, Der Village Pantry, is open. This may be the only place in Sugarcreek where you can buy gasoline for your vehicle on this day. Goshen Dairy is also open for business downtown. Two shops, Kuntry Korner and Victoria's Country Store and Christmas Shoppe, do business on Sundays June-Nov..

If you're hungry when you get to Sugarcreek, you can grab something to eat at McDonald's, The Pizza Parlor & Family Restaurant, Subway Shop, Crossroads Pizza, or downtown at the Swiss Hat.

Broad Run Cheese House and Der Marketplatz are good places to stop. The only drawback at Der Marketplatz is that you can't buy any of their 32 wines on the seventh day of the week.

COSHOCTON COUNTY

New Bedford and Crawford Twp.

There's no better day to see Coshocton County's great scenery. And that picnic I suggested? Mohawk Dam's got that lovely picnic area waiting for your arrival. Don't forget to drive by Fender's Fish Hatchery while you're in the area.

Well, that's about it for our tour of Amish country. I hope I've answered most of your questions along the way. I also hope you've had a relaxing, enjoyable visit and want to return soon to discover something new—with a copy of *BACK ROADS & BUGGY TRAILS* in hand, of course!

ALPHABETICAL INDEX OF BUSINESSES

Shell Food Mart, 107
Shetler's Bulk Food and Book Store, 79
Shreve Dari-Bar, 210
Shreve Hardware, 208
Shreve Lake Wildlife Area, 213
Shreve Storage Barns, 57
Shreve Used Furniture, 208
Silly Goose Emporium, 209
Sleep on the Farm, 148
Sleepin Inn Charm, 64
Smith's Bulk Foods, 190
Smith's Pleasant Valley Family
     Campground, 101
Sol's Exchange, 35
Sol's Palace, 35
Sommer's General Store, 35
Sommerset Tourist Rooms, 40
Sonia Lee's Coffee Haus, 48
Spector's, 31, 200, 235
Spookhollow New & Used Furniture, 79
Spoonful of Sugar, 142
Squash Blossom Square, 92
Squaw Valley Country Barn &
     Greenhouse, 129
Stan's Meats, Inc. 47
Stitching House, The, 36
Stoltzfus Woodcrafts, 165
Stonehedge Fabrics, 165
Stonehedge Guest Cottage, 168
Stony Mountain Botanicals, 92
Stony Point Belgians, 243
Stutzman's Buggy Shaft & Wheel Works,
     253
Stutzman's Nylon Shop, 182
Subs-n-Such, 97
Subway, 85, 238
Sugar Valley Meats, 243
Sugarcreek Antiques, 243
Sugarcreek Blacksmith Shop, 235
Sugarcreek Candles, 233
Sugarcreek Livestock Auction, 235
Sugarcreek Storage Barns, 243
Summit Valley Fabrics, 182
Sunflower Mercantile, 48
Sunny Slope Farm, 72
Sunny Slope General Store, 152
Swan Lake Retreat, 154
Swartzentruber Bakery, 165
Sweet Shoppe, 85
Swiss Country Lawn Furniture, 144
Swiss Hat Restaurant, 238
Swiss Hobby Shop, The, 233
Swiss Valley Fence, 144
Swiss Valley Furniture and Crafts, 144
Swiss Village Bulk Foods, 235

Swiss Village Chocolates, 235
Swiss Village Country Store, 236
Swiss Village Quilts & Crafts, 236
Swiss Village Time Shop, 236

T-Town Mart, 79
Tea Rose Bed & Breakfast, 148
Three Feathers Pewter, 107
Thoughts That Count, 107
Thunderbird Indian and Western Wear,
     93
Time and Treasure Trove, The, 158
Tina's House, 25
Tiverton Dish Farm, 152
Tom Miller Gallery, 236
Top Dawg Pizzeria, 210
Towne House Bed & Breakfast, 41
Trail Furniture & Appliances, 145
Traveler's Country Loft, 51
Traveler's Rest Motel, 113
Trillium House, 158
Tripp's Chips, 243
Troy Acres Crafts, 124
Troyer's Arrow & Supply, 64
Troyer's Arts, Inc., 124
Troyer's Bargain Store, 72
Troyer's Brookside Guest House, 126
Troyer's Cabinet, 145
Troyer's Country Store, 72
Troyer's Furniture, 236
Troyer's Genuine Trail Bologna, 138
Troyer's Harness Shop, 47
Troyer's Home Pantry, 174
Troyer's Homemade Candies, 79
Troyer's Lawn Furniture, 124
Troyer's Windmill Sales, 72
Twin Oaks Barns, 165
Twinsberry Tree Farm, 209
Two Rivers Indian Shop, 93

Uncle Burt's Kase Haus, 36
Under the Grape Arbor, 158
Upholstery A New, 203

V-W Woodcraft, 47
Valley Blacksmith Shop, 182
Valley Bulk Foods, 253
Valley Furniture, 73
Valley Harness Shop, 125
Valley View Inn Bed & Breakfast, 253
Valley View Oak, 125
Valley View Woodcrafts, 73
Victoria's Country Store and Christmas
     Shoppe, 237
Victorian House, 108

Village Antique Mall, 189
Village Bears & More, 209
Village Floral, 209
Village Pantry and Soda Shoppe, 97
Vintage Collectibles, 218
Vogt General Store, 139

Wal-Mart, 108
Walnut Creek BP Food Mart, 136
Walnut Creek Cheese, 145
Walnut Creek Country Store, 136
Walnut Creek Furniture, 30
Walnut Creek Woodworking, 145
Walnut Valley Greenhouse, 146
Watchman's Cottage, The, 65
Weaver Woodshop, 182
Weavers of Sugarcreek, 244
Weaver's Bulk Foods, 114
Weaver's Produce, 125
Weaver's Shoe Shop, 176
Wendell August Forge, 165
Wendling's Custom Cabinets, 146
Wengerd Furniture, 79
Wengerd Wood Shop, 57
Whispering Hills Campground and RV
    Park, 58
Whitmer's Store, 158
Whittlers & Weavers, 203
Wilderness Center, Inc., The, 218
Willie's Sports Stuff, 108
Willow Lane Nursery & Greenhouse, 196
Wilmot Pizza, 219
Wilson's Country Creations, 84
Windmill Village, 47
Windsong Acres, 196
Winesburg Antiques (And Stuff), 159
Winesburg Carriage, 159
Winesburg Collectables, 159
Winesburg Craft House, 159
Winesburg Dari-ette, 160
Winesburg Family Restaurant, 160
Winesburg Meats, Inc., 159
Winklepleck Grove, 245
Wooden Craft and Toy Shop, The, 36,
    237
Woodland Rocker Shop, 24
Woodland Tarp Shop, 57
Woodland Woodcrafts, 146
Woodlyn Coach Co., 125
Woodside Furniture, 166
Woodwind Hollow Bed & Breakfast, 115
Woolen Mill, The, 36
World Crafts, 189
Woven Memories, 130

Y & M Chair Co., 177
Yankee Workshop, 36
Yarn & Bead Shop, 55
Yoder Bakery, 80
Yoder Bargain Store, 183
Yoder Mfg. & Lumber, 58
Yoder's Amish Home, 146
Yoder's Archery, 58
Yoder's Baskets, 213
Yoder's Blacksmith Shop, 166
Yoder's Canvas Shop, 213
Yoder's Country Meat, 242
Yoder's Country Store, 37
Yoder's Craft Store, 57
Yoder's Greenhouse & Nursery, 177
Yoder's Market, 108
Yoder's Nylon Halter Shop, 166
Yoder's Porch Swings, 125
Yoder's Produce, 183
Yoder's Rocker Shop, 24
Yoder's Shoes and Repairs, 58
Yoder's Tarp Shop, 253
Yoder's Upholstery, 80
Yoder's Valley Pottery, 237
Yoder's Variety Shoppe, 160
Young Music & Sound, 108

Zimm's Drive Inn, 98
Zinck's in Berlin, 37

SUBJECT INDEX

Ice Cream, 33, 37, 106, 142, 175, 188, 189, 232 (See also Dining)
Indian Crafts, 83, 89, 93
Inns, See Lodgings

Jewelry, 30, 32, 33, 83, 89, 91, 93, 107, 142, 189, 216
Jewelry Boxes, 24, 237

Kayaks, See Canoeing
Kidron-Sonnenberg Heritage Center, 185
Kitchenware, 37, 136, 161, 216, 252 (See also General & Variety Stores)

Lamp Shades, 142, 208
Lamps, 30, 47, 142, 203
Lawn Ornaments, 30, 127, 159 (See also Furniture, Lawn)
Leather, 42, 118, 140, 233
Llamas, 123
Lodgings, 25, 38-41, 50-51, 64-65, 73-74, 85, 94, 98-99, 111-113, 114-115, 120, 125-126, 131, 137-138, 147-149, 153-154, 160-161, 167-168, 191, 203, 219-220, 239-240, 244, 253

Mailboxes, 29, 30, 142, 225, 231
Mantels, 157
Manure Spreaders, 68
Maps, Where to Order, 14
Mattresses, 43, 72, 176, 180
Meals, See Dining
Meats, 36, 47, 66, 138, 159, 179, 224, 242, 243
Mennonite Relief Sale, 186
Mills, 46, 212, 224
Miniature Golf, 67, 82, 91, 136
Moccasins, 93
Mohican Tourist Association, 88
Motels, See Lodgings
Movie Theater, 82, 91
Museum, 45, 61, 83, 89, 108, 135, 230
Music, 108, 173, 232
Music Boxes, 233
Muzzle Loaders, 124, 195 (See also Hunting)

Newspaper, 232

Ohio Agricultural Research & Development Center, 172
Ohio Light Opera, 171
Orchard, 136

Percherons, 72, 196
Perennials, 35, 114, 121, 129, 130, 146, 196, 201, 225, 251
Pewter, 30, 107, 230
Picnic Tables, 66, 165, 182 (See also Furniture, Lawn)
Plaques, 71
Potato Chips, 243
Pottery, 29, 30, 32, 34, 35, 36, 56, 64, 83, 88, 92, 189, 207, 237
Produce, 79, 122, 125, 143, 183, 201, 243
Putting Green, 67

Quilts, 33, 42, 46, 63, 92, 107, 119, 123, 141, 163, 165, 186, 187, 189, 194, 201, 208, 217, 218, 236

Rafting, See Canoeing
Railroad, 234
Restaurants, See Dining
Rockers, 34, 67, 77 (See also Hickory Rockers and Furniture)
Rolltop Desks, See Desks
Rugs, 29, 32, 41, 64, 68, 93, 130, 160, 186, 207, 217

Saddles, 140, 202, 233, 250
Sand Boxes, 140
Sand Volleyball, 67
Satellite Dish, 152
Saws, 159
Sewing Machines, 139
Shoe Repair, 42, 57
Shoes, 42, 57, 62, 65, 68, 78, 118, 176, 202, 225, 250
Silver Chest, 24
Slates, 92, 159
Sleeping Bags, 176
Spinning Wheel Repair, 69
Sports Cards, 108, 157
Stained Glass, 84, 158
State Park, 93
Storage Barns, 45, 46, 57, 113, 161, 165, 190, 243, 244
Stoves, 48
Sugarcreek Tourist Bureau & Information Center, 230
Sweatshirts, 29, 48, 91, 135, 143, 216
Swings, 23, 66, 70, 80, 125, 140, 158
Swingset, 48, 113, 140, 165

Tack, See Harness
Tarp Shop, 57, 78, 140, 163, 176, 213, 253